JAMES BURNHAM

JAMES BURNHAM

AN INTELLECTUAL BIOGRAPHY

DAVID T. BYRNE

NORTHERN ILLINOIS UNIVERSITY PRESS
AN IMPRINT OF CORNELL UNIVERSITY PRESS
Ithaca and London

Copyright © 2025 by Cornell University

All rights reserved. Except for brief quotations in a review, this book, or parts thereof, must not be reproduced in any form without permission in writing from the publisher. For information, address Cornell University Press, Sage House, 512 East State Street, Ithaca, New York 14850. Visit our website at cornellpress.cornell.edu.

First published 2025 by Cornell University Press

Library of Congress Cataloging-in-Publication Data

Names: Byrne, David T., author.
Title: James Burnham : an intellectual biography / David T. Byrne.
Description: Ithaca : Northern Illinois University Press, an imprint of Cornell University Press, 2025. | Includes bibliographical references and index.
Identifiers: LCCN 2024038939 (print) | LCCN 2024038940 (ebook) | ISBN 9781501780042 (hardcover) | ISBN 9781501780059 (epub) | ISBN 9781501780066 (pdf)
Subjects: LCSH: Burnham, James, 1905-1987. | Burnham, James, 1905-1987—Political and social views. | Burnham, James, 1905-1987—Philosophy. | Conservatism—United States—History—20th century.
Classification: LCC JC251.B87 B97 2025 (print) | LCC JC251.B87 (ebook) | DDC 320.52092 [B]—dc23/eng/20240925
LC record available at https://lccn.loc.gov/2024038939
LC ebook record available at https://lccn.loc.gov/2024038940

For TJ

Contents

Acknowledgments ix

Introduction	1
1. The Young Burnham	10
2. Embracing Marxism	16
3. Leaving Marxism	33
4. The New Elite	47
5. The Truth about the Elite	61
6. Samuel Francis, George Orwell, the Bureaucratic Elite, and Power	75
7. Using Power against Communism	82
8. A Strategy for Liberation	104
9. Thought and Action	117
10. *National Review*, *Congress and the American Tradition*, and *Suicide of the West*	136
11. Vietnam Failure and the Non-Western World	165
Epilogue: Burnham Today	187

Notes 193

Index 233

Acknowledgments

Many people have made important contributions to this book. Amy Farranto at Northern Illinois University Press provided indispensable guidance in preparing the manuscript. I am grateful to scholars Michael Kimmage, Jennifer Burns, and an anonymous reviewer for suggestions that were incorporated into this book. Editors Jon Harrison, Liz McKibbin, Allister Thompson, and Michael S. improved drafts of the manuscript. This book fortunately landed in their hands at early stages of writing.

I could not have completed the research by myself. The research staff at Hoover Institute Library and Archives was particularly helpful in making Burnham's archives accessible. The librarians at Southern New Hampshire University acquired countless *National Review* articles for me. Ryan Rebstock at Canterbury School also retrieved an article.

JAMES BURNHAM

Introduction

James Burnham began his intellectual career in the 1930s as one of Leon Trotsky's leading American exponents and ended it as a senior editor for America's preeminent conservative magazine, *National Review*. In between, he penned two of the most successful political works of the 1940s: *The Managerial Revolution* and *The Machiavellians*. During his lifetime, Burnham's writings influenced figures across the political spectrum—from George Orwell to Barry Goldwater, from Arthur Schlesinger Jr. to Ronald Reagan, from C. Wright Mills to Karl Popper. In the twenty-first century, Burnham has been called a neoconservative and a proto-Trumpist. In fact, two James Burnhams did exist: one an embryonic neocon, and the other a paleoconservative paragon.

The emergence of these two James Burnhams will be described in chapter 1. The teenage Burnham penned an essay extolling World War I, and his belief that violence could regenerate the world appeared in his writings for almost a half-century. First as a Marxist and later as a Cold Warrior, this James Burnham optimistically argued that democracy could prevail if force and power—sometimes even violence—were properly used. A second James Burnham who was skeptical and gloomy appeared during his college years. This side of Burnham, in its mature form, questioned true democracy and its future, maintaining it was always stifled by the ruling elite. Both James Burnhams remain politically significant.

Burnham first gained prominence as a thinker in the 1930s when he embraced Marxism in the wake of the Great Depression. The newly minted Marxist trumpeted Trotskyite positions to the American working class. In chapter 2, I show how the two James Burnhams manifested themselves during this time because according to cynical Marxists, the United States is a sham democracy in which the wealthy and powerful conspire against the masses. Violent revolution would sweep away this decrepit system, however. From 1933 to 1940, Burnham wrote dozens of articles for socialist journals expressing these viewpoints while attempting to foment socialist revolution.

Burnham began questioning Marxism in the late 1930s in the wake of Joseph Stalin's purges. The Nazi-Soviet Pact and the Soviet invasion of Poland further eroded his faith. He pivoted by challenging Trotsky's assumption that the Soviet Union was a state for the working class and openly disavowed Marxist concepts like the dialectic, the unity of opposites, and the inevitable victory of the proletariat. Stalin was not the problem in the USSR, he wrote. Marxism was. Trotsky fired back. Consistent with ideas that he had presented in his classic *The Revolution Betrayed* (1937), Trotsky had refused to fault Marxism. The revolutionary declared that Stalin and his bureaucratic clique had perverted the revolution. He blamed Burnham's inability to correctly interpret Soviet affairs on his bourgeois American upbringing. In chapter 3, I examine this dramatic breakup that was codified in important Trotskyite texts, such as "A Petty-Bourgeois Opposition in the Socialist Workers Party" (1939) and "An Open Letter to Comrade Burnham" (1940).

Burnham, now an apostate Marxist, embarked on a new intellectual journey. Yet he did not completely abandon the Marxist framework in the early 1940s—he just denied Marx's contention that the future belonged to the working classes. Burnham's new imminent ruling elite differed from Marx's because they were not defined by their economic class; according to Burnham, they took many forms. His book *The Managerial Revolution* (1941) foretells the rise of a new powerful caste composed of dreary bureaucrats, corporate managers, and technicians. In this work, Burnham describes their quest for power and the limitations they imposed on democracy. Some remnants of his Trotskyism can also be found in the book, such as the idea that a privileged bureaucratic elite held the levers of power. In chapter 4, I discuss *The Managerial Revolution* and its significance.

Burnham's next book, which I analyze in chapter 5, was a gloomy work titled *The Machiavellians* (1943). This treatise details the works of four thinkers the author called Machiavellians because of their realistic attitudes about human nature and society. Gaetano Mosca, Vilfredo Pareto, Robert Michels, and Georges Sorel were the subjects of this book, particularly their ideas about the elite and power. Burnham proclaims: "The Machiavellians present the complete record: the primary object, in practice, of all rulers is to serve their own interest, to maintain their own power and privilege. There are no exceptions."[1] Darkly reducing politics to a struggle for power, *The Machiavellians* teaches the reader to ignore the words of the ruling elite. It insists that democracy may be an unattainable ideal, but it must be fought for lest tyranny prevail. Burnham asserts that the perilous quest for some measure of democracy can be achieved only by resisting those in power because "only power restrains power."[2]

The Managerial Revolution and *The Machiavellians*, as I show in chapter 6, remain important texts. They inspired parts of George Orwell's *1984*, such as the dystopian book's idea that elites exercise power by manipulating the masses with words. And Burnham's two books have influenced a sect of conservatism called paleoconservatism. Members of this movement believe that the elite and bureaucratic state have gained too much power, at the expense of the people. Paleocons—asserting realism—claim that the struggle for power is natural in politics and society. Democracy is achieved by exercising power and resisting those with excessive power.

After World War II, Burnham turned his attention to foreign affairs and became one of America's foremost anticommunists. He wrote *The Struggle for the World* (1947), a classic in early Cold War history. In chapter 7, I describe how the former Marxist warns against Soviet expansion and insists that the United States must use power—possibly even violence—to confront the Soviet behemoth because a defensive strategy could never win. Contending that Americans need to be educated about the evils of communism and the threat it posed to Western civilization, Burnham argues that provincial isolationism no longer suffices in the dangerous postwar era. The new hardliner demands an American empire, specifically a soft empire through which the United States exerts its power and influence around the world against communism, not one that placed foreign nations under a US yoke. According to Burnham, parts of an American empire already existed in Europe, Japan, and the Philippines. To ensure success, the United States had to embrace its allies and make them recognize that they benefited by following it. He maintains that the US military must also be strengthened because it showed American resolve. Defeating the USSR was his ultimate goal because "the danger of this war will not disappear until the present

Soviet regime is overthrown, and world communism as a whole rendered impotent."[3] This work displays little optimism for the future as it suggests that all American political leaders could do in the struggle for the world was vacillate.

A cross-country trip in the late 1940s allowed Burnham to study Americans more intimately, and this led to some optimism. He began to believe that ordinary Americans did recognize that war raged. And that it had to be won. This positive view was displayed in his next Cold War work titled *The Coming Defeat of Communism* (1950). In chapter 8, I show how this book provided a road map for American Cold War triumph. Burnham asserts that the goal of US foreign policy should be to liberate the people of Eastern Europe from Soviet communism by employing both hard power and soft power—the latter he called political warfare—against the Soviets. Leaders within satellite states and the Catholic Church should be utilized because they provided an oppositional force to communism. Divides within the Soviet leadership must be provoked. The positive Burnham predicted that the United States would defeat communism; he proclaimed that the victory of democracy was inevitable.

Burnham was also a man of action. While composing important Cold War polemics, he worked for the Central Intelligence Agency (CIA). Here his mind teemed with ways to undermine communism, as I show in chapter 9, from planting rumors of Stalin's imminent assassination to capturing Soviet secret agents and injecting them with truth serum. He also became a critical figure in the CIA-funded Congress for Cultural Freedom, where Burnham and noncommunist liberals collaborated in their efforts to recruit intellectuals to their side of the Cold War. With Burnham's help, the congress sponsored anticommunist conferences and writers worldwide.

Burnham's staunch anticommunism extended domestically. He wanted to outlaw the Communist Party and he refused to condemn Joseph McCarthy or his congressional investigations. As McCarthyism became one of the central political issues of the age, Burnham called himself "anti-anti-McCarthyite." Another dramatic breakup followed because his neutrality toward McCarthy ended friendships and limited writing opportunities with left-wing journals. He was forced to resign from the editorial advisory board of *Partisan Review* over the issue and even the CIA grew wary of him. A colleague said that he had committed professional suicide.

Fortunately for Burnham, just as he was burning bridges with liberals, William F. Buckley was eager to start a new conservative magazine, one with a strong anticommunist and free-market slant. Burnham agreed to become a senior editor at *National Review*, and he became its second-most-important figure for the next twenty-three years. He would never have to criticize McCarthy here. Burnham's primary responsibility was to analyze foreign affairs, which for him meant emphasizing the Soviet threat. He wanted to raise consciousness about the raging power struggle—one he thought that the Soviets were waging more successfully. Burnham usually portrayed US foreign policymakers as bumbling; he lambasted containment and détente policies, believing that they benefited only the Soviets. He called for the United States to invest heavily in its military because the Soviets could not win an arms race. As the Vietnam War escalated, the Cold Warrior demanded that the United States show strength. Disarmament was counterproductive for Burnham. He believed that US security—and hence its national interest—was promoted by using hard power in Vietnam. Burnham later explained America's failure by claiming she had not used enough force. As I reveal in chapters 10 and 11, geopolitical affairs dominated his attention, but he occasionally wrote about America's turbulent domestic scene from 1955 to 1978.

Despite his position at America's most important conservative magazine Burnham never considered himself a conservative Republican. He preferred the liberal Nelson Rockefeller over Barry Goldwater. Distrusting ideologues on both sides of the political spectrum, unlike most of his *National Review* colleagues, Burnham's economic philosophy revealed his skepticism of what he called "the theoretical world of von Misean abstractions."[4] He showcases his distrust of US liberal ideology in *Suicide of the West* (1964), another bleak work predicting that if liberalism prevailed, the West was doomed. He argues that communism posed the greatest threat to Western civilization and that only by defeating communism could the West survive. Burnham, however, questions liberalism's ability to thwart communism because liberals did not view communists as their enemies. Challenging a myriad of liberal assumptions, the book attempts to show liberalism's irrational side. Adopting positions from Edmund Burke, Burnham denounces what he called liberalism's incessant need for reform.

Burnham may have eschewed ideology, but various conservatives drew from his thought after his writing career ended in 1978. Ronald Reagan, for example, evoked Burnham's writings on multiple occasions before and after becoming president. One contemporary writer called Burnham "Reagan's Geopolitical Genius."[5] Reagan followed Burnham's advice by pursuing an arms race, insisting the Soviets could not keep up.

Containment did not suffice for the fortieth president, either. Consistent with the first James Burnham, Reagan optimistically believed that the Soviet Union could be defeated if the United States properly showed its strength.

The fall of the Soviet Union suggested to some that the United States could promote democracy in other parts of the world. Irving and Bill Kristol helped bring Burnham's ideas to the neoconservative movement that gained momentum in the aftermath of the Cold War. A former Trotskyite and colleague of Burnham's, Irving Kristol is considered a founder of neoconservatism, and his son Bill is recognized as one of the leaders of the movement. In 1996, Bill Kristol and Robert Kagan wrote "Toward a Neo-Reaganite Foreign Policy" for *Foreign Affairs*. The article could have been titled "Toward a Neo-Burnhamite Foreign Policy" because it contained the central ideas from *The Struggle for the World*: explicitly rejecting neo-isolationism, it demanded American leadership in the world.[6] The most powerful nation on Earth could not retreat in the post–Cold War era. Kristol and Kagan advocated a "benevolent hegemony," one whereby the United States would exert disproportionate power around the world.[7] They argued that the United States already exerted tremendous influence globally, such as in the Persian Gulf, Haiti, and the former Yugoslavia, and that Americans needed to be better educated about the nature of the global leadership position that had fallen to them. The article insisted that "America's allies are in a better position than those who are not its allies."[8] Kristol and Kagan also recommended a more robust military budget.

At the same time, certain paleoconservatives continued to advance the ideas of the less idealistic and gloomy second James Burnham. This Burnham has been identified as a forerunner to Donald Trump's rise to power.[9] One link between Burnham and Trump supporters is Samuel Francis. Francis was inspired by *The Managerial Revolution*, *The Machiavellians*, and *The Suicide of the West*, not his mentor's Cold War writings. Focusing on Burnham's realism and his emphasis on the human need for power, Francis considered Burnham a paleoconservative, like himself. He stressed Burnham's defense of Congress (as opposed to neoconservatives who, for Francis, favored an active executive branch); Burnham's support for tradition; and, finally, Burnham's criticism of liberal universalism. Francis also distrusted the elite, a group he associated with corporate managers and bureaucrats, believing that they posed a threat to the American middle class, the American way of life, and even American democracy.

The same month in which Kristol and Kagan argued in the *New York Times* that the United States must use power to remove Saddam Hussein, the paleoconservative Francis wrote about a group he called "Middle American Radicals."[10] The pessimistic Francis suggests that democracy was an illusion for them because as American ruling elites (with the help of the bureaucracy) thrive in Washington, DC, these Middle Americans are "excluded from meaningful political participation."[11] Disproportionally White and middle-class, this group feels powerless as globalization threatened their way of life and their nation. While Kristol and Kagan used Burnham's ideas to justify a more aggressive and international US foreign policy, Francis demands an "America First" approach. This means promoting US economic and geopolitical interests above any cosmopolitan or humanitarian ideals. Pat Buchanan initially carried his political torch. It would be passed to Trump. The president harnessed sentiments that can be found in Burnham's and Francis's writings, even some Trotskyite ones, such as the idea that a privileged bureaucratic elite hold the levers of power. They need to be thwarted in the name of democracy.

Scholarly writings have tended to focus on the two Burnhams separately, with some asserting that he was a neocon in embryo, while others (particularly in the wake of Trump's election) stress his theory of elites. Christopher Hitchens, also a one-time leftist who moved to the right, was in the former group. He called Burnham, "the real intellectual founder of the neoconservative movement."[12] Hitchens described what he believed to be Burnham's foremost contribution to neoconservatism: the necessity of an "American Empire."[13] Along similar lines, an academic article titled "The First Neo-conservative: James Burnham and the Origins of a Movement" argues that Burnham displayed the "psychological signatures of the neo-conservative mind: an abhorrence of containment and a willingness to seize the offensive moment and a respect for 'empire.'"[14] In this article, the author accurately describes Burnham's "aggressive, Manichean language" and emphasizes links between Burnham's ideas and those of other neoconservatives, like Bill Kristol and Kagan.

Another neoconservative interpretation came from former *National Review* staffer Daniel Kelly. His *James Burnham and the Struggle for the World* (2002) interprets Burnham as progenitor of the neoconservative movement. According to Kelly, Burnham's "general stance—secular, empirical, modernist, resigned to the welfare state as inevitable in a mass industrial society, emphatic on the need for victory in the struggle for the world—afforded a preview of the neo-conservatism of the 1970s."[15] In his book,

Kelly quotes the *National Review* senior editor Richard Brookhiser's description of Burnham as "the first of the neocons."[16] Kelly's book is a solid personal biography that successfully introduces the reader to Burnham's life, but it was published more than twenty years ago. Much has changed in the United States since 2002, such as the war in Iraq, the COVID-19 pandemic, and the rise of a political figure who promised to make America great again by limiting the power of the elites.

Donald Trump's unexpected rise inspired new interest in the alleged paleoconservative Burnham. Michael Lind assesses Burnham in *The New Class War: Saving America from the Managerial Elite* (2020). Lind's work is admittingly a neo-Burnhamite treatise in that it interprets politics as a power conflict between classes, but these classes are not defined by their wealth. Lind describes the "native working-class populism" of groups who have been excluded from the political process, especially non-college-educated Americans.[17] They struggle against "technocratic neoliberal elites" with college degrees.[18] Over the past half-century, Lind maintains, the elites have gained too much power and democracy has withered. Enter Trump.

Burnham's seeming culpability in the rise of Trump has earned him the wrath of left-wing writers. The scholar Alan Wald, for example, wrote in 2017: "How seriously should we take the head-spinning makeover of an upper-class philosophy professor? Shouldn't we laugh at James Burnham, who started out lecturing Leon Trotsky on revolutionary strategy and ended up running a rogue CIA operation with mobster Frank Costello to kidnap American communists and pump them full of sodium pentothal?"[19] Wald describes Burnham's attempt to help orchestrate the 1953 coup in Iran, his belief that the United States should use chemical weapons in Vietnam, and his support for colonialism. This recent criticism of Burnham underscores his contemporary significance.

Unlike these works, in this intellectual biography, I show the historical significance of James Burnham by exploring his main books and their historical importance in depth. This book analyzes thinkers that inspired Burnham, such as Aquinas, Marx, Lenin, Trotsky, Machiavelli, and, at his most mature, Edmund Burke (Burnham was a Europhile). For example, *The Managerial Revolution* was partly a neo-Trotskyite treatise that shaped some contemporary conservative attitudes. And Burnham's Cold War polemics, which neoconservatives have appropriated, largely inverted Marxism-Leninism-Trotskyism. I describe how diverse writers, such as Aquinas, Marx, Lenin, Trotsky, Machiavelli, and Burke, have nourished the two James Burnhams who remain important for twenty-first century American political discourse.

Burnham's broader political philosophies will not be defended or condemned in this book. Although it is about a political philosopher, this is not a work of political philosophy. Any seeming sympathy for Burnham's ideas—whether his Marxism or his anticommunism—are attempts to explicate his ideas so they can be understood. Readers can determine the validity of these ideas on their own.

Chapter 1

The Young Burnham

James Burnham was born in Chicago in 1905 into a wealthy family. His father Claude immigrated from England in the 1880s and settled in Chicago where he became a successful railroad executive.[1] In 1904, Claude married Burnham's mother, Mary Mae Gillis.[2] Claude was Protestant, Mary Mae was Catholic, and James was reared in the Catholic faith.

The life of the teenage James (Jim to those who knew him) Burnham bears an uncanny resemblance to one of the most famous protagonists of his youth, Amory Blaine of F. Scott Fitzgerald's *This Side of Paradise*. The novel took the nation by storm when it was published in 1920. Burnham would have easily identified with Blaine because Burnham was also a teenage, second-generation, Upper Midwesterner who was raised by a Catholic mother in relative wealth. Like Fitzgerald's character (or maybe because of him), Burnham aspired to be a writer. The year after *This Side of Paradise* was published, Burnham even moved to Connecticut to attend the same type of posh Catholic high school that Blaine had attended. It was called Canterbury School (John F. Kennedy briefly attended the school in 1930).

Burnham arrived there in 1921. The school probably appealed to the Burnhams because although it was Catholic, it still promoted Ivy League colleges, which traditional Catholic schools rarely did due to their Protestant heritage. Canterbury was unique for its time because it was run by Catholic laymen. Burnham would go on to receive some of the highest grades and test scores in Canterbury's school's history.[3]

An essay Burnham wrote as a student in 1923 was a harbinger of some of his significant political views. Burnham and his fellow classmates were asked, "Do present conditions in America stimulate the production of literature?" Burnham answered in the affirmative, predicting that the United States would be transformed by World War I. He wrote: "The Great War produced an upheaval of all economic and social conditions. It changed life in every way; it revivified existence; it gave renewed impetus to everything."[4] Optimistically he wrote: "Present conditions in America, however, are perhaps the greatest stimulus there has ever been to literature, to the production of real literature."[5] Burnham contended that young people especially would live to write.[6]

The essay's most remarkable feature, given Burnham's future intellectual development, is the idea that war leads to progress. Although nothing in the essay question about American literature suggested anything about war, the future Cold War hardliner makes this connection. During the early 1920s, most Americans saw World War I as a catastrophe—more than one hundred thousand Americans had died seemingly for nothing, but the teenage Burnham found redeeming features in the conflict. The idea that war could improve the world would be a hallmark of his thinking for almost a half-century.

After graduating high school, Burnham (like Fitzgerald's character Blaine) attended Princeton. This traditionally Protestant university was changing during the early twentieth century as Protestantism began losing its cultural, political, social, and intellectual hegemony in the United States. The influx of Jewish and, like the Burnhams, Catholic immigrants from Europe in the second half of the nineteenth century contributed to this change. By the 1920s, Princeton went from exclusively to mostly Protestant; Catholics and Jews by now made up almost 15 percent of the university's freshman class.[7]

Along with religious pluralism, secularism became widespread among American college students during this time. Religious unbelief spread like an epidemic. During the Roaring Twenties, many young adults rebelled against the Victorian values that seemingly led to the World War I calamity. Regular attendance at chapel services, which had been mandatory at Princeton since its birth, were reduced. Required biblical classes were jettisoned shortly before Burnham's arrival, too. A survey in 1927 (the year Burnham graduated) by the *Daily Princetonian* found that although most Princeton students rejected atheism, they slightly preferred agnosticism to theism.[8] Around this time, Burnham would be in the minority who espoused atheism.[9]

Apolitical during his college years, the soon-to-be scholar invested much of his time in the study of literature and philosophy. In *This Side of Paradise*, Blaine remarks, "I'm in a superior class. You are, too. We're philosophers."[10] Burnham, like Fitzgerald's character, wrote for Princeton's *Nassau Literary Magazine*. One of his stories, titled "Through a Glass, Darkly," was written in 1925 when Burnham was nineteen. Flashes of the second gloomy James Burnham appear in this essay. It describes a man desperate to find a wife to bear him a child so he can pass on the family name and farm. In his thirties, the man meets a wonderful woman named Helen whom he marries, only to have her pass away during childbirth.[11] For this James Burnham, any ray of light (such as the birth of a child) became a precursor to night; one would have to accept life's darker shades.

Burnham excelled at Princeton. One of his literary professors wrote that he had "without any question one the finest brains I have encountered in all my years at Princeton."[12] His extracurricular activities included tennis, golf, bridge, and a Catholic club.[13] He boxed, too, and apparently threw a strong punch.[14] Burnham never really stopped throwing punches; attacking others would become part of his writing style. He needed sparring partners.

After graduating from Princeton at the top of his class, the budding intellectual matriculated at Balliol College, Oxford, where he studied with one of the twentieth century's great Catholic thinkers, Martin D'Arcy. By now Burnham had left the Catholic faith, but the Jesuit priest still influenced him. D'Arcy wrote *St. Thomas Aquinas* (1930), *The Nature of Belief* (1931), and *Belief and Reason* (1946). D'Arcy used Aquinas's style of syllogisms when teaching.[15] For Aquinas, reason buttressed faith, and the great Catholic scholastic employed the method of reason to understand the world several centuries before Enlightenment philosophers. Aquinas (drawing from Aristotle) would posit an argument, such as the following: "It seems that God does not exist; because if one of two contraries be infinite, the other would be altogether destroyed. But the word God means that He is infinite goodness. If, therefore, God existed, there would be no evil discoverable; but there is evil in the world. Therefore God does not exist."[16] He would then refute the argument, using reason. D'Arcy continued this approach, and so would the mature Burnham.

The emphasis on logical reasoning in the works of Aquinas and D'Arcy molded his intellectual development because Burnham would fashion himself a logician. More so than most intellectuals, Burnham excelled at exploiting logical weaknesses in others. He routinely employed syllogisms. And he practiced the scholastic method of disputation that involved presenting arguments that he may or may not have agreed with as a means to stimulate debate in search of truth. Burnham became steeped in the method of Aquinas and taught courses on him at New York University.[17]

The influence of Aquinas and D'Arcy may explain why although Burnham professed atheism for most of his adult life, he was not antireligion. He condemned many social phenomena in his life, but religion escaped his wrath, even as a young Marxist. His attitude toward religion resembled that of George Santayana, who, although an atheist, deemed religion a benign force with some redeeming characteristics. He respected spiritual life. For Santayana, religion had a social benefit, like poetry. He believed it should not be studied scientifically any more than should other pieces of literature. Santayana called himself an "aesthetic Catholic," which was a good way to describe Burnham, who certainly read some of Santayana's works on religion at Princeton and Oxford.[18]

While Burnham was at Oxford, his father died at the early age of forty-seven. Burnham was twenty-two. His father's unexpected death was a shock, so Burnham had no time to prepare and say his goodbye. The event did provoke Burnham's brother, David, to write a quasi-biographical novel titled *This Is Our Exile*. Biographer Daniel Kelly called it a "literary semiportrait of [James] Burnham."[19] F. Scott Fitzgerald did not like the book, but it did interest Santayana, who wondered if the pessimism depicted in the book was a realistic depiction of American culture.[20]

The novel details the patriarch's death and its impact on the family. James Burnham provided inspiration for the character Fred, who is away studying in Europe at the time.[21] Fred handles his father's death philosophically. He advises his mother shortly after his father's passing: "It's quite natural for you to feel a certain despondency. I don't ask you to go around humming dance tunes. Your life has lost what, rightly or not, was its chief interest. The thing to do now is to develop other interests."[22] Like a young graduate student studying philosophy and literature, Burnham tried to rationalize his emotions. Given that he was beginning to enter a life of mind, the death of his father became just another topic to smugly apply the philosophical method.

Burnham's own apparent stoicism did not fool his family, however. His brother wrote in *This Is Our Exile*, "You have never heard Fred's motto: 'Let nothing be necessary to you.' Fred prides himself on the fact that he doesn't want anybody. Fred has no emotions."[23] In response to this, another character perceptively replies: "You mean you can watch how excited he can get over a little horse-race and still not realize that, whatever he tries to do or tries not to do, Fred's one of the most emotional people—directly emotional—we know; much more so than your mother even."[24] The future philosophy professor may have presented himself as an even-keeled intellectual, but those closest to him knew better. His passions were never really concealed. Writing gave Burnham an outlet to release his emotions, always at the expense of some individual or idea.

In the summer of 1929, Burnham completed his schooling at Oxford and returned to the United States. The ensuing Great Depression had no direct impact on him. He secured a teaching position at a New York University satellite campus where he initially taught courses on Aquinas, Dante, aesthetics, and the Renaissance.[25] Burnham also published one textbook, cowritten with his former philosophy professor Philip E. Wheelwright, titled *Introduction to Philosophical Analysis* (1932). Intended to train aspiring philosophers in the art of reasoning, the work is a study of basic philosophical concepts. It includes chapters on "Logical Structure," "Factual Reasoning," "Moral Values," and "Religion." The book calls Marx's dogmatic approach the opposite of the philosophical approach.[26] Even the dialectal method is challenged.[27] It would be Burnham's sole academic work.

He also collaborated with Wheelwright on *Symposium*, a journal intended to provide a forum for critical discussion about contemporary intellectual issues. This journal was his first real intellectual outlet after finishing school. Its inaugural issue, published in 1930, stated that its purpose was to study "ideas rather than events, with analysis rather than consequences."[28] The journal initially pledged not to promote any sect or cause, but the persistence of the Great Depression and American suffering changed this. One of Burnham's political overtures in 1931 was the study of Marxism. It condemned the philosophy as "perhaps the most degrading ideology that has ever been imposed on a large section of mankind."[29] The editor's opinion about the antibourgeois ideology would soon change.

This next phase in Burnham's intellectual development baffled his friends and biographers; many have wondered how someone so genteel could embrace revolutionary Marxism.[30] One explanation is the Great Depression: economic crisis radicalized the young man. But personal circumstances should also be at least partly considered. In 1931,

Burnham met a vivacious young woman named Martha Dodd, and they were engaged to be married.[31] He wrote to her: "I remember your kisses soft light like a petal brushing like the wing brushes Dante's forehead . . . these times I remember."[32] But it was not to be. The engagement was broken off in early 1932 as she had been having an affair with another man.[33] It seems Dodd never took Burnham and their engagement too seriously. It was the second time in four years that he had been abruptly abandoned by someone he loved. Could this trauma have helped radicalize the soon-to-be Marxist's political thought? Burnham himself insisted at the very end of his intellectual career that "political man . . . is seldom a rational animal. Confronting a political issue, most of us try to present our point of view with a respectable overlay of rational-sounding rhetoric, but you can still hear the drumbeats throbbing underneath."[34] Burnham, who would go from Marxist to one of America's most hardline anticommunists, insisted that deeper irrational forces guide the political writer.

Chapter 2

Embracing Marxism

In 1932, Burnham began to entertain political ideas, even some radical ones. On the surface, the bourgeois professor was the epitome of balance and moderation. He was a dapper dresser, and his smooth, calm writing style seemed to match his ostensible temperament. But intellectually, Burnham went to extremes, albeit with the flat rhetoric of a logician. Instead of promoting the New Deal policies of Franklin D. Roosevelt (FDR), Burnham sprinted left, embracing Marxism. Revolutionary Marxism—the idea that human salvation required the activity of leading individuals—seduced Burnham, like it did so many others, because it gave him a cause to fight for, a way to change the world. He dove in headfirst.

Burnham's first source on revolutionary Marxism was Sydney Hook, a philosophy colleague at New York University (NYU). Burnham could not have found a better mentor if he wanted to leave armchair philosophy. Hook's interpretation of Marxism can be found in the July 1931 edition of *Symposium*, in which his essay "Towards the Understanding of Karl Marx" appeared.[1] Late nineteenth- and early twentieth-century German socialists used the voting booth to gain some concessions for the working classes. Hook contended that this pacified workers and even Marxist leaders. Seeking to exploit the turmoil of the Great Depression, Hook maintained in *Symposium* that revolutionaries were required because "power is bestowed neither by God nor the economic process. It must be taken. When Marx spoke of communism as being a result of 'social necessity,' he was referring to the resultant of the whole social process, one of whose components was the development of objective social conditions, the other, the assertion of a revolutionary class will."[2] Hook insisted that economic determinism did not mean that all human affairs are preordained. He believed that political activity is good, but revolutionary activity is better.

Hook pulled Burnham away from the metaphysics of Aquinas and toward the world of politics and revolution by championing Marxist revolutionaries, such as V. I. Lenin, Rosa Luxemburg, and Leon Trotsky. Insisting that Marxism was more than a determinist philosophy, they all demanded action in what for them was a daily struggle against capitalism. Something always had to be done for Burnham, too. For the next forty-five years, he would emulate Lenin, Trotsky, and Luxemburg by preaching ideas that inspired action. And he always argued against those who wanted to wait. The struggle must always occur everywhere. All that changed over the decades was the opponent.

This call for action was just one theme from "Towards the Understanding of Karl Marx" that Burnham would employ for the rest of his intellectual career. Other specific concepts from the essay that the new man of action would utilize include Hook's argument (based on the ideas of Luxemburg) that the goal of the proletariat movement was not the establishment of socialism, but the *"conquest of political power."*[3] Power was at the heart of the struggle; it was the beginning and the end. And this seizure of power primarily depended on "will and organization."[4] Determined individuals must lead. Burnham always exhorted these themes, in one form or another.

Hook's works on Marxism piqued Burnham's intellectual interest in the movement, but Leon Trotsky's *History of the Russian Revolution* (1932), which had just been published in English, started a fire. Trotsky's three-volume tome is relentlessly Marxist; it reduces even worldviews to economics. It extols the prescience of Lenin, who recognized that Russian workers were poised to revolt, and the Bolshevik Party, which "created not only a political but a moral medium of its own, independent of bourgeois social opinion and implacably opposed to it."[5] For Trotsky, the 1917 revolutions saw the masses fulfill their historic destiny by becoming rulers.[6] What about his biases? The revolutionary scorned historians who sought to "stand on the wall" with "objective" works of history; they only promoted reactionary forces.[7]

Trotsky's classic cast a spell over the Burnham. In his review for *Symposium*, the editor gushed at the book's style, describing it as a "rapid succession of events, concisely given persons, clear analogies in the form of similes and metaphors . . . compact, logical structure, and throughout the powerful dialectic of historical materialism."[8] Giving life to large historical forces and protagonists, Trotsky's historical method provided the philosophy professor a new way to analyze the past. Whereas history traditionally had been written about great figures, Burnham recognized that this method provided limited understanding of society in an industrial age when impersonal forces shaped the world as much or more than individuals. Trotsky's Marxist method was an alternative. For example, Russia seemed the least likely European country to advance to socialism. Burnham asserts that Trotsky explained her progress without resorting to great figures. Trotsky argues, according to Burnham, that Russia's belated industrial development meant that during World War I "a much larger percentage of Russian workers were employed in giant industries than in other countries, and these workers were conscious of themselves as a class, better trained in political strikes, more aware of the inadequacy of the bankrupt bourgeoisie."[9] Parroting Trotsky, Burnham claims that the seemingly backward Russian nation became the vanguard of the proletarian revolution because its working class was most affected by the imperialist war of 1914–1918. A class possessed, the Russian proletariat surged ahead.

Burnham's review notes that although Trotsky believed in the inevitable victory of the proletariat, he was not a rigid historical determinist.[10] The dialectic did not equate fatalism. Trotsky wanted to create a space for great men to participate on the historical stage. Not bound by determinism, they could become historical protagonists. The Russian Revolution showed that leading individuals—with free will—could propel history forward.

Burnham grappled with this issue of free will versus historical determinism his entire writing career. Like most Marxists, he would usually mix some form of historical inevitability with the notion that individuals mattered, too. Sometimes the first James Burnham would optimistically predict that with the assistance of determined individuals willing to use force, inexorable historical trends were blowing the world toward some form of democracy. More often, the second James Burnham expressed little confidence for democracy's future, although he occasionally left a small window open for the same resolute individuals to alter its course. Burnham's world was always moving somewhere. All that changed was where, and would anyone do anything about it?

The world was changing dramatically when the next issue of *Symposium* appeared in April 1933 as the Roosevelt administration launched the New Deal. Over the next five years, dozens of new government agencies were created along with a cast of bureaucrats who would alter the American social, economic, and political landscape. In response, Burnham and Wheelwright cowrote "Thirteen Propositions," a statement of the journal's principles and how they related to current affairs. Rejecting communism but embracing some Marxist language, Burnham and Wheelwright declared that capitalism had failed. The piece argues that its degrading effects "threaten to destroy all vestiges of Civilization in a series of increasingly violent imperialist wars," and that capitalism cannot reform itself.[11] Collectivization must be applied to property relations, even if it means revolution. Like Hook, the authors believed that parliamentary means might not suffice; violent and nonlegal measures may be required.[12] The exact details will be left "for history to decide."[13] The editors rejected Soviet communism because conditions in the United States in 1933 differed from those in Russia in 1917. Nonetheless, they insisted that profound change must occur, even beyond the New Deal.

By July 1933, Burnham's writing style had changed. It began to resemble the Marxist style that would characterize his articles for the next seven years. His articles became less precise and more dogmatic. The kind of unequivocal declarative statements that he cautioned against in *Introduction to Philosophical Analysis* became routine. An example comes from the July1933 edition of *Symposium* in which he reviewed *The Modern Corporation and Private Property* (1932) by Adolf Berle and Gardiner Means. A classic in management and corporate law, the book describes the decline of firms in which the same group of people controlled all aspects of the corporation. Berle and Means describe how, in the early 1900s, individual capitalist owners began relinquishing control of businesses to managers, thereby losing direct control of the means of production. Now, corporations existed with two important and different groups: the stockholders who invested in the company, and the managers (or experts) who actually ran the company. The latter had little economic investment in the company, so they would be less likely to resist government intervention in the corporation, as long as their professional interests were not threatened. The book also notes the increased concentration of wealth that had occurred in the United States during the 1920s.

Burnham praised the work, claiming that no more significant book had been published in the United States in years.[14] He declared, "The negative conclusions of the book are inescapable, incontrovertible; and they are faced by the authors with complete and admirable clarity. In three short brilliant chapters... they smash the 'American Myth' beyond its restorative ability of even the most skillful bourgeois surgeon-economist."[15] The review contends that Berle and Means had shown that wealth was increasingly being concentrated into the hands of "economic autocrats."[16] For Burnham, the book provided evidence for the Marxist theory of surplus value because the appendix showed that 0.4 percent of the population received 78.9 percent of stock dividends. He maintained that Berle and Means had effectively used the dialectic in showing that the changes in the American capitalist system had created an "objective opposition" that gave rise to an "active struggle of interests."[17] What the authors did not understand was that the changes they described were not changes within capitalism—they were changes from capitalism toward a new social order.[18]

The review also foreshadowed another hallmark of Burnham's writings: an incisive criticism of President Roosevelt and his administration. Burnham argues that the president reduced unemployment by merely hiring workers at the lowest possible wages. Sure, Roosevelt desired a *just wage*, but who determines what a just wage is? The burgeoning Marxist argues that because there were two main classes, the state must always favor the dominant class. He laments that big banks and Wall Street did not have to fear Roosevelt.[19] Burnham predicts that class consciousness would continue to grow; the president and his allies could not stop what was coming.

His October 1933 contribution to *Symposium* expressed even starker Marxist sentiments. It partly responded to T. S. Eliot, who critiqued the editors of *Symposium* for placing political and economic issues above moral ones in "Thirteen Propositions."[20] Burnham argues that the primary distinction between himself and Eliot was that Burnham wanted to overthrow bourgeoisie property rights, whereas Eliot defended them.[21] The young editor asks, why tell the worker to be a good family man when his whole subsistence depends on the profits he could generate? How could one tell a woman to go to church on Sunday when she could not afford a coat or shoes?[22] Burnham states that although he did not support everything the Communist Party stood for, he still supported it, much more so than he had six months earlier.[23] He even proclaims that he accepted the dictatorship of the proletariat.[24]

A new Burnham emerged in the fall of 1933. He wrote that until this time his Marxism had been merely "theoretical."[25] Now, his support for the ideology was "unequivocal."[26] Burnham attributed this change to personal experiences, writing in the *Symposium* that his travels to places like Detroit and cities in Illinois showed him class struggle in action as factory workers struggled with owners.[27] During the Ford Hunger March of 1932, several thousand Detroit autoworkers marched to Dearborn, where clashes followed between the police and protesters. Four men were killed.[28] In the spring of 1933 in Chicago, after working for weeks without pay, thousands of teachers stormed and desecrated banks. Armed with textbooks, the teachers were beaten with clubs.[29] In the throes of the Great Depression, the revolution seemingly loomed. Burnham even began mentoring members of the Young Communist League in hopes of hastening revolution.[30] By 1933, the philosophy professor had become radicalized. A personal rift developed between Burnham and Wheelwright. The year 1933 would be *Symposium*'s last.

At the behest of Hook, the neophyte Marxist joined the American Workers Party (AWP) in late 1933.[31] It was an American-centered, less authoritarian alternative to the Moscow-directed Communist Party of the United States of America (CPUSA), and one that the professors believed could actually ignite revolution in America.[32] The AWP's Statement of Programmatic Orientation called the CPUSA a failure.[33] It accused the Communist Party of failing to radicalize American workers and advance their interests. The party had even brought discredit to communism.[34] Promising to succeed where the CPUSA had failed, the statement pledged to establish "a free workers' democracy."[35]

Creating an alternative to the CPUSA allowed Burnham to establish his independent Marxist identity. Through the AWP, he could use his intellectual talents to influence the world. The party was originally led by A. J. Muste, a former clergyman who became radicalized during World War I. He still used Christian concepts to buttress his Marxist viewpoints. In an essay called "Pacificism and Class War," he compares the working classes to Jesus: although Jesus was deemed a social disturber, it was really those in power who disturbed the social order.[36] The strikers could be blamed for violence and upheaval, but it was those in power who founded a system based on violence and created social upheaval.[37] Muste asserts, "In a world built on violence, one must be a revolutionary before one can be a pacifist."[38] Under certain circumstances, Muste rationalized violence. Burnham would do the same.[39]

Burnham became a respected member of the new party, but he always seemed a bit detached. Reluctant to subordinate everything to the imminent revolution, he continued teaching at NYU.[40] By now married, he lived in an upscale area of New York City where he mostly associated with his old college friends and family.[41] Burnham gave to the party, yet he did not give everything. Fellow Marxist intellectual James Cannon called him the classic "petty-bourgeois intellectual," meaning he wanted to teach the workers without fully integrating himself in the movement.[42] As Hook recalled decades later, "there was something bizarre about this scion of a wealthy Midwestern Catholic industrialist, a product of Princeton and Oxford, who had delivered his oration as a class valedictorian in Latin, entering the lists as a protagonist of the working class."[43] Like Superman, Burnham had a dual identity: on one hand, he was an even-keeled, modest philosophy professor, and on the other, he was a radical revolutionary, trying to save the world from bourgeoisie capitalism. (Except Burnham sometimes did not change his wardrobe; he would travel from upscale cocktail parties to communist committee meetings dressed in formal dinner attire.)[44]

The new party member never connected with the average American worker, either personally or intellectually. Workers he addressed found him condescending.[45] Hook stated that whenever Burnham spoke, he lost support for his cause.[46] The young philosopher was too consumed with reason because he assumed that human beings would naturally gravitate toward logical arguments, regardless of how they were presented. The mature Burnham would know better; he would recognize that nonrational impulses could steer human thought. He would even go on to teach courses on irrationalism at NYU.[47]

Burnham was more persuasive with the typewriter; he wrote forcefully using Marxist terminology. Burnham's first Marxist polemic for a national magazine appeared in a 1934 issue of *The Nation*. It responded to a piece called "Was Europe a Success?" by Joseph Krutch. Krutch argues that the rise of the Nazis and communists meant the death of Europe because they rejected traditional European values, such as freedom, democracy, and Christianity. Therefore, Europe was dead. But had it been a success? In a piece that appeared in the same section as responses from Albert Einstein, Bertrand Russell, H. L. Mencken, and Aldous Huxley, the new socialist avers that the revolution in Russia did not reject traditional European values but fulfilled them.[48] Krutch championed freedom as a European value and Burnham agrees while insisting that freedom had no "absolute" meaning; it existed only in the abstract. And because Krutch wrote as a capitalist, he interpreted freedom in a way promoted by capitalists. The socialist championed the socialist conception of freedom—freedom from exploitation and economic insecurity. Krutch's worldview—his definition of terms—would disappear.

Burnham insists that only by embracing socialism could Europe fulfill her true destiny. Only by embracing socialism would it be possible to achieve real civilization.[49]

Roosevelt always bore the brunt of Burnham's attacks. He relentlessly attacked the administration and its policies in a series of articles titled "THEIR Government."[50] Noting in one article that Roosevelt had recently dined with J. P. Morgan, Burnham interprets this meeting as symbolizing a "new stage" of Roosevelt's capitalism. The first stage was characterized by presidential rhetoric that sounded sometimes "liberal" and even "radical" because the public demanded change.[51] It frustrated the capitalists, however, who now forced Roosevelt to promote the interests of the bankers. This would characterize the next stage of Roosevelt's plan. Burnham cynically maintains that Roosevelt shrewdly used liberal slogans as cover for his reactionary program. He would emphasize the disconnect between words and actions for the next forty years.

In another article, the rising Marxist star declares that the depression had not yet killed capitalism, but it had left it "bruised and broken."[52] Burnham states that Roosevelt was merely playing the role of doctor, with the Agricultural Adjustment Act being a cast and the Civil Works Administration being iodine. The capitalists would use any tactic to preserve their system. Laws were flouted merely to protect the bourgeoisie; they were enforced when they benefited the ruling class and ignored when they did not. Burnham opined that capitalism may not be worth saving—maybe it should be killed now to put it out of its misery.[53] For the communist sympathizer, it was time to sweep aside capitalism and its representatives, like Roosevelt.

The revolution had to be led by great men. Burnham loved this idea, too. He idolized Lenin and Trotsky. In *What Is to Be Done?* (1902), Lenin demands that full-time, dedicated, professional revolutionaries prepare the masses for revolution because "no revolutionary movement can endure without a stable organization of leaders that maintains continuity."[54] Worker advancement needed external assistance. The book asserts that training and preparing the masses was the intellectual's moral duty. Burnham always believed that the masses must be led by the elite, wherever he found himself on the political spectrum. Like Lenin, he always viewed himself as part of the intellectual elite whose writings were intended to inspire the masses.

Burnham showed his affinity for the great man in history in his review of *Lenin*, written by British Communist Party member Ralph Fox in 1933. The review venerates Lenin by contending that the world's greatest leader had orchestrated its greatest revolution.[55] Lenin's new student argues that the Bolshevik successfully subordinated everything to the interests of the working class, making him the opposite of demagogues, like Hitler or Roosevelt. The latter exploited the masses for their own interests, whereas Lenin showed the masses their strength. Burnham concludes that a man as great as Lenin deserved an equally fitting biography. Fox's work did not suffice because despite presenting many facts about Lenin, it failed to use them judiciously to describe the historical background that shaped Lenin.[56]

The young Burnham's apathy about politics evaporated after studying Hook, Lenin, and Trotsky. The November 1934 midterm elections piqued his interest. Despite his criticisms and the persistence of the Great Depression, FDR's Democratic Party gained seats, something neither party had done since the Civil War. Burnham minimized the results by declaring in a "THEIR Government" article that elections under capitalism resembled prisoners electing new wardens. The prisoners could choose from among a few candidates, and they would be told this was freedom and democracy. Burnham asserts that one warden may be kinder than the other, but the inmates remained in jail. The election changed nothing; revolution was still needed to displace Roosevelt.[57]

In December 1934, the AWP merged with the Trotskyite Communist League of America (CLA), led by James Cannon and Max Shachtman, to form the Workers Party of the United States (WPUS). Cannon viewed the union as an opportunity to expand communist propaganda and activities.[58] Shachtman recalled that both sides were united over their interest in theoretical questions, internationalism, and a struggle against Stalinism.[59] The merger also increased Burnham's proximity to Trotsky, something that may have motivated his support. Burnham had gained Trotsky's attention with his review of *The Russian Revolution*.[60] Alan Wald wrote of the now twenty-nine-year-old Burnham: "To the Trotskyite movement he brought some special qualities: a breadth of cultural knowledge, a writing style free of Marxist cliches, an aura of objectivity and impartiality, and a fresh perspective on indigenous political issues."[61] Burnham often used the pen name John West, again suggesting a dual identity.

When Burnham entered the WPUS, a divide existed between Trotsky and Stalin, one precipitated by Lenin's death. Trotsky appeared to be the superior candidate to replace Lenin, but Stalin outmaneuvered him. Portraying himself as Lenin's designated heir, Stalin exploited Trotsky's association with the Mensheviks; Trotsky had not even joined the ranks of the Bolsheviks until 1917. The Georgian also used his own position as secretary of the party to strengthen his hand—because most Communist Party members owed their position to Stalin, they remained loyal to him. The exiled and outcast Trotsky—who still considered himself Lenin's true heir—had to repudiate the leader of the first socialist society from afar. Many American communists, repulsed by Stalin, joined Trotsky's intellectual army in the late 1920s and early 1930s.

Trotsky and the Soviet leader were also divided over how to build socialism in the Soviet Union and abroad. Lenin believed that the 1917 Bolshevik Revolution would spark successful socialist uprisings across Europe. This never happened. Questions began to be asked, such as could socialism be built by the Soviet Union alone, or was international help needed? Should socialists direct all of their efforts toward promoting socialism in the USSR, or should they work toward promoting socialism abroad? Stalin conceptualized his response as "socialism in one country" by arguing that the Soviet Union needed to strengthen itself before promoting worldwide revolution.[62] The Soviet Union could and should advance toward communism, alone if necessary. Trotsky argued for "permanent revolution," or the belief that socialists needed to promote revolution everywhere—even in countries with primitive economies—because economic systems should be interpreted globally, not nationally.[63] He wrote: "a national revolution is not a self-contained whole; it is only a link in the international chain."[64] Trotsky's holism denied the existence of isolated nationalist economies. He maintained that genuinely nationalistic economies did not exist because all economies are shaped by global forces. Burnham had to side with Trotsky against Stalin.

He did so as coeditor (with Shachtman) of the Trotskyite *New International*. Burnham used his position to bring Trotskyite ideas to American workers and other Marxist intellectuals. For example, in a piece called "The Question of Organic Unity," Burnham insists that "if we examine the political meaning of the resolutions and speeches of the Seventh Congress, we naturally enough find it resting firmly on the doctrine of socialism in one country, the heart and lungs of Stalinism. That is to say, it rests on the denial of revolutionary internationalism."[65] The author continues that the gangrene of Stalin's "socialism in one country" was afflicting the whole body of communism, demonstrated by a mutual assistance treaty between the USSR and France.[66] According to Burnham, the pact disregarded the Marxist theory of the state—the belief that government merely managed the affairs of the bourgeoisie.

Rather than fighting for workers around the world, Stalin had collaborated with the bourgeoisie. The new Trotskyite argues that by abandoning true Marxism and permanent international revolution, Stalin had poisoned the entire organism.

While Burnham was showing his fidelity to Trotsky, the winds of war were blowing across Europe. Unwilling to submit to the Versailles Treaty, Hitler was reconstructing the German Wehrmacht and demanding more living space for his people. Benito Mussolini was doing the same in Italy. He glorified his army and suggested that the Italians may need more living space, too.[67] No one thought this would be accomplished peacefully. In response to this militarism, pacifist movements burgeoned across the West. Millions of people signed "peace pledges" and "peace ballots." "Peace Leagues" became fashionable.

Burnham would have none of this. One of his first articles as a formal Trotskyite (using the pseudonym John West) reviewed Richard B. Gregg's *The Power of Non-Violence* (1934). Burnham rejects the book's thesis that nonviolent resistance was the best way to promote social change. He asserts that the Marxist contention is that institutions, themselves based on material forces, determine the thoughts and feelings of people.[68] To create a just and peaceful society, the institutions must be overthrown. For Burnham, as Gregg had admitted, these institutions had been founded on violence; therefore, they must be eradicated with violence.[69] The review argues that because of the corrupt nature of the world, violence was a necessary precondition for a better world, a socialist world, stating that "Marxists are not worshippers of violence, but Marxists deal with the society that confronts them, not with hopes and dreams."[70] In it, Burnham acknowledges that Marxists promoted war, but Marxists promoted only class warfare, and Burnham argues that his was justified because it overthrows the class that by its nature starts war.[71]

The antipacifist began an article for the socialist *New Militant* by declaring that the revolutionary movement seeks to eliminate the expansion of capitalism, the real cause of war.[72] For capitalists, new capital investments must be made, and new markets found. The inability of capitalists to find new markets, however, leads to conflicts between them. The best way to end these conflicts? End capitalism. Burnham continues in the next week's issue that socialism will end the contradictions that lead to war.[73] In the meantime, the workers had to participate by provoking revolution, thereby obtaining power.[74] Burnham decries pacificism, proclaiming that every strike and militant demonstration was worth one-thousand Peace Leagues.[75] Only revolution on behalf of the working classes can bring peace.[76]

Burnham loved the idea of violent revolution. Matthew Josephson, a journalist who met Burnham in the early 1930s, described him this way: "In expanding the doctrines of Marx, Lenin and Trotsky he sounded implacable; he became a true fanatic carried away by vast blood baths that would attend the overthrow of our society. I felt the cold flame behind the tortoise-shell glasses of that composed and well-mannered young man of twenty-six."[77] Josephson also described the internal passion that guided the seemingly calm philosophy professor. Peaceful ideas and movements always earned his ire. Many of his future critics would note the apocalyptic nature of his thought.

Trotsky's worldview was also apocalyptic. Lenin had argued that imperialist nations inevitably competed against one another in search of ever-scarcer raw materials and markets to export their goods, provoking conflicts. Trotsky continues this argument in a 1934 essay titled "War and the Fourth International" by predicting that the same imperialist contradictions that caused World War I would ignite another European conflagration, and soon. The League of Nations was helpless to do anything about it. Trotsky calls the League "a secondary figure on the chessboard of imperialist combinations," and asserts that the real levers of diplomacy were being pulled by the imperialist powers, not by the international governing body.[78] The geopolitical strategist argues that the important diplomatic work went on "behind the back of Geneva."[79]

How should Marxists respond when (not if) the imperialist Nazi state attacked the USSR? Trotsky argues that when the time came, the Soviet Union had to be defended because it was a "workers' state."[80] The USSR was a state for the workers, by the workers, and of the workers. Therefore, it had to be defended. It was part of a broader worldwide conflict.

Burnham heralds these ideas to his American audience in a 1935 piece titled "The Bands Are Playing." He writes that Stalin's usage of the phrase "defend the Soviet Union"—one that gives priority to the Soviet Union over other working-class movements—misapplied the concept because workers around the world needed assistance: "What does the slogan, 'Defend the Soviet Union!' mean to a Marxist? The essence can be summed up quickly. It means: 'Extend the October revolution.' It means to strengthen the economic and political organizations of the world proletariat, to carry the class struggle on a world basis to ever higher levels, to drive toward workers' power."[81] Burnham promotes a

Trotskyite holism: no class struggle could take place in isolation; they were all linked. Defending the revolution meant extending the revolution worldwide.

This universalism was crucial idea for Burnham's future intellectual development. He applied this idea on the eve of World War II by maintaining that workers around the world must unite in their battle against capitalist countries: revolution for democracy everywhere. He would turn this idea on its head as a Cold Warrior because in about thirty years, he would distinguish himself from some other American Cold Warriors by demanding that the fight against communism be fought everywhere—it was a constant struggle. The universal nature of the conflict never left Burnham. And consistent with Lenin and Trotsky, it would not be peaceful.[82]

The Italian invasion of Ethiopia in the fall of 1935 confirmed what Burnham already knew: the world raged in violence and aggression. Burnham explains this in a piece called "War and the Workers," which had been influenced by Rosa Luxemburg's article of the same title. World War I had provided the context for her piece. Luxemburg argues that socialism would not descend from heaven; it could only follow a violent contest between the two competing classes. World War I was bad, although not necessarily because of the violence. Hoping the conflict would prepare the workers for their destiny, Luxemburg asserts they should not fight one another, but rather should aim their aggression against imperialism.

Burnham agreed. Running to almost fifteen thousand words, "War and the Workers" provides his most complete Marxist statement. It proclaims that war had begun: the Italian campaign in Ethiopia was part of a broader global imperialist struggle, from which the workers' revolution must emerge.[83] A workers' revolution eliminates the causes of war: contradictions inherent in capitalism that spawn imperialism.[84] Burnham favored war, but he demanded war by workers against their oppressive government and its representatives like Roosevelt. He castigated peace movements that bloomed across the United States on the eve of World War II, contending that this pacifism benefited the American capitalists. Their representatives may have talked about peace and neutrality, but they simultaneously increased military spending. As the workers suffered, the US army was modernized.[85] The apocalyptic Trotskyite insisted that pacifism should never be the response to war; the response had to be revolution. The working classes could save the world by directing violence against their imperialist rulers, not each other.[86]

"War and the Workers" also contains a theme that Burnham advanced his entire writing career: a critique of disarmament. Here he draws from Lenin. As World War I raged, some European Social-Democrats recommended universal disarmament, even among socialist groups. Lenin dissented. The leading Bolshevik declares: "And in face of this fact, revolutionary Social-Democrats are urged to 'demand' 'disarmament'! That is tantamount to complete abandonment of the class-struggle point of view, to renunciation of all thought of revolution. Our slogan must be: arming of the proletariat to defeat, expropriate and disarm the bourgeoisie."[87] Opposing pacifism in this piece, Lenin argued that disarmament meant running away from an unpleasant reality rather than fighting it. For Lenin, an armed proletariat would lead to peace because upon eliminating the bourgeois class by using force, armaments could then be consigned to "the scrap-heap."[88]

Whereas Lenin criticized disarmament in the midst of World War I, World War II provided the context for Burnham's initial attitudes. He argues that pacifist demands for disarmament favored the reactionary classes that were preparing the world for war.[89] Fascist powers tried to "disrupt, weaken, and disarm the revolutionary struggle against war, which can be carried on only and under all circumstances against the state and the class enemy."[90] Any socialist who promotes disarmament "betrayed" the class struggle (betrayal is an important concept in this essay that appeared as Trotsky was writing *The Revolution Betrayed* in 1936).[91] For Burnham, disarming in the midst of a raging struggle benefited only the enemy. He would always believe this.

What could the League of Nations do to prevent the impending conflict? Following Trotsky and beginning another theme that would characterize his mature writings, in "War and the Workers," Burnham harangues the world's international governing body. Founded in the ashes of the last imperialist war and designed to create peace, he maintains that the UN's architects demanded adherence to its principles of collaboration.[92] Trotsky's American disciple deems the League a sham because it promoted only the interests of Europe's imperialist states, so it only perpetuated war.[93] It did nothing to stop the war between Bolivia and Paraguay, nothing to stop the Japanese invasion of Manchuria, nothing to stop German rearmament, and nothing to stop the Italian invasion of Ethiopia.[94] According to Burnham, "every lesson of history since the foundation of the League serves to confirm this analysis. Whenever an international conflict rises above diplomatic maneuvering, it immediately and automatically goes outside the League framework."[95] The League worked against the interest of the working class and those who promoted it were traitors. Burnham named socialist Leon Blum, Stalinist Maxim Litvinov, and Stalinist Earl Browder as conspirators.[96]

Throughout his writing career Burnham loved to name names, often turning the intellectual struggle into a personal one against some (usually unfortunate) opponent. More so than most intellectuals, the irascible Marx had a poisonous pen that he used to condemn rivals. He bequeathed this style to his disciples, including Lenin and Burnham. Not only did Marxists seek to tear down capitalism, but they also tore down individuals, including their comrades. No group engaged in infighting and personal castigations the way Marxists did. Burnham continued this tradition; many writers, diplomats, and politicians would be left in the wake of his verbal assaults.

One of Burnham's first targets was Max Eastman. It was Eastman whom Trotsky had contacted when trying to learn more about Burnham after reading his review of *The Russian Revolution* in *Symposium*.[97] Twenty years Burnham's senior, Eastman's and Burnham's lives ran like a double helix, sometimes together, sometimes apart, but usually parallel. Like Burnham, Eastman studied philosophy and literary theory. He taught philosophy at Columbia and was a rising star in Marxist circles two decades before Burnham. He also edited leading socialist journals. It was Eastman who translated Trotsky's *The History of the Russian Revolution* into English (Burnham lauded Eastman's prose and translation in his review of the work). Eastman had also lived in the Soviet Union. Unlike most Marxist intellectuals who did the same, he was not impressed. Sooner than most, Eastman recognized that futility of the Soviet system, and, again sooner than most, he questioned Stalin. In 1925, Eastman wrote one of the first anti-Stalin pamphlets titled "Since Lenin Died," and it was Eastman who smuggled Lenin's "Last Will and Testament" out of the USSR. Eastman became part of the "Left Opposition" to Stalin that was led by the marginalized Trotsky. But he was becoming disenchanted with the revolutionary around the time Burnham became a trusted disciple.

Eastman also had a contentious relationship with Hook. Eastman's *Marx, Lenin and the Science of Revolution* (1927) spurred the rivalry. The work asserts that Marxism resembled Freudian psychology in many respects because it recognized that ideas have suppressed motives: "The economic interpretation of history is nothing but a generalized psychoanalysis of the social and political mind."[98] From Hook's perspective, this turned Marxism into a metaphysical philosophy. Hook preferred to see Marx as a pragmatist. Arguing that Marxism was a flexible method applicable to society, Hook asserts that Marx provided instruments that the working class could use to overthrow capitalism. Eastman responded by literally ripping out pages from Hook's *Toward the Understanding of Karl Marx*, contending that Marx's metaphysics could never be reconciled with pragmatism.[99] The feud simmered for years. Burnham showed his loyalty to Hook and Trotsky by disparaging Eastman.

In a piece titled "Max Eastman's Straw Man," Burnham argues that Eastman uses a "deceptive" critical method when analyzing Marx.[100] Burnham writes that according to Eastman, Marx insisted in *The German Ideology* that Hegelianism marked the end of philosophy so now, only scientific philosophy could lead to human liberation. According to Burnham, Eastman argues that Marx's thought was in fact philosophical, as was proven by his use of the philosophical method to reject Hegelian idealism. Burnham responds that Eastman misinterpreted Marx because Marx did not reject philosophy, just Hegelian philosophy—philosophy that reasoned deductively using abstract concepts. Burnham maintains that Marx's scientific philosophy instead used the empirical method, distinguishing it from Hegelianism.

Another of Burnham's favorite targets was Earl Browder, a loyal Stalinist who led the US Communist Party from the early 1930s to the mid-1940s.[101] In a February 1938 piece, Browder defends what was called "collective security," or the belief that the United States should take an active role in international affairs. Opponents favored isolationism or neutrality because to them US involvement in world affairs only meant US involvement in war. Browder argues that the warmongers were Germany, Italy, and Japan. The rest of the world should not suffer the burdens of imperialist war. Browder urges cooperation between the USSR and the United States because both their people and their leaders desired peace.

Burnham responded in a piece titled "Browder Defends Imperialism." The piece contends: "Naturally enough, Stalinists pretend to their own followers that they write from the point of view of the international proletariat. Even a brief survey of Browder's article in the New Republic can demonstrate beyond any doubt that he is reasoning and writing from the point of view of the defense of U.S. Imperialism."[102] Burnham argues that Browder's position was consistent with Roosevelt's policy. The Trotskyite then asks, what about class struggle? The Marxist must always promote class struggle. Because Browder says little about the class struggle, and because this leads him to adopt the same foreign policy as FDR, and because FDR is an imperialist, Burnham reasons that Browder is therefore an imperialist.[103]

Roosevelt remained Burnham's bête noire as he even faulted Roosevelt for the persecution of Jews in Nazi Germany: "The blood of the German Jews, dripping from the hands of Goebbels and Goering and their gangs of maddened sadists, drips also from the white hands of Chamberlain and Roosevelt and from the whole international association of cut-throats and murderers who sustain in life a system whose price for humanity is now measured only in a daily and continuous increase of torment and death."[104] Burnham argues that the contradictions that begat Hitler's racial hatred were inherent in the capitalist system; Hitler incites hatred toward the Jews as a means to distract the German people from the failings of capitalism. And Roosevelt defends capitalism.

Burnham deemed Roosevelt to be an imperialist spokesperson. He states that the president sought an "American League of Nations" through which the United States would assert authority over the two continents. In "U.S. Imperialism at Work," Burnham suggests that Latin America was already a colony because its basic industries were financed by US capital, evidenced by the fact that the American United Fruit Company handled most of Central America's orchards, railroads, and communications.[105] That did not mean the United States did not have worldwide territorial aspirations; capitalists required outlets everywhere.[106] What could Marxists do? Burnham begs workers and revolutionaries across the continent to unite in their quest to overthrow the imperialists and their spokesperson.

This position revealed the merging of the two James Burnhams during his Marxist phase. The first James Burnham was attracted to the apocalyptic nature of the socialist movement that optimistically predicted that real democracy would follow revolution. And the revolutionary violence had to be directed against America's faux representatives like Roosevelt. Marxism gave the second James Burnham a megaphone to decry the United States as a sham democracy, ruled by a corrupt elite who governed against the interests of the people. Burnham cynically argues that its rulers would use any means necessary—even war—to advance their interests. For democracy to succeed, the political elite had to be resisted and toppled. Soon, these two James Burnhams would become more distinct. They did not disappear.

Chapter 3

Leaving Marxism

Marxism allegedly improves the human condition, provides a rational understanding of history, and even allows its adherents to predict the future. James Burnham, like many early twentieth-century intellectuals, found these prospects appealing. But critical events during the 1920s and 1930s caused some writers to reject the philosophy, or at least parts of it. During Burnham's tenure as a Marxist, evidence continued to mount that the Soviet Union—a society theoretically built on Marxist principles—was a tragedy. Joseph Stalin's purges of 1930s and famine killed millions of Soviet citizens. Millions more were sent to the Gulag. Most of the leaders of the 1917 Revolution had perished. Important Soviet military leaders had succumbed, too (a fact not lost on Adolf Hitler). Twenty years after the Bolshevik Revolution, things seemed bleak. But was it Marx's fault? How should Marxists interpret the Soviet Union? All Marxist intellectuals wrestled with what was called the "Russian question."

Leon Trotsky tried to explain what went wrong in *The Revolution Betrayed: What Is the Soviet Union and Where Is It Going?* (1937). He argues in his characteristic dramatic style that initially the Soviet Union had developed an advanced, productive, socialist economy. The revolutionary proclaims that socialism had won, "not on the pages of Das Kapital, but in an industrial arena comprising a sixth part of the earth's surface—not in the language of dialectics, but in the language of steel, cement and electricity."[1] He contends that at first, socialism had animated the USSR. Unfortunately, a bureaucratic class hijacked the revolution by transforming state property back into private property. The privileged bureaucracy moved Russia backward; counterrevolutionary, regressive forces prevailed. Trotsky insists that Bolsheviks should not be blamed. His old Bolshevik party was dead.

Trotsky maintained that Stalin was temporary. Like Marx, Trotsky used history to explain social reality: Stalin should be compared to the Napoleonic phase of the French Revolution because both perverted the true nature of the revolution. What began progressively turned violent and regressive under dictatorship, or the "Soviet Thermidor." The Soviet Union was still a workers' state.

Burnham was growing skeptical. No longer seduced by all of Trotsky's arguments, he replied to a 1937 party resolution designed to show support for Trotsky's positions with a piece titled "From Formula to Reality." He asks: "We ask them, what kind of state is the Soviet Union? They answer, it is a workers' state. We ask, why is it a workers' state? They answer because there is nationalized property. We ask, why does nationalized property make it a workers' state? And they answer, because a workers' state is one where there is nationalized property."[2] Burnham continues that this was, in form, the same as arguing that the Bible is the word of God because God says it is, and God never lies.[3]

The wavering Marxist boldly argues that "the Soviet Union is at the present time neither a bourgeois state nor a workers' state: that is, neither the working class nor a consolidated bourgeois class is the ruling or dominant class within the Soviet Union in any intelligible sense that can be given to the conception of a ruling or dominant class."[4] Burnham suggests that this may seem surprising, yet V. I. Lenin had described "a dictatorship of the proletariat and peasantry."[5] He conceived of a state that was neither exclusively bourgeois nor proletarian. Calling the committee's description of the Soviet Union a workers' state a "verbal habit," Burnham now asserts that it may not be a workers' state, and it did not have to be unconditionally defended.[6]

In 1938, Burnham publicly introduced motions to clarify the positions of the new Trotskyite Socialist Workers Party (SWP).[7] Privately, his doubts continued to mount. In a letter to Sydney Hook, he muses about "the nature of democracy, and its relations to Russia, to socialism, to what [it] is worthwhile in general."[8] He writes that democracy typically meant the will of the people; and communists insist that their form of government is for the masses. However, what if only a small group of people in a society wants communism?[9] Burnham asks, should communism still be advanced?[10] What if the United States goes communist, but only a small minority in Canada want communism? Should the US army be used to spread communism to Canada? By 1939, these theoretical questions would have answers for Trotskyites.

Some of Burnham's questions were fostered by Max Eastman, or at least Burnham used Eastman's ideas to justify an escape from Marxism. Eastman earned Trotsky's censure by calling Marxism a "dialectical faith" and by arguing that the dialectic was not a form of science, but rather philosophy in the very way Marx denounced philosophy.[11] Eastman replied to Trotsky's *The Revolution Betrayed* (a work he translated into English) by penning a piece for *Harper's* called "Russia and the Socialist Ideal." Claiming the status of a detached observer now that he had left Marxism, Eastman contends that he could see more clearly than those still under the spell of the dialectic.[12] His conclusion was unequivocal: the Soviet Union was one of the greatest tragedies in human history. What was supposed to become a free and equal socialist society had morphed into bureaucratic despotism. The culprit? Not Stalin, but Marxist philosophy.[13] Eastman argues that Marxism resembled Christian beliefs or political beliefs, such as natural rights.[14] Socialists whom Marx deemed "utopian," such as Robert Owen, Henri de Saint-Simon, and Charles Fourier at least created a blueprint based on man's nature that made the construction of socialism realistic. Marx, however, never asked what it was about man that ensured "each according to his ability, each according to his need."[15] Eastman writes that Marx just assumed this, based only on the dialectic. No wonder Marxists were surprised by the Soviet catastrophe. Eastman singled out Trotsky for his inability to adjust his attitude toward socialism and the dialectic.[16]

Trotsky requested that Burnham reply, and the latter obliged in "Max Eastman as Scientist." The piece condemns Eastman while only partly defending Marxism. Burnham insists that Eastman's new position as a nonbeliever did not make his analysis superior; it just meant he had less knowledge of the facts than Trotsky.[17] Burnham concedes that Marx's scientific method may lack rigor, but that did not invalidate Marx's political philosophy. Eastman misunderstood the scientific method, anyway. Burnham argues that science never provides a complete blueprint because too precise a blueprint suffocated the agent, leaving no room for creativity.[18] For Burnham, too perfect a blueprint was utopianism.[19] Notably, this piece never refutes Eastman's ideas about the dialectic. In fact, it does not even use the word.

Eastman recognized this in his response titled "Burnham Dodges My Views," published in the August 1938 edition of *New International*. He theorizes that Burnham probably knew the dialectic was a metaphysical as opposed to scientific concept, but, fearful of Trotsky's wrath, would not admit it.[20] To deny the dialectic would end his Marxist career. Instead, Burnham resorted to word games, misinterpretations, and distortions.[21]

Burnham's reluctance to defend the scientific nature of Marxism was also influenced by Karl Popper. Popper employs the concept of confirmation bias to undermine both Freudian psychology and Marxism as any sort of sciences. He maintains that everywhere Marxists looked, they found economic explanations for phenomena. Psychologists displayed the same tendencies. Take the concept of resistance: if the patient accepts the theory, it is confirmed. If the patient resists, the psychologist asserts resistance, confirming his or her initial theory. This does not refute the concepts of economic determinism and resistance because sometimes economic factors determine events and sometimes resistance occurs. Instead, Popper rejects the scientific status of these theories.

What methodologies must scientists then use? Popper introduced the concept of falsification into the lexicon of scientific philosophy: a scientific theory must have a testable way to be falsified. For example, Newtonian physics says that every body exerts a force of attraction on every other body, so it would be falsified if we observed one body repelling another body. That has not happened. If it did, everyone would abandon classical Newtonian physics. For Popper, Marxism was different. Marx predicted that socialist revolutions would begin in the most industrialized nations. Instead, the first socialist revolution took place in Russia. Therefore, because Marxism was falsified, everyone should have abandoned it, at least as some form of science. Instead, Marxists just created ad hoc explanations.

Hook was having doubts, too. In a 1938 article titled "Reflections on the Russian Revolution," Hook questions some contentions made in *Revolution Betrayed*.[22] For instance, Trotsky suggested that the USSR was moving progressively toward socialism. Hook asks, is the Russian worker better off than twenty years ago? Trotsky said yes, but Hook argues that the answer depended on which year one was comparing with 1917. Certainly not 1933, when several million Russians starved to death. The period 1936–1938 had not been great either. Moreover,

Hook maintains that worker standards of living had risen everywhere. Maybe capitalism promoted economic development more than socialism; nothing that had happened over the previous twenty years suggested otherwise.[23] Did Stalin really betray the revolution? Hook agrees that despotism reigned in the USSR. Stalin's corruption of communist ideals needed no explication. Yet Burnham's first Marxist mentor saw Stalin's dictatorship as a result of Bolshevik theory: "That the identification of the dictatorship of the party and the class is an integral part of Bolshevik theory, and not a removable appendage, must be the inescapable conclusion of any critical inquiry into its party documents and historical practice."[24] Party dictatorship characterizes Bolshevik thought and this led to political dictatorship.[25] Given this, there were no reasonable assurances that Trotsky's rule would be any different than Stalin's. Yes, the two disagreed on some philosophical questions, but Hook argues that the same conditions that spawned Stalin—the death of Lenin, the weak productive forces, the absence of world revolution, and declining morale—would have existed if Trotsky had followed Lenin.[26]

By the late 1930s, Trotsky was beset by personal problems. Besides being abandoned by former comrades, the society he had helped found was floundering. Usually in ill health, the "Old Man" had been exiled from numerous European countries to a small village in Mexico. He was Stalin's bête noire, essentially a death sentence not just for him but also for his associates. His sons-in-law were arrested, grandchildren were displaced, an ex-wife was deported, and a son was executed.

A commission led by John Dewey and Hook informally acquitted Trotsky in 1938 of the charges brought against him by Stalinists during the rigged Moscow trials. However, his personal reputation was still suffering because many on the left began wondering about his culpability in the rise of Stalin. Trotsky had explicitly rejected civil rights and parliamentary democracy, believing them to be tools whereby the bourgeoisie exploited others. During the October Revolution of 1917, he ordered the execution of resisters. During the ensuing Russian Civil War, Trotsky massacred innocents and the Kronstadters. American writer Selden Rodman denied any significant difference between Stalin and Trotsky, arguing that if Trotsky were in the Kremlin, he would be no less ruthless than Stalin because of their shared Marxist beliefs and dependence on violence.[27] Henry Wallace contended that Thomas Jefferson was hated as much as Trotsky, but the third American president, unlike the Bolshevik leader, "kept his sense of balance."[28] George Orwell opined that Trotsky "is probably as much responsible for the

[Soviet dictatorship] as any man now living, and there is no certainty that he as a dictator would be preferable to Stalin."[29] Both Stalin and Trotsky rejected parliamentary democracy, and once on that path, the kinship between the men becomes clear.

Trotsky replied to some of these criticisms in a June 1938 with a piece titled "Their Morals and Ours." The "reactionaries," he declares, see similarities everywhere: similarities between czarism and Bolshevism, Hitler and Stalin, Stalin and Trotsky, Lenin and fascism.[30] And there are similarities, just as two armies in combat look similar; they have to act similarly or neither side would strike a blow. Trotsky argues that the mere fact that the reactionaries falsely call him complicit in the Soviet tragedy shows their weakness.[31] The communist in exile asserts that Marxists differ because they assert the importance not of blood, honor, or immaculate conception, but class struggle. Marxists are superior because their means and ends come from the dialectic, with the goal of human liberation.[32]

Trotsky still employed Burnham as his bulldog, despite his growing skepticism with Marxism. Burnham used this opportunity to continue lifting his Marxist veil and to reveal a new identity in a piece titled "Intellectuals in Retreat" (January 1939), cowritten with Max Shachtman. It begins with Burnham's style of calling out his opponents: "WE ARE, IN THIS ARTICLE, writing particularly about the following persons: Group I: Max Eastman, Sidney Hook, Charles Yale Harrison, James Rorty, Edmund Wilson, Philip Rahv, Benjamin Stolberg, James Farrell, Louis Hacker, and others. Group II: John Chamberlain, Louis Adamic, Eugene Lyons, John Dewey, George S. Counts, Ferdinand Lundberg."[33] Both groups were anti-Stalinist intellectuals whom Burnham and Shachtman condemn for failing to advance any program. Desperate times called for some political measures. Calling their writings "negative," insisting that they only criticized other programs, Burnham and Shachtman deem them "irresponsible" and "unprincipled."[34] Eastman was singled out: "Eastman, as so often, gives the show away. At the end of his polemic against Burnham (*New International*, August 1938) he confesses openly that he has no (conscious) program. 'If I live,' he promises, 'I will complete my thesis. But he 'would not hurry.' To him, it seemed like a good time in America for 'deliberation.'"[35] Burnham and Shachtman believed deliberation would not defeat fascism, war, and unemployment.

Hook especially earned Burnham's and Shachtman's wrath, particularly his notion that the Bolshevik idea of party-dictatorship inevitably led to one-person dictatorship. The authors argue that no historical precedent exists for this argument.[36] It was just one case. Hook notes that Russia became a dictatorship, and he then asserts a relationship between this and Lenin's ideas about dictatorship. Yes, Lenin preached party-dictatorship, and yes, Stalin emerged from this, but Stalin's dictatorship did not necessarily relate to Lenin. Lenin's ideas could lead in different directions, proven by the fact that Trotsky, also a disciple of Lenin, disagreed with Stalin on a myriad of issues.[37] In fact, many of the writers named earlier broke from Stalin. Alternative avenues existed. Lenin could lead to Stalin *or* to Trotsky.

Yet in "Intellectuals in Retreat" Burnham and Shachtman hesitate when it came to defending the scientific nature of the dialectic, framing and answering the question this way: "Let us assume that the entire attack of our subjects on dialectical materialism is correct. Dialectical materialism is 'contrary to science,' an 'idealistic metaphysics,' a theology.' Then let us ask: So what? What follows, politically?"[38] The authors argue that one could promote revolution and not necessarily accept all the details of Marxist philosophy. Marxists routinely disagreed about Marxism. That did not invalidate any of their revolutionary political activity. This article, however, never denies the metaphysical nature of the dialectic. Popper's influence can be seen in part of the article: dialectics is not a science because "scientific hypotheses are tested by the predictions that are made on their basis."[39] The dialectic's inability to formulate clear and consistent laws about society revealed the nonscientific nature of the dialectic for Burnham and Shachtman.[40]

The piece naturally provoked a response from the Old Man. Divorcing politics and thought—claiming to support Marxism's revolutionary side but not the dialectic—was impossible for Trotsky. He wrote in a letter to Shachtman shortly after the article appeared expressing his dismay: "Comrade Burnham says: 'I don't recognize the dialectic.' It is clear and everybody has to acknowledge it. But you say: 'I recognize the dialectic, but no matter; it does not have the slightest importance.' Re-read what you wrote. This section is terribly misleading for the readers of the *New International* and the best of gifts to the Eastmans of all kinds."[41] Burnham and Shachtman never rewrote their words.

Burnham's growing antipathy toward Marxism became clearer in a spring 1939 book review for *Partisan Review*, a journal that reflected developments in American communist thought. It originated in 1934 as its founding editors believed that the changing economic conditions during the Great Depression required a new literary style.[42] *Partisan Review* tried to distinguish itself from other socialist publications by focusing on more than pressing political issues using Marxist jargon.[43] It employed literary criticism, even embracing "reactionary" writers such as T. S. Eliot.[44] By the late-1930s, its editors had to grapple with the fact the Soviet Union was faltering. The journal responded by providing a haven for American anti-Stalin leftists. Trotsky recognized it, stating that he hoped *Partisan Review* would "take its place in the victorious army of socialism."[45] Editors and frequent contributors included Dwight Macdonald, Arthur Koestler, George Orwell, and Hook.[46] Burnham became a member of its editorial advisory board.

He helped turn the magazine away from any Trotskyite pretenses with a caustic book review titled "A Belated Dialectician." The review analyzed *The Marxist Philosophy and the Sciences* by J. B. S. Haldane, a mathematician and Marxist neophyte. Burnham pulled no punches with the new convert as the review begins: "This is a naïve and rather pathetic book."[47] Haldane opens his book modestly, stating that he was by no means an expert on Marxism; Burnham retorts, then why write the book? Haldane continues by noting the Hegelian principle "the unity of opposites." Burnham replies in true-Burnham fashion:

> What are opposites? We use the word loosely in common sense, relying on the context to give us a rough approximation to our meaning. Logic and science must be more precise. The word "opposites," among its other meanings, may refer to: (1) "contradictories"—i.e., two sentences in such a logical relation that of them must be true and both cannot be true; (2) "contraries"—i.e., two sentences in such a logical relation that one of them must be false and both may be false; (3) points, angles, lines and other geometrical terms having certain geometrical relations with each other; (4) two human beings (or other animals) or groups of humans who are in physical conflict with each other; (5) or simply two particulars which are "different" from each other.[48]

Burnham implied that no one really knows what the principles of opposites meant. And the whole concept of dialectical materialism is neither true nor false.[49] It certainly is not scientific because it could not be tested.[50] Burnham recognizes that the vague nature of the dialectic was not Haldane's fault; he suggests that it was the fault of every Marxist writer since Engels (this tacitly included Trotsky). Marxists had to abandon their scientific pretenses and recognize that Marxism was a philosophy.

Burnham began offending other Marxists, too. Intellectual disputes were turning into personal feuds between Burnham and his comrades.

Philip Rahv, a cofounder of *Partisan Review*, declared that Burnham acted as if he were giving out cards, determining who were real and fake Marxist revolutionaries.[51] Burnham nearly came to blows with Hook.[52] A feud simmered with Cannon, too, as Burnham tried to thwart his power in 1939.[53]

The Nazi-Soviet pact of August 1939 exacerbated this dispute. It was a traumatic event for Marxists because Hitler was considered an opposite, an enemy, like all other capitalist leaders. Supposedly a bulwark against fascism, the USSR now collaborated with fascists. Moreover, Marxists were disproportionately Jewish, creating more confusion; how could Jews possibly collaborate with the Nazi regime? It only got worse when on September 1, the Nazis invaded Poland, igniting World War II. The Soviets soon did the same, invading from the east as prescribed in a secret clause. Within two weeks, the Soviets had secured eastern Poland. Burnham's theoretical question (Should a communist United States invade a sovereign nation where communism was unpopular to spread socialism?) now had a Marxist answer.

Trotsky believed that the Soviet Union was justified and socialist gains in Poland should be defended. In a September 1939 piece titled "The USSR in War," he states that private ownership of land would be eliminated in Poland, so socialism would spread: "Our *general* appraisal of the Kremlin and Comintern does not, however, alter the *particular* fact that the stratification of property in the occupied territories is in itself a progressive measure. We must recognize this openly."[54] Trotsky saw progress: socialism and the abolition of private property would soon exist in Poland. It was just another victory for the proletariat. Maintaining that his defense of the USSR did not relate to the deeds and crimes of the Kremlin, Trotsky insists that his views are determined by his "conception of the interest of the Soviet state and world revolution."[55]

Burnham called the invasion Soviet imperialism—a confiscation of land by Stalin. The seizure led Burnham to widen the increasing gap between himself and Trotsky. Knowing that Trotsky would disagree, Burnham recommends in a piece titled "On the Character of the War and the Perspective of the Fourth International" that the SWP condemn the Soviet invasion of Poland.[56] He declares that "far from defending the Soviet state . . . we call upon the workers and peasants of Russia to overthrow and to re-establish their own socialist power."[57] These were fighting words. Exchanges between Burnham and Trotsky (and their followers) went on for months, leading Cannon to write, "For such a brief space of time, this is already the most voluminous party discussion in the history of mankind."[58] This was not the last conflagration that Burnham would help provoke among his intellectual peers.

Trotsky tried to defend himself against Burnham in a December 1939 article, "A Petty-Bourgeois Opposition in the Socialist Workers Party." The piece asserts that two sides existed: on one hand, the antidialecticians, Burnham and Eastman, who represented the bourgeoisie; and on the other, Trotsky and Cannon, who moved with the dialectic and represented the workers. Trotsky proclaims that the dialectic was a "science of forms of our thinking" that allowed the follower to understand the material developments of society.[59] He continues that dialectical thinking recognizes that everything changes—so A ceases to be A—depending on the material conditions.[60] If the American philosophy professor would have employed dialectical thinking, he would have pondered the origins of the USSR, what changes it had undergone, and most important, whether these changes caused the rise of an exploitative class. If Burnham had asked these questions, he could have concluded only that the USSR was a "degenerated workers' state."[61]

Why did Burnham, Eastman, Hook, and Shachtman deny the dialectic? Trotsky noted their "pragmatism," a distinctly American philosophy. In no other Western nation but the United States—the beacon of capitalism—had Marxism failed to grasp the minds of intellectuals and workers.[62] This could not be a coincidence. For Trotsky, the rejection of the dialectic by American writers revealed not Marxism's weakness, but its strength because Marxism recognized the sway of economic forces in determining thoughts and ideas. The ideas of Burnham, Hook, Shachtman, Eastman, and their ilk merely represented the ideas of the ruling classes. Trotsky predicted that all of this would crumble.[63]

When asked for a reply, Burnham quipped to a comrade, "I stopped arguing about religion a long time ago."[64] After Trotsky learned of this, he fired off another article titled "Open Letter to Comrade Burnham." It ran about ten thousand words. Burnham's assertion that the dialectic was a religious concept stung Trotsky. The subtitle reads: "Is There Logic in Identifying Logic with Religion?" Trotsky argues that two types of logic existed: Aristotelian logic (syllogism) and Hegelian logic, the dialectic. The dialectic, like Aristotle's syllogism, provides knowledge:

> As I understand this, your words imply that the dialectic of Marx, Engels and Lenin belongs to the sphere of religion. What does this assertion signify? The dialectic, permit me to recall once again,

is the *logic of evolution*. Just as a machine shop in a plant supplies instruments for all departments, so logic is indispensable for all spheres of human knowledge. If you do not consider logic in general to be a religious prejudice (sad to say, the self-contradictory writings of the opposition incline one more and more toward this lamentable idea), then just which logic do you accept?[65]

Trotsky feared that Burnham was right. And Burnham *was* right: the dialectic had become the providential god for Marxists. As Trotsky asserts in "A Petty-Bourgeois Opposition in the Socialist Workers Party," it guides everything—a spring that moves the clock.[66] Following the dialectic leads to human liberation from this wretched world. Human beings must subordinate their individual interest to become followers; everything must be abandoned, save what conforms to the dialectic (e.g., class struggle). For believers, it produces knowledge and essence. There can be no truth, wisdom, or logic without it. Nor can there be any social reality—past, present, or future. It, and only it, allows the believer to understand the world. You do not directly see the dialectic, of course. You just see it in action, everywhere and always. The mere existence of reality is evidence of their existence.

Burnham, obviously frustrated with Trotsky, replied three days later in "The Politics of Desperation" that he had never believed in the dialectic in the first place.[67] Burnham continues that Trotsky knew of his agnosticism toward the dialectic, yet still employed him to promote Marxism. Trotsky trusted him to edit Marxist works, at Burnham's discretion. Using the syllogism-style logic that Trotsky advocated, Burnham reasons: if the dialectical method was fundamental to understanding everything, and Burnham questioned the dialectic, then why did Trotsky trust him to interpret Marxism?

In February 1940, Burnham discharged another lengthy piece called "Science and Style." One biographer notes: "In contrast to Trotsky, Burnham never lost his composure. He replied to Trotsky's tirades in an even tone that sometimes hinted at sadness."[68] Another describes Burnham's "controlled prose."[69] But Burnham's seemingly calm and detached prose belied his anger. Burnham was not stoical, despite appearances. Reminiscing how he had first been mesmerized by Trotsky's *History of the Russian Revolution*, the repentant Marxist now realized it was Trotsky's style, his marvelous literary skills, that seduced him—not his method or logic. Burnham declares: "Comrade Trotsky, I will not match metaphors with you. In such a verbal tournament, I concede you the ribbon in advance.

Evidence, argument, proof: these only are my weapons."[70] Burnham proceeds with an assault that began:

I will now summarise your argument:

With reference to your own position, you assert the following:

A. The philosophy of dialectical materialism is true.
B. Marxian sociology, in particular the Marxian theory of the state, is true.
C. Russia is a workers' state.
D. A tactic of defence of the Russian state in the present war is correct.

With reference to the position of the opposition—or, more exactly, of Burnham who you claim expresses the "essence" of the opposition—you assert the following:

1. Burnham is a bourgeois democrat.
2. Burnham rejects dialectics.
3. Burnham rejects Marxian sociology, in particular the Marxian theory of the state.
4. Burnham denies that Russia is a workers' state.
5. Burnham's practical politics are "abstentionist."
6. Burnham rejects Bolshevik organization theories and methods.[71]

Burnham suggests that Trotsky was a great historian and political scientist, but his philosophy lacked rigor, especially scientific rigor. The fact that Trotsky continues to rely on the nineteenth-century philosopher G. W. F. Hegel proved his lack of interest in more contemporary logicians, such as Bertrand Russell, A. N. Whitehead, and C. I. Lewis. Burnham thus deems Trotsky's idea of logic "incorrect" and "out of date."[72]

In April 1940, Trotsky's view of the Soviet Union was endorsed by the SWP.[73] It was, indeed, a workers' state. Opponents could no longer hold party posts.[74] This intentionally marginalized Burnham. Another party of outcasts quickly formed, but Burnham resigned the following month.[75] His resignation announcement kicked Marxism where it counted. In his letter of resignation, he calls Marxist economics "false or obsolete or meaningless."[76] He declares: "Not only do I believe it meaningless to say that 'socialism is inevitable' and false that socialism is 'the only alternative to capitalism'; I consider that on the basis of the evidence now available to us a new form of exploitive society (what I call 'managerial society') is not only possible as an alternative to capitalism but is a more probable outcome of the present period than socialism."[77] Burnham would expand on this idea of a "managerial society" soon. He concludes by defending his bourgeois upbring. He asks, did his upbringing lead to confused thinking that kept him from embracing Marxism, or did it lead to clear thinking that kept him from embracing Marxism?[78]

There were several ways to poke a Marxist in the eye and Burnham chose all of them. First, he denied that Trotsky and his brand of Marxism were "progressive." Second, he disagreed that Marxism was any sort of scientific socialism. Third, he not only rejected the existence of the dialectic but also called it a religious concept. These were not jabs, but right-hooks. This relationship—like so many of Burnham's relationships—was a boxing match. And this time, he fought a great historical figure. Burnham provoked rebukes because it was only a boxing match if both sides got punched. Trotsky was one of the foremost Marxist theoreticians of the twentieth century and, at one level, his attacks must have stung Burnham, like a professor who shuns a student, or even a parent who shuns a child (the Old Man was about the same age as Burnham's father).

It was painful for both sides. Burnham burned his correspondence with his former mentor. Trotsky called his former disciple "an educated witch-doctor" who succumbed to "petty-bourgeois fatheadedness."[79] William Troy, who knew Burnham personally and contributed to *Partisan Review*, wrote that Burnham "inclines to be strongly influenced in an intellectual sense by people, and then to turn on them drastically... Father D'Arcy. Then Wheelwright. Then Hook."[80] Now Trotsky. Sometimes people sabotage relationships so they do not have to confront the pain of being left—a self-fulfilling prophecy, at least the relationship ends on their terms.

The immediate catalyst for this fallout shaped Burnham's future political philosophy in two important ways. First, Trotsky's attempt to justify the Soviet invasion of Poland in accordance with Marxism showed Burnham the weakness of ideology. He began to believe that ideologies attempted to explain reality in accordance with their principles, but reality was messier and more complex than ideology suggested. Ideologies led people to distort reality—to misinterpret the facts—to ensure everything conformed to ideology. This spelled disaster. Second, the Soviet invasion of Poland underscored the role that power played in politics. Regardless of what Stalin and Trotsky said, the invasion of Poland was nothing more than a naked power play. Ideology could not explain this; it masked truth. Recognizing that power dominated human impulses could reveal the true nature of the world. Words meant nothing. These ideas would be expanded in future works by the more cynical Burnham.

Burnham was a Marxist in mind only; his heart was never in it. As a young intellectual, he may have believed that only mind mattered. Moreover, Burnham had invested—maybe wasted—seven years of his intellectual energy on his relationship with Marxism. He had left the party and felt alienated by one of its leaders. Yet like any serious relationship, it left an indelible impact on Burnham, one that would shape his future intellectual relationships.

Chapter 4

The New Elite

When James Burnham left Marxism in 1940, World War II was raging. Nazism seemed to be the wave of the future in Central and Western Europe. Joseph Stalin, in concert with a bureaucratic clique, controlled the Soviet Union. Fascist Japan occupied important Chinese cities like Beijing and Nanjing. In the liberal-democratic United States, the New Deal had become a permanent feature of American life. Burnham's *The Managerial Revolution: What Is Happening in the World* (1941) explains these events by arguing that fascism, communism, and the New Deal were not distinct phenomena; they represented a larger, predictable trend in human history. They were the wave of the future.

The book does not completely jettison Marxist, Leninist, and Trotskyite principles. In fact, the title of the first chapter is one that V. I. Lenin and later Leon Trotsky regularly used: "The Problem." Lenin wrote pieces called "The Balkan Problem," "The Problem of the New Economic Policy," "The Problem of Resettlement," "The Liberals and the Land Problem in Britain," "The Essence of the Agrarian Problem," and "Fundamental Problems of the Election Campaign." Trotsky would later write pieces titled "Problems of the British Revolution," "Problems of the Spanish Revolution," "Problems of the Chinese Revolution," "Problems of the Soviet Regime," and "Problem of the Ukraine."

CHAPTER 4

Part of the problem for Burnham was social revolution. Consistent with Marx, Lenin, and Trotsky, *The Managerial Revolution* preaches revolution and the imminent dawn of a new era. It asserts at the beginning, "We must be careful not to permit historical judgement to be distorted by the staggering emotional impact of war itself. If a major social revolution is now in fact occurring, the war is subordinate to the revolution. The war in the final analysis—and future wars—is an episode in the revolution."[1] War signaled revolution and a new age; they all remained inexorably bound.

In *The Managerial Revolution*, Burnham predicts that capitalism would disappear, probably within a couple of decades.[2] Capitalism's greatest fault is its mass unemployment.[3] This defines sick civilizations, such as Athens in its dying years, Rome before its fall, and even displaced serfs and villeins characterized the late medieval period.[4] Mass unemployment crushes society, bleeding it to death. Moreover, public and private debt were skyrocketing. And farmers were struggling to produce food. Consistent with Karl Marx, Burnham asserts that capitalism could no longer organize human affairs. Describing the recent rise of "technological unemployment," he insists that not even technology could help; it only contributed to capitalism's failure.[5] What about war? Burnham suggests that not even total war could solve this problem.[6]

Burnham argues in *The Managerial Revolution* that the waning of capitalism was also demonstrated by the decrepit nature of its dominant ideology. Liberalism (Burnham meant classical liberalism here) was passe, as shown by the fact that England and France could not thwart the advance of Nazism. The former Marxist believed that the social sciences showed that bourgeois ideologies were just temporary expressions of a particular time period, not universal values.[7] The bourgeoisie have lost faith in their ideologies. For Burnham, nothing established liberalism's failure more clearly than the fact that England and the United States had to impose a draft when unemployment surged, as the fate of their nations hung in the balance.[8]

Until this point, Burnham's analysis preserves elements of Marxism: he relates economics and ideology, he insists that capitalism is outmoded, and he argues that technology will facilitate its collapse. He even writes that violence signaled the dawning of a new era in history. But Burnham deviates from Marxism by declaring that capitalism would not be replaced by socialism. Chiding Marxists for thinking that socialism was the only alternative to capitalism, he contends that myriad economic systems could replace capitalism.[9] Burnham argues that Russia provided an example of a society that experienced a socialist revolution yet saw little real progress toward a classless society.

So, if the decline of capitalism was inevitable, yet the victory of the proletariat unlikely, what would happen next? Burnham predicts the rise of what he called a managerial class led by a group that included "operating executives, production managers, plant superintendents and their associates."[10] This class will supplant the bourgeoisie owners. Managers may run factories or a department within a factory. Or they may run mines, newspapers, railroads, or even government offices. The managers will work either with the state or for the state because Burnham assumes that private industry will fall under some form of state control. Yet, significantly, managers determine the policies by controlling production.[11] This makes them the ruling class.

Burnham invokes *The Modern Corporation and Private Property* to explain how managers relate to the capitalists. According to Burnham, the authors show that most corporations were in fact "management controlled," meaning that—unlike the capitalist stockholders—managers owned just a small percentage of shares of their corporations. But capitalists yield daily operations to managers because managerial expertise generates the capitalist profits. Managerialism is a natural result of the historical development of capitalism. Like Marx, Burnham believes that the capitalists have in fact birthed their own gravediggers. They are just managers, not workers.

While trying to explain why managers and not workers represent the wave of the future, Burnham argues that in the waning capitalist era, the working classes had not gained control of any of the instruments of production, unlike the capitalists in the late feudal era.[12] Marxists had suggested trade unions could fix this; Burnham calls this argument an illusion because experience showed that trade unions were not anticapitalist.[13] Instead, the former Marxist predicts that the managers would rule society and conquer the state: "The state—that is, the institutions which comprise the state—will . . . be the 'property' of the managers. And that will be quite enough to place them in the position of ruling class."[14] The victory of the managers over state and society is inevitable.

Launching a theme that would become central for his future political philosophy, Burnham dedicates a chapter to "The Struggle for Power." He asserts as an axiom that in modern societies, a small group of men exercise most of the power.[15] During the medieval era, says Burnham, the ruling class of feudal lords owned the most land and had power. During the capitalist era, the ruling capitalists had the most money and obtained power. Now, an ascending class struggles against the decaying capitalist class in their quest for power: "What is occurring in this transition is a drive for social dominance, for power and privilege, for the position of the ruling class, by the social group of class called managers.... This drive will be successful. At the conclusion of the transition period the managers will, in fact, have achieved social dominance, will be the ruling class in society."[16] This power-struggle rages between the capitalists and an incipient class that was poised to rule over society.

According to Burnham, however, the managers will not necessarily make the most money; they were more concerned with power and privilege than profits.[17] Separating the managers from wealth is important because it distinguishes Burnham's powerful ruling class from Marx's. For Marx, the powerful elite control the means of production, and this generates them wealth. For Burnham, the new ruling class holds various positions in the state and society that allow them to exercise power over the production of goods.[18] Some are executives. Some are technicians. Some are corporate managers. Some are bureaucrats. They are privileged and they direct the economy, but they are not necessarily the wealthiest, at least not immediately.

The Managerial Revolution conceives of an elite privileged class that would use the state to advance its social, economic, and political interests. Burnham compares this class to the Catholic College of Cardinals, a separate group that determines who has power in the Catholic Church.[19] And they control who enters their ranks. The managerial elite self-perpetuates because its dominance means it controls recruiting.[20] Potential disrupters can easily be excluded.

Managerialism was progress. It would be slightly better than capitalism for the masses because the production of goods would increase.[21] For Burnham, a managerial economy would not prevail if it could not solve some of capitalism's problems.[22] Economic recessions and depressions that characterized capitalism would wane since managerial society would more effectively utilize manpower because of greater centralization.[23] A centralized managerial economy could plan more effectively, "in a way that is not possible for a capitalist economy, with its system of divisive and uncoordinated control."[24] Writing in the early stages of World War II, Burnham extolls the virtues of a centralized, planned economy. Collectivist rule of the managers will dominate the future of society.

So, too, would their corresponding ideas. The new managerial era will lead to new modes of thinking, as Burnham suggests: "In place of capitalist concepts, there are concepts suited to the structure of managerial society and the rule of the managers. In place of the 'individual,' the stress turns to the 'state,' the people, the folk, the race. In place of gold, labor and work. In place of private enterprise, 'socialism' or 'collectivism.' In place of 'freedom' and 'free initiative,' planning. Less talk about 'rights' and 'natural rights'; more about 'duties' and 'order' and 'discipline.'"[25] The ruling class (the managerial elite) foists ideology upon the people for the ex-Marxist. They prepare the "psychic atmosphere" (culture) for managerial rule.[26]

Burnham highlights the expanding role of the bureaucracy, a class he predicts will become nearly indistinguishable from the managers because the managers will wield power through the growing bureaucracy.[27] *The Managerial Revolution* contains details about how the New Deal had created a new class of bureaucrats who played a critical role in the new American society by assuming roles previously reserved for the private sphere. Predicting that the power of the bureaucrats would grow immeasurably, Burnham contends that no fundamental difference will exist between the managerial state and the bureaucratic one as both will have the same type of economy, ideology, and political institutions.[28] They cooperate.

Burnham holds that political power will shift from elected representatives to these unelected managers and bureaucrats. The latter were already usurping political power from Congress, evidenced by the fact that "laws" were no longer made by Congress, but rather by government agencies, such as the "NLRB, SEC, ICC, AAA, TVA, FTC, FCC, the Office of Production Management (what a revealing title!), and the other leading 'executive agencies.'"[29] Most recent laws passed by Congress in fact had increased the power of government agencies.[30] Burnham concedes that the United States had yet to reach the same stage as the USSR and Nazi Germany—Congress would occasionally discipline or even abolish an agency.[31] But present trends favored the bureaucrats.

Burnham's ideas about the bureaucracy and its importance largely come from Trotsky. Marx, Engels, and Lenin and even Marxist theoretician Nikolai Bukharin grappled with the concept of bureaucracy, but Trotsky's analysis was the most complete. He had struggled politically with the bureaucracy in his efforts to thwart Stalin—and lost. Even before Lenin's death, Trotsky wrote that the bureaucracy was the enemy of the party, implying that the bureaucracy was the enemy of the people.[32] In 1927, Trotsky wrote that the USSR was increasingly coming under the control of "an innumerable caste of genuine bureaucrats."[33]

In *The Revolution Betrayed*, he partly blames the bureaucracy for socialism's wayward path in the USSR: "The new ruling caste soon revealed its own ideas, feelings and, more important, its interests.... The bureaucracy conquered something more than the Left Opposition. It conquered the Bolshevik party."[34] Trotsky suggests that a new bureaucracy could replace the decaying bourgeoisie as a new oppressor class, meaning it had to be resisted in order for democracy to succeed.[35] He interprets the bureaucracy as a politically independent force—neither left nor right. It pursues only its own interest and seeks to maintain its privileges. And it could—at least temporarily—rule the Soviet Union.

The Managerial Revolution is partly a neo-Trotskyite treatise. Burnham based his predictions about the powerful managerial-bureaucratic class on Trotsky's interpretation of the Soviet Union. Burnham first presented his notion that a society can be neither capitalist nor socialist while emphasizing the bureaucracy in his 1937 response to *The Revolution Betrayed*, in which he describes the Soviet Union in Trotskyite terms: "The Soviet State at present is primarily the instrument of the privileged strata of Soviet society—the bureaucracy, Army (particularly the upper ranks), the GPU, the richer collective peasants, the technicians, intellectuals, better-paid Stakhanovites, etc.; and the instrument also of the sections of the international bourgeoisie toward which the State gravitates. Is this not the *fact*?"[36] Adhering to Trotsky's view of the Soviet Union, Burnham argues in this 1937 article that the real rulers would be more subtle managers and bureaucrats. Bland, nameless and faceless, they controlled the levers of power. Burnham continues, "Is this a 'no-class' state? Of course not. It is simply not, primarily, the instrument of either of the two major classes in contemporary society."[37] He agrees with Trotsky that the Soviet Union was ruled by a privileged bureaucracy.

Trotsky believed this was a temporary stage in Soviet development until the workers prevailed, whereas Burnham speculates in *The Managerial Revolution* that this was the next stage in human history. Everyone was traveling along the same road, albeit at different speeds. Significantly, he did not distinguish between Nazism and communism—they were both already managerial societies because Stalin and Hitler had dismantled capitalism and were coordinating policies with the managers.[38] The Nazi-Soviet Pact of 1939 showed that the two nation-states could collaborate; economic and social relations between them swelled as German managers and goods moved east.[39] At the same time, Russian boundaries expanded west.[40] Burnham places Japan in the camp of managerialism, too. He even suggests that Russia could split in two parts: a European West and a Siberian East that would cooperate with Asia.[41]

The Managerial Revolution is determinist. It holds that the United States was a burgeoning managerial society and although geographically separate from Europe, the United States cannot resist worldwide trends.[42] The New Deal was displacing capitalism; it represented a new stage on the road to managerialism. Agriculture had become dependent on state subsidies and the state was now the "greatest banking establishment."[43] Burnham argues in *The Managerial Revolution* that no one could deny that the New Deal "moves in the same direction as Stalinism and Nazism. The New Deal is a phase of the transition process from capitalism to managerial society."[44] The forecaster adds that he did not necessarily like where the world was going, but he had to report what was true.[45]

Written mostly in 1940 when the future seemed to belong to Germany, USSR, and Japan, *The Managerial Revolution* predicts that this trend would continue, with the United States maintaining its privileged position in the Western hemisphere. The rest of the world would coalesce around these hegemonic centers. This tripartite division of the world is based on the ideas of Halford Mackinder, a turn-of-the-century geographer and geopolitical strategist. Burnham does not cite him in *The Managerial Revolution*, but he does refer to Mackinder in future writings. Mackinder insisted that geography played a pivotal role in international relations. Believing that Europe and Asia were one great continent, he divided the world into three strategic regions: (1) the World Island, consisting of Europe, Asia, and Africa; (2) the Offshore Islands, comprising Japan and Britain; and (3) the Outlying Islands, North and South America. The World Island, the largest and richest of all land combinations, had at its center the "Heartland." This was roughly Eastern Europe (and subsequently the Soviet Union). Mackinder declared that whoever controlled it controlled the world. This idea would dominate Burnham's post–World War II writings.

Would these managerial societies be totalitarian like Nazi Germany and the USSR? Or would they be democratic? Before answering, Burnham waxes philosophical by critiquing ideology and political concepts. He holds that ideologies are often "the expression of hopes, wishes, fears, ideals, not a hypothesis about events—though ideologies are often thought by those who hold them to be scientific theory."[46] He gives the examples of Marxism, the doctrines of the US Constitution and Declaration of Independence, Nazi racial doctrines, and even some religious beliefs. Burnham chastised popular political concepts, too. For Burnham, freedom was a term better used as "freedom." He contends, "Freedom is by itself an incomplete term; there is no such thing as freedom, pure and simple; it must always be freedom from things and for something."[47] He continues: "If you want to be free of hangovers, you must restrict your freedom to drink larger amounts of alcohol. When slaves were freed in the South, planters were no longer free to own slaves."[48] Freedom is not an absolute value, but a relative one.

When it came to explaining the totalitarian or democratic nature of future managerial societies, Burnham equivocates. He argues that totalitarianism, impossible in past ages, had been facilitated by modern technology as it allowed the state to intimately control the lives of its people.[49] Privacy has been vanquished. Burnham predicts that the executive branch would expand in concert with the bureaucracy, at the expense of institutions, such as congress and parliaments.[50] A managerial society, however, cannot be completely totalitarian because it must be attuned to popular demands to satisfy them.[51] A totalitarian government separates itself from the needs of the people, so it cannot thrive. It lacks knowledge of what its citizens needed because everyone was afraid to provide true and unbiased information; the USSR proved this.[52] Democracy, in contrast, leads to openness, and knowledge of the people's needs. Moreover, democracy allows the masses to "let off steam" without ruining the social fabric of managerial society.[53] Revolutionary fervor builds in totalitarian systems because no other outlets exist. Given all of this, Burnham asserts that the totalitarian managerial societies were just transitory phenomena. More democratic managerial societies would emerge.

Yet they would not necessarily be democratic in the modern sense of the word. Providing ideas he would explore in more depth in future works, Burnham theorizes that not everyone can have equal political rights because the ruling classes always keep their privilege.[54] They must maintain control of the "instruments of production."[55] Moreover, opposition groups, so important in democracy, would wane in managerial society because they required different factions to position themselves for and against, such as labor against capital, or light industry against heavy industry.[56] Burnham acknowledges that this was all speculation. Managerial society could produce some sort of democracy that simultaneously accorded some power to the people while also allowing the managerial class to maintain its privileged status.[57] The purported prophet did know this: the democracy of capitalist society was moribund, and a new society was emerging.[58] World War II was just the birth pains.

The Managerial Revolution represents a broader trend in American political and social life in the 1930s and 1940s: the shift toward centralism. The tendency began with the onset of the Great Depression and the ensuing government responses, such as the New Deal. The pace quickened during World War II when Western governments wrested even more economic and social power away from private interest. Ensuring that it produced everything needed to win the war, the US government created numerous agencies that directed the production of the economy. Civilian goods, such as automobiles and nonessential foods and textiles, were shuttered for state purposes. The question was whether these were temporary, makeshift solutions to the problem of Nazi and Japanese expansion, or whether they represented (and should they) a permanent trend in world history? For left-wing socialists, the days of unregulated, unplanned economies were over. Right-wing fascists agreed.[59] And so did James Burnham.

Burnham may have been influenced by Bruno Rizzi, author of *Bureaucratization of the World* (1939). Published in France under the name "Bruno R.," many copies of Rizzi's work were confiscated by the French state, but his ideas still circulated among Marxists. Trotsky made numerous allusions to "Bruno R." in 1939 and even called Burnham a "semi-follower" of Rizzi's.[60] Rizzi adhered to Trotsky's position that the Soviet Union was not really a socialist state, but rather a bureaucratic one: "The Soviet state, rather than becoming socialized, is becoming bureaucratized; instead of gradually dissolving into society without classes, it is growing immeasurably."[61] The Soviet Union was merely bureaucratic collectivism. The bureaucrats exploit the masses, too. Trotsky believed that the Soviet Union's path toward bureaucratic collectivism was a temporary aberration. Rizzi disagreed. He argued two years before *The Managerial Revolution* that Stalinism, fascism, and even the New Deal were all manifestations of a single trend that represented the future.

Accusations of plagiarism emerged shortly after *The Managerial Revolution* appeared, even by Rizzi himself.[62] Burnham said he had heard of Rizzi through Trotsky but had not read his work.[63] Rizzi claimed Burnham was lying.[64] Over ten years after the publication of *The Managerial Revolution*, Rizzi and Burnham exchanged cordial letters. Telling Burnham that he presented his ideas to Trotsky in 1938, Rizzi inquired where Burnham had first learned of him.[65] Burnham replied that he could not remember that exact piece in which Trotsky had referred to Rizzi, but he was certain it was in 1939.[66] Burnham maintained that he had tried for many years to obtain a copy of Rizzi's work and requested a copy of the *Bureaucratization of the World*.[67]

Burnham acknowledged his debt to Thorstein Veblen's *The Engineers and the Price System* (1921).[68] This collection of essays analyzes America's economy in the aftermath of World War I. Declining industry and rising unemployment meant for Veblen the dawn of a new economic era. What would come next? Veblen predicts the rise of expert engineers—a class separate from the factory owners—who would and should guide production. He asserts, "This incoming industrial order is designed to correct the shortcomings of the old."[69] Veblen stresses concepts like "collective ownership" and "absentee owners" when attempting to explain how the new class would effectively allocate resource in the next stage of economic development.[70]

The Managerial Revolution was a hit. One review called it "the most widely read essay in social theory and philosophy of history to appear in recent years."[71] The *New York Times* spent multiple days reviewing the book, concluding that it was "extraordinarily impressive in some respects" and that "its scope and implications are enormous."[72] Noting that its readers hotly debated the book's prognostications, *Fortune* magazine called it, "the most debated book published so far this year."[73] *Time* magazine called it "one of the top books of 1941."[74] *Foreign Affairs* opined "in spite of its inconsistencies, schematic dogmatism and other faults, this provocative book may have a deep influence on the social and political thought of our time."[75]

The reviews were not consistently favorable. Numerous reviewers slammed the book. Dwight Macdonald (also a former Trotskyite and now editor of *Partisan Review*), in an eight-page review titled "The Burnhamian Revolution," spent most of the space criticizing the work. Macdonald wrote: "Logically fallacious, Burnham's thesis is also historically baseless. Although he frequently claims that the revolution it describes has already taken place to a large degree, he mentions only one specimen of the manager in the whole book ... and not a single managerial party, program or even a group."[76] Criticizing his former comrade for his lack of data, MacDonald insisted that a vast gulf existed between what the author said and what the author did. Burnham discussed the scientific method, but he never employed it.[77] McDonald even wrote the work resembled propaganda.[78]

Marxists were even less impressed. Trotskyite Albert Glotzer (using the pseudonym Albert Gates) dismissed Burnham's book by arguing that its popularity stemmed from its prediction that socialism was not the wave of the future. Loving this argument, the bourgeoisie promoted Burnham's work, ensuring its popularity.[79] Marxist economist Paul Sweezy wrote a full-length article reviewing the book. Titled "The Illusion of the 'Managerial Revolution,'" it too took issue with Burnham's contention that some sort of new economic system had emerged in Germany under Hitler. Yes, Hitler directed more state control of the economy, but profit margins had returned to, or surpassed, their pre-depression levels for German industrialists, showing that the capitalists had benefited from the Nazi regime.[80] And, yes, the Soviet Union had not achieved socialism by most measures, at least not yet. But Marx's and Engels's theory of revolution "makes specific allowance for a period of transition, significantly called 'the dictatorship of the proletariat.'"[81] There was no timetable for the completion of revolution. Joseph Hansen, a Trotskyite, wrote: "As Trotsky predicted, this petty bourgeois snob has swiftly completed his evolution into a rabid enemy of Marxism . . . The essence of Burnham's alternative is borrowed—without acknowledging the source—from Bruno R., an Italian who developed the theory that capitalism is being replaced by a new kind of exploiting society."[82]

Mixed reviews and inconsistencies aside, Burnham became a respected public intellectual. John Kenneth Galbraith maintained that *The Managerial Revolution* was more popular than Berle's and Mean's *The Modern Corporation*.[83] Burnham's predictions about the collectivization of Western society prompted a litany of responses over the next several years. Some of these books became classics in twentieth-century thought, especially among conservatives. *The Managerial Revolution* provides part of the context for Peter Drucker, Ludwig von Mises, Fredrich Hayek, and Karl Popper. *The Future of Industrial Man* (1942), *Bureaucracy* (1944), *The Road to Serfdom* (1944), and *The Open Society and Its Enemies* (1945) must, to some degree, be understood as rejections of the collectivism that Burnham predicted would sweep around the world. Written during World War II, the authors of these books had agreed with Burnham that Nazism and communism were related ideologies. Unlike Burnham, however, they had feared both; the authors had left Central Europe in hopes of finding economic and social freedom. Insisting nothing was inevitable, they champion free economies and open societies.

Peter Drucker reviewed *The Managerial Revolution* in 1941 and recognized that the book continued Marxist themes, such as the idea that social, political, and economic development followed advances in technology. He ends his review by proclaiming, "All in all, it is one of the best recent books on political and social trends; it will probably become the Bible of the next generation of neo-Marxists."[84] Drucker's *The Future of Industrial Man* (1942) contests Burnham's thesis by arguing that modern industrial society should be—and could be—free. One way to achieve this was through decentralization: Drucker suggests that the managerial elite held too much power, and to curb it, businesses and corporations needed more decentralizations. He also questions Burnham's thesis about inevitability by reasoning that if Germany had developed along pacificist lines instead of militarist, this would have been seen as the logical outgrowth of the Reformation, Kant, and Beethoven. If tyranny had swept across England, it would have been the logical culmination of Cromwell, Hobbes, and Bentham.[85] Drucker maintains that Nazi victory in World War II was not assured.[86] He offers a more optimistic vision of the future than Burnham, one at least less collectivist, rigid, and determinist.

Another émigré, Ludwig von Mises, lauded the freedom that capitalism seemingly promoted. His *Bureaucracy* (1944) refutes the idea that we should passively accept that the world was moving toward managerialism. Von Mises summarizes Burnham's position as follows: "Managers, responsible to nobody, will become a hereditary aristocracy; the government will become mere puppets of an omnipotent business clique."[87] Noting that for adherents this phenomenon was inevitable, *Bureaucracy* challenges this by demonstrating that bureaucracy can be foiled by restraining government interference.[88] Von Mises continues that bureaucracy is not inherently bad because government needs it to function; only when bureaucracy interferes with all aspects of human life does the system becomes totalitarian.[89] Capitalism thwarted this because no industry will ever fall prey to bureaucratic collectivism as long as it remains profit motivated.[90]

Von Mises's colleague, Friedrich Hayek, reviewed *The Managerial Revolution*. He notes that for its author, although Roosevelt is the face of the New Deal, the real representatives are "administrators, technicians, bureaucrats, who have been finding places through the state apparatus."[91] Hayek's *The Road to Serfdom* (1944) describes *The Managerial Revolution* as a "significant book."[92] In his book, Hayek reduces economic theorists to two groups: individualists (like himself) and collectivists (or totalitarians). The latter tacitly included Burnham, Nazis, and communists because they favored a state-centered economy designed to promote the greater good.[93] Hayek insists that this paved the road for totalitarianism: "The authority directing all economic activity would control not merely the part of our lives which is concerned with inferior things; it would control the allocation of the limited means for all our ends. And whoever controls all economic activity controls the means for all our ends must therefore decide which are to be satisfied and which not. This is really the crux of the matter."[94] The economic philosopher contends that economic planning meant controlling the people, so whereas Burnham analyzes the rise of centrally planned economies neutrally, Hayek laments the phenomenon. Not accepting Burnham's ideas that freedom was relative and arbitrary, Hayek holds that expanding government should be feared because the more government grows, the more restrictions it will impose on personal freedom.

Hayek's friend Karl Popper also feared Burnham's predictions might come true. He refers to Burnham in the introduction of *The Open Society and Its Enemies* (1945), writing that "those minor prophets who announce that certain events, such as a lapse into totalitarianism (or perhaps into 'managerialism'), are bound to happen may, whether they like it or not, be instrumental in bringing these events about."[95] Burnham may not have realized it, but for Popper, his predictions about the inevitability of managerial collectivism fueled the totalitarian fire; they became self-fulfilling prophecies. Popper contends that these ideas discouraged individuals from fighting against totalitarian regimes, which he equates with collectivism.

Burnham continued *The Managerial Revolution*'s pessimism about the prospects of real democracy in a 1941 article titled "Is Democracy Possible?" The more skeptical Burnham rears his head here. He contends that democracy's biggest enemy is always whatever force dominates society—this can be the Church, or military, or landowners, or capitalists.[96] Currently in advanced civilizations, it was the state.[97] And who controlled the state? He continues to predict that state and society are headed toward some sort of centralized managerial or bureaucratic control.[98] What about the people—those who have power in democracy? Burnham announces that they always lose, so real democracy can never prevail: "Democracy can never win. Democracy always loses, because the forces of democracy, in winning, cease to be democratic."[99] Burnham suggests that it was a law of nature that most people could not be winners.[100] Thus, democracy could never prevail.

CHAPTER 4

After leaving Marxism, the cynical Burnham rarely envisioned a future that belonged to the people. He always distrusted the ruling elite, but any faith he had in the masses collapsed, too. In fact, he even questioned how much the masses really cared about democracy, anyway. Weren't they more concerned with patriotism, morality, and economic security?[101] He reduced politics to a power struggle between competing elites. Any semblance of democracy was fleeting. These ideas were expanded in his next work, a work inspired by one of the most cynical of all thinkers.

Chapter 5

The Truth about the Elite

The Managerial Revolution predicted the inevitable collectivization of society. When Burnham wrote the book, collectivist Germany, the USSR, and Japan seemed destined to rule their regions of the world. The United States was technically neutral. But Pearl Harbor changed everything, both in the United States and in Burnham's mind. The United States now fought against the managerial collectivism Burnham believed represented the future. He went from a detached observer of events in Europe to a proponent of war.[1] In *The Machiavellians: Defenders of Freedom* (1943), Burnham expresses concern for the centralization that he believed was the wave of the future. The book provides specific ways to resist this process—even contending that thwarting tyranny depended on it.

Written in the same flat yet straightforward manner as Machiavelli's *The Prince*, *The Machiavellians* is a practical analysis of politics. It specifically seeks to raise consciousness about the raging power struggle that Burnham asserts existed in all societies. Using Machiavelli's method, Burnham tries to scientifically study how rulers obtain, use, and lose power. After all, politics is based on observable events, and these events can be recorded and analyzed. Subsequent theories can emerge, which can then be tested through future events. Burnham suggests that this empirical method reveals truths about the nature of power.

The work continues the reductionism that characterized Marxism. For Marxists, the history of the world can be reduced to a class struggle. For the new Machiavellian, the history of the world can be reduced to power struggle. The Machiavellians were the only ones with the wisdom and courage to tell the people the real truth: that everything was about power. Priests, humanitarians, soldiers, business leaders, bureaucrats, presidents, and feudal lords sought power.[2] These people exercise power and will not give it up.

The Machiavellians is a product of the gloomy James Burnham. After leaving Marxism, Burnham found a thinker that allowed him to project cynicism toward individuals, society, and politics. Machiavelli wrote in *Discourses* that the founders of any state must assume "that all men are bad, and will always, when they have free field, give loose to their evil inclinations."[3] Burnham adopted this assumption, applied it to the ruling classes, and provided a method to resist the duplicitous power-seekers in hopes of curbing extreme authoritarianism.

Franklin Delano Roosevelt (FDR) was Burnham's first subject. Before becoming president, FDR preached limited government, and the Democratic Party's 1932 platform demanded cuts in spending and a balanced budget. In *The Machiavellians*, Burnham calls these words the "formal meaning."[4] They were deceptive because, in reality, FDR expanded the power of government. His words masked his true intentions. Dante Alighieri's *De Monarchia* provided another example for Burnham. Dante preached a universal empire based on peace (the formal meaning). Burnham calls this "politics as a wish."[5] Although Dante employed concepts like peace, unity, and harmony, they meant nothing. In reality, Dante was a warmongering partisan. His work was a propagandist defense of a Renaissance political faction, the Ghibellines.[6]

Burnham argues in *The Machiavellians* that the "real meaning" of words and texts was often disguised in the formal meaning.[7] He insists: "It is characteristic of *De Monarchia*, and of all similar treatises, that there should be this divorce between formal and real meanings, that the formal meaning should not explicitly state but only indirectly express, and to one or another extent hide and distort, the real meaning. The real meaning is thereby rendered irresponsible, since it is not subject to open and deliberate intellectual control; but the real meaning is nonetheless there."[8] Disputes about the nature of God at Nicaea were really about the authority of Rome over the Mediterranean region.[9] Debates about balanced budgets were really about who regulated the distribution of currency.[10] Discussions about movement in seas were really about who controls the seas.[11]

The Machiavellians taught the people to distrust the words elites use because rulers seek to "confuse and hide."[12] Burnham asserts that examining the action of rulers, not their rhetoric, reveals their true motivations because the ruling class never tells the truth. He declares: "In the hands of the powerful and their spokesman, however, used by the demagogues or hypocrites or simply the self-deluded, this method is well-designed . . . to deceive us, and to lead us by easy routes to the sacrifice of our or own interests in the service of the mighty."[13] The real levers of government are pulled by the elite. And they will do anything to maintain their positions of power, even resorting to force and fraud.[14]

Burnham continues by examining four thinkers he calls "The Machiavellians." Like their forefather, these thinkers wrote during a time of social and economic upheaval. Noting that Machiavelli lived during the opening of the New World, Burnham contends that the first half of the twentieth century was equally transformative. According to Burnham, this explained Machiavelli's new-found popularity, after so long having been ignored or misunderstood.[15] As World War I raged—one of the great power struggles in human history—ideas analyzing power relations bloomed. The Machiavellians Gaetano Mosca, Vilfredo Pareto, Georges Sorel, and Robert Michels were power theorists who wrote around the time of the Great War. Unlike Machiavelli, these men had four hundred years of human experience and scientific development at their disposal, allowing them to create a science of politics.[16]

Gaetano Mosca, an Italian political scientist and author of *Elementi di Scienza Politica* (1923, translated in 1939 as *The Ruling Class*), was Burnham's first Machiavellian, and the one he felt most sympathy toward.[17] Mosca argued that societies were composed of two groups: the minority who rule and the majority who do not.[18] True democracy was impossible because the masses cannot rule themselves; an elite inevitably emerges. Mosca maintains that this holds true in every conceivable form of government, including feudal, capitalist, socialist, collectivist, democratic, and aristocratic.[19]

In Mosca's view, the official head-of-state may not even be part of the real ruling class. He believed that below the highest stratum of society, a larger, more numerous group of people existed whose power often eclipses that of the rulers.[20] They direct the activities of the masses. Their integrity was vital because "any intellectual or moral deficiencies in this second stratum, accordingly, represent a graver danger to the political structure, and one that is harder to repair, than the presence of similar deficiencies in the few dozen persons who control the workings of the state machine."[21] This level of government that can supplant the rulers may be called the bureaucracy. It remained crucial for Burnham.

Burnham wrote that, according to Mosca, the best societies have an open pool of rulers, representing various classes and interests. The elites circulate from the masses to positions among the ruling class. How does one become part of the ruling class? The rulers and their spokesmen will insist that the rulers are wiser, or they have inherited superior traits, or they possess altruism, or they are willing to sacrifice for the community.[22] Burnham writes that the Machiavellians know to distrust words. Ambition, hard work, and luck will propel one into the ruling class more easily than intelligence and virtue.[23] Most important, rulers will have an attribute that the society esteems. A skilled warrior will rise to prominence in a military society; an able priest in a religious society.[24] Mosca did not make moral judgments; he just studied things the way they really are.[25]

For Mosca, all ruling classes display two tendencies: autocratic and liberal.[26] These principles regulate social and political life. They never exist in isolation, for all societies have some liberal and some autocratic features that inspire the ruling classes. According to Burnham, the United States may proclaim itself a democracy (or even a republic), but the bureaucracy and federal judiciary demonstrate autocratic features because its members are not elected.[27] Liberal and autocratic elements are indispensable because a completely autocratic society will be tyrannical, and a completely democratic society will not have security.[28] In the traditional of Aristotle, extremes must be avoided.

Following Mosca, Burnham affirms that both forms of government have strengths and weaknesses. Autocracies recognize that social hierarchies are natural. This explains their popularity throughout history among diverse civilizations, and why they tend to last longer.[29] They thrive when the rulers really are the best members of societies. But autocracies limit social activities and forces. Burnham argues in *The Machiavellians* that Classical Athens and Western Europe never could have prospered as autocracies.[30] Yet democracy had deficiencies, too. Parroting Mosca, Burnham insists that political leaders in democracies merely point out "with exaggerations, of course, the selfishness, the stupidity, the material enjoyments of the rich and the powerful; to denouncing their vices and wrongdoings, real and imaginary; and to promise to satisfy a common and widespread sense of rough-hewn justice."[31] Elected politicians have little choice but to play to the crudest instincts of the masses, making promises they could never really keep.

Whatever type of political system exists, the elite must be restrained or tyranny reigns. Mosca preached "juridical defense" as a means to check the powerful. This social mechanism helps rulers and the masses control their "wicked instincts."[32] It is a form of power against the elite that consists of the hallmarks of contemporary democracy: private property; due process; and freedom of assembly, speech, and religion.[33] Checks against the ruling elite lead to balance between the aristocratic and democratic tendencies. Without checks and balances, an aristocracy "produces a closed and inflexible caste system," whereas extreme democracy leads to social disorder.[34] Citing Mosca, Burnham contends that history has revealed that civilizations thrive when guided by various political and social forces.[35] Freedom comes from conflict, not unity.[36]

Burnham contends that Mosca was not utopian. In fact, Burnham maintains, Mosca believed that political doctrines that promise utopia are the worst of all. Justice is good, but not absolute justice. Those who prescribe it should be looked at skeptically. Again quoting Mosca, Burnham continues: "The idealists, utopians and demagogues always tell us that justice and the good society will be achieved by the absolute triumph of their side. The facts show us that the absolute triumph of any side and any doctrine whatsoever can only mean tyranny."[37] When leaders of the governing class, without opposition, claim to be the exclusive interpreters of the will of the people in a democratic society, or the will of God in a religious society, oppression will ensue.[38]

What governments most successfully promote freedom? Burnham suggests that Mosca argued that nineteenth-century parliamentary forms of government most effectively provided safety from tyranny. They had aristocratic elements, but these were checked by the "unprecedented ease with which vigorous new members were able to enter the ruling class."[39] Consequently, commerce, arts, literature, science, and technology flourished.

Burnham's second Machiavellian was George Sorel, a *fin de siècle* French socialist and political theorist who authored *Reflections on Violence* (1908). Burnham states that Sorel, as a political extremist, cannot be a true Machiavellian. The Machiavellians repudiated any political extremism because they generally eschewed political activity and ideology to scientifically study the way things really are. Burnham, however, contends that Sorel did influence Machiavellians like Michaels and Pareto, so he must be examined along with them.[40]

In *The Machiavellians*, Burnham writes that Sorel recognized humankind's desire for power.[41] Sorel believed that the conquest of the political state by one party over another does not fundamentally change the state; it just changes who has power. The conquest of power by socialist parties, for example, will not give power to the people. It will just give power to socialist parties.[42]

Burnham also notes that, according to Sorel, myths must exist to sustain civilization.[43] For Sorel, great myths should never be confused with the Noble Lie because the great myth can never be proven or disproven. Christianity and its ideas that Jesus will return, Marx's imminent socialist revolution, and Mazzini's nationalist propaganda all constitute great myths for Sorel. Contending that the successful myth binds the members of society together by arousing their energies toward a solution for any problem, Sorel held that the myth guides action.[44]

The myth must be accompanied by violence. One section of *The Machiavellians* is titled "The Function of Violence." Burnham argues that Sorel defended violence, especially on the part of the working classes. The elite, who rule by fraud, feign revulsion at violence so they can protect themselves.[45] Violence provides the best means for the masses to reclaim power, but they have been deluded by what the ruling classes deem humanitarian pacifism.[46] Sorel believed that strikes and violence were necessary for socialism because this was the only way to overthrow the existing power structure. He rationalized violence used in the context of class struggle.

The Machiavellians rejects any sort of idealistic approach to violence. Burnham holds that Sorel believed humanitarian and pacificist movements only cause social degeneration because they fail to recognize that "force is always a main factor regulating a society."[47] These movements merely redirect force in more subtle ways, such as fraud, bribery, and deception. This can only lead to the destruction of society, either from without or within. Consistent with Machiavelli, elites who practice benevolence only get overthrown, to the detriment of all.[48] Their benevolence harms themselves and their societies.

Citing Sorel, Burnham insists that societies need violence to sustain themselves and their values: "An open recognition of the necessity of violence can reverse the social degeneration. . . . Myth and violence reciprocally acting on each other, produce not senseless cruelty and suffering, but sacrifice and heroism."[49] Violence and force are ubiquitous in societies. Pacifists can do nothing to curb this, just as a doctor who ignores the existence of germs does not weaken their effects.[50] Burnham asks: what had pacifism actually accomplished? The eighteenth-century French aristocracy preached humanitarianism; revolutionary bloodshed followed. Peace movements swept across the West on the eve of World War I and World War II. This stopped nothing. In fact, pacifists had only made things worse because "they have, rather, in those countries where they were most influential, brought about a situation in which many more men have been killed than would have been if policy had been based on the fact that wars are a natural phase of historical progress."[51] As a Marxist, Burnham condemned pacificism. Here, as a Machiavellian, he uses Sorel to condemn it.

Sorel also allowed Burnham to project his usual pessimism. Burnham notes that Sorel decried optimists as a danger to society because they cannot understand the true nature of its corruption.[52] This leads them to pursue misguided courses of action to correct things.[53] The Reign of Terror of the French Revolution took the lives of those who dreamed the most. The pessimists, in Machiavellian fashion, see things most clearly, and so they are the wisest. They will most successfully overcome obstacles.[54]

Sorel's one-time friend and collaborator Robert Michels was Burnham's third Machiavellian. Burnham begins his chapter on Michels by contending that those who write about democracy operate under the assumption that democracy is good.[55] All books about democracy imply this, analyze why democracy has not been achieved, and then explain how it can he achieved. The same is true with peace, justice, and a host of other concepts. Burnham argues that the Machiavellians were different because before declaring an allegiance to a concept, they made clear exactly what the concept means.

As realists, the Machiavellians knew that real democracy—defined as the people having power—was impossible. According to Burnham, Michels recognized that if everyone tried to have an equal say in any committee or organization, nothing would get done.[56] Michels believed that every society must have an elite class because as soon as leadership emerges—and it inevitably does—democracy ceases. Rousseau recognized this first when he argued that democracy should mean more than just voting for whoever rules over you.[57] The will of the people is not transferable to a single individual, despite what the despots want us to believe.[58] Moreover, decisions must occasionally be made quickly during times of crisis, yet real democracy can never move quickly.

According to Michels's "iron law of oligarchy," in any group of people, only a small number of them will actually make decisions, regardless of how power is formally vested. The masses can never really rule.

Michels, Burnham tells his reader, proclaimed that even within democracy those with power will seek to extend it.[59] Burnham argues that the struggle against these power-lovers should continue.[60] Burnham quotes Michels: "Nothing but a serene and frank examination of the oligarchical dangers of a democracy will enable us to minimize these dangers, even though they can never be entirely avoided."[61] Consciousness must be raised. Oligarchical and aristocratic elements dominate political systems, but Burnham, like Michels, insists that extreme measures have to be resisted.

The book's final Machiavellian thinker is Vilfredo Pareto, the author of *Trattato di Sociologia Generale* (1916, translated in 1935 as *The Mind and Society*). Burnham writes that Pareto sought to uncover the "general laws" that guided society.[62] Pareto, in Burnham's description, favored an objective study of society based on empirical data, not a utopian philosophy.[63] This was preferable, Burnham argues, because anyone can tell us how to save society; only a rare few can tell us real truths about society.[64]

Burnham points out that Pareto emphasized the irrational side of man. Taboos, superstitions, myths, and even "empty verbalisms" pervade all civilizations.[65] Every civilization has its own irrational beliefs that it needs to thrive. Whether a society rises or falls depends little on its ability to use reason.[66] Pareto did not believe that reason could be used to improve society because most people were not rational.

Burnham writes that Pareto argued that the character of society was the character of its elites; the accomplishments of society are the accomplishments of its elite class.[67] A society must ensure that the elite class is open to everyone, equally.[68] According to Burnham, like Mosca, Pareto advocated an open rulership with circulating elites. This ensures dynamism and strength. Democracy promotes an open elite system more than aristocracy, in which elite status is merely acquired at birth. Elites can be found in all segments of society.[69]

The Machiavellians promotes a pragmatic approach to political science. Values and ideals by themselves cannot effectively guide human conduct. For example, Burnham asks, what does freedom mean? There is no general freedom, just freedom from or for certain things. If I am free not to be murdered by individuals, then you are not free to murder me.[70] President Roosevelt, Burnham writes, described "freedom from want" as one of his central goals, but man is a wanting animal, so achieving this goal was impossible.[71] Burnham maintains that the same holds true with equality: all men are equal in some respects, but men in general cannot be completely equal.[72] These concepts sound nice and they do guide action, but rational action in the real world cannot be based strictly on concepts: "Thus, in all cases—and these include the majority that is relevant to social change—where goals are vague or ambiguous or meaningless, human conduct is non-logical."[73] For Burnham, these so-called ideals resembled religious values. Each in its own way makes positive contributions to society, but their relevance to society is still limited because they remain subjective.[74]

Burnham later characterized the writing of *The Machiavellians* as a form of post-Trotsky education that showed him the weakness of ideology, which prevented the acquisition of wisdom: "Having come to know something of the gigantic ideology of Bolshevism, I knew that I was not going to be able to settle for the pygmy ideologies of Liberalism, social democracy, refurbished laissez-faire or the inverted, cut-rate Bolshevism called 'fascism.' Through the Machiavellians I began to understand more thoroughly what I had long felt: that only by renouncing all ideology can we begin to see the world and man."[75] Ideology was guided by core values, but Burnham makes clear that Machiavellians assumed nothing—they questioned all values. He argues that "peace," "democracy," and "justice" must constantly be examined to determine their usefulness.[76] Before advocating a concept, the Machiavellians always clarified what the concept means and what it will lead too.[77] Obviously, peace was not always desirable, or the United States would not have engaged in World War II. And true democracies can never really exist, so why call them that? And what is meant by justice? The Machiavellian did not base their philosophy on vague, abstract principles.[78]

Does this mean that the Machiavellians and by extension Burnham reject all human ideals and morality? Burnham answers in the negative. In fact, he points out that the Machiavellians try more than anyone else to study real human ideals, such as truth, not artificial ones like "freedom," "justice," and "equality." Recognizing the futility of studying humanity based on subjective, empty concepts, the Machiavellians study the true nature of humanity, not a romanticized version.[79]

Some of Burnham's expositors have interpreted him as an amoral thinker.[80] This is incorrect. Burnham's morality revolved around seeing human nature as it really is. Liberating humans from their naivete was a moral act for the Machiavellian Burnham. His writings for the next three and a half decades following the publication of *The Machiavellians* tried to do exactly this. He begs his readers to see things the way they really are, not how they wished them to be. Burnham believed that no moralist could support disillusionment. His experience with Marxism taught him that utopianism was worthless—and it made the world a worse place for everyone involved. Jettisoning idealism from one's thought was moral for Burnham.

Sidney Hook called Burnham's *The Machiavellians* "the least known and most important of his books."[81] Another colleague deemed it "the key to everything he subsequently wrote."[82] And it is, particularly the end of the work. The last chapter of *The Machiavellians* titled "Politics and Truth" summarizes the relevance of the Machiavellian thinkers for the author, and it describes ways for the masses to resist tyranny, allowing for a small measure of democracy.

The concept of democracy vexed Burnham more than any other during the first part of his writing career. In *The Machiavellians*, he acknowledges that true democracy as traditionally defined—such as "self-government" or "government by the people"—was impossible.[83] But Burnham contends that something called "Bonapartism," in which a leader or small group claimed to embody the will of the people, was gripping nations.[84] Stalin and Hitler provided recent examples. Their despotism allegedly is democratic because it is an expression of the people.[85] The rulers slyly use words to maintain their rule: "The century of the common man" instead becomes "the people's state" and the "classless society."[86] But words belie reality. In truth, according to Burnham, this tyranny of the minority in the name of the people was the worst of all possible systems.

Burnham felt obliged to define democracy again, insisting that it had different meanings for different people. In *The Machiavellians*, he relates democracy with liberty. Democracy exists when there is liberty: "Democracy so defined, in terms of liberty, of the right of opposition, is not in the least a formula or myth."[87] Everyone can agree that more liberty exists in the United States than in Germany or Russia.[88] This means it can be empirically studied, allowing for a science of politics.

The Machiavellians knew that social development depended on liberty.[89] And freedom must come from below. Machiavelli wrote in *Discourses* that elites seek to dominate, but "when the commons are put forward as the defenders of liberty, they may be expected to take better care of it."[90] Only the people can defend their liberty. Liberty must include the ability to express one's thoughts, even when it goes against prevailing opinion because "even when [liberty] offends the sentiments of the few or of the many, even when it is generally reputed absurd or criminal, [it] always proves favorable to the discovery of objective truth."[91] Without liberty, Burnham suggests, societies only advance in ways that are consistent with fascism. A religious fascism will lead to advances in religion. A military fascism will lead to advancements in war. Overall, however, conformity will prevail, stultifying any "creative freshness."[92]

How can the powerful be restrained so liberty and democracy can triumph, even transitorily? Burnham proclaims in *The Machiavellians* that only power restrains power.[93] Public opposition to government is the best way to ensure freedom and therefore any semblance of democracy; it is the most effective check against the ruling elite.[94] The power theorist insists that "liberty or juridical defense, moreover, is summed up and focused in the *right of opposition*, the right of opponents of the currently governing elite to express publicly their opposition views and to organize to implement those views."[95] Without opposition, tyranny thrives. Fortunately for Burnham, an opposition group can exert more power than its apparent strength because even a few thousand protesters can thwart the inevitable power grab by government.[96]

Burnham emphasizes in *The Machiavellians* the public nature of the opposition because it destroys "the prestige of the governing élite by exposing the inequities of its rule, which it knows much better than do the masses."[97] To curb public opposition, the ruling class makes concessions to the nonelite, limiting abuse.[98] The iron law of oligarchy means that the masses can never directly possess political power, but unless the people resist the elite, totalitarianism flourishes.[99] Burnham suggests that if the people do not exert force against the government, then it can be assumed that the government is exerting force against the people, limiting democracy.

The seemingly even-keeled philosophy professor wanted to raise consciousness about the raging power struggle and its relationship with democracy. He insists that to confront their enemies, the people must realize that those in power love power. Any benevolent act on the part of the government would be accidental.[100]

Burnham predicted in *The Managerial Revolution* that an increasing amount of power would accrue to the state. As US armies advanced against nations with strong centralized states, he now asserts that the future of liberty depended on those who resisted. Without continued resistance, the powerful would swallow up small outposts of resistance.[101] No one class or group preserves liberty; everyone who resists the government preserves liberty.[102] Those fighting against government may be deemed extremists, or even traitors, but Burnham argues that it is their extremism that preserves freedom. Now defending extremism, he provides several examples: extremist "Black Republicans" during the Civil War exerted force against Lincoln, enabling the North to win the Civil War more quickly.[103] During World War I, more oppositional force in England would have led the English to adopt the tank sooner, thereby saving lives.[104] More freedom for an oppositional force in Germany would have prevented some Nazi strategic errors, such as the Russian campaign.[105] Burnham suggests that extremism in defense of liberty is no vice.

The defender of liberty believed that liberty and democracy require an armed citizenship because arms strengthen the citizens (Machiavelli says the same in chapter 14 of *The Prince*).[106] Burnham, however, maintains that force should never be used individually and arbitrarily. The Machiavellians know never to trust individual men because all men are guided by ambition and power.[107] For liberty to be preserved, Machiavelli recognized that no one person can be above the law, whether ruler or a citizen.[108]

Burnham declares that only the Machiavellians speak the truth; they are the real defenders of freedom. He provides what he believed was the clearest description of Machiavelli's philosophy of power:

> In any case, whatever may be the desires of most men, it is most certainly against the interests of the powerful that the truth should be known about political behavior. If the political truths stated or approximated by Machiavelli were widely known by men, the success of tyranny and all the other forms of oppressive political rule would become much less likely. A deeper freedom would be possible in society than Machiavelli himself believed attainable. If men generally understood as much of the mechanism of rule and privilege as Machiavelli understood, they would no longer be deceived into accepting that rule and privilege, and they would know what steps to take to overcome them.[109]

For Burnham, Machiavelli's pernicious reputation among the powerful proves his verity.[110] Possessing much skill in sizing up their opponents, the powerful ruling elite recognize an intransigent enemy. Burnham argues that Machiavelli must be placed in the same category as an executed Bruno, an imprisoned Galileo, and an exiled Einstein.[111] He asserts that while those men teach us about the universe, Machiavelli teaches us about ourselves.

The Machiavellians was Burnham's response to disenchantment with Marxist political philosophy, as applied in the USSR. Instead of being ruled by the working masses, a corrupt elite ruled the country. Regardless of what its rulers said, it was a sham democracy. Burned by Marxism, Burnham lashed out against many philosophical concepts at this time. He certainly opposed Marxism, socialism, communism, and even laissez-faire capitalism. Freedom and even democracy were simultaneously critiqued and defended. Burnham's thinking after Marxism could be inconsistent, and it opposed most political values. The one exception was power and the human desire to exercise power.

In this sense, *The Machiavellians* represented another synthesis for Burnham because, in it, he preserves the Marxist theme of power and conflict between groups, but he abandons the emphasis on the wealthy economic elite. Power was not economically determined. It became an independent force. Now, the powerful may appear in an array of costumes. No longer is reality reduced to a power struggle between the capitalist and bourgeoisie, instead a power struggle rages between the elites in society who have power and the masses who do not. Force and power struggles are ubiquitous in society, and in contrast to Marxist illusions, there was little reason for hope or optimism; no socialist revolution would wipe the old world away.

The book lacks the historical determinism that usually underlies Burnham's writings. The world was not moving toward the rule of the duplicitous elite; it had always been here. The pessimist suggests in *The Machiavellians* that the sin-ridden world was here to stay. The best one could hope for would be that he or she apply the force, instead of it being applied against him or her.

One wonders if, at least at some level, Burnham realized that his fundamental premises were open to the same critiques he levied against Marxism. Power, too, is an abstract concept that the alleged Machiavellian never fully defined. It resembles concepts such as freedom and democracy; Burnham recognized that these could be defined in different ways. His attempt to scientifically study society was fraught with inadequacies. His Machiavellian approach was philosophy, not science.

The Machiavellians may have been directly inspired by Sidney Hook's "The Fetishism of Power" (Hook claimed decades later that he introduced Burnham to Machiavelli's thought in the late 1930s).[112] Hook's 1939 article for *The Nation* reviewed the new English translation of Mosca's *The Ruling Class*. Writing in the midst of the Soviet tragedy, Burnham's former collaborator wrote: "Mosca, Pareto and Michels, writing in an age when optimism was as general as pessimism is today, raised all the crucial problems which have now come to the fore."[113] Hook defined politics as the process by which the minority ruling elites attempted to satisfy their own interests.[114] Contending that the rulers play the role of saviors under the guise of new myths, Hooked argued that the masses always lose, however, because although the form of the rule changes, the content stays the same.[115] He also asserted that checks against corruption and oppression could and should occur. One safeguard that would protect the masses against the worst abuses of tyranny is "conflict" in social life. Hook held that it would "require a treatise" to explore this theme fully.[116]

The Machiavellians, like *The Managerial Revolution*, was widely reviewed. *The Atlantic* called it "a work of high quality in its political and philosophical analysis" and praised Burnham for studying the conditions that maintained liberty.[117] Benedetto Croce found Burnham's ideas about the nature of power and rulers plausible.[118] He wrote that Burnham, however, focused too narrowly on the political; he analyzed liberty only in the context of politics while ignoring man's moral nature.[119] For Croce, power was guided by morality; it was not an independent force. Reinhold Niebuhr was also critical in his review titled "Study in Cynicism." Niebuhr reduced Burnham's "science of politics" to cynicism about all things political, particularly rulers and their words.[120] But if Burnham's premises are true—if everyone dissembles merely to acquire power—then how can we trust Burnham? Do not social scientists seek power? Niebuhr argued that if political leaders are subject to the laws of human nature, then so is everyone else. If Burnham is correct, then Niebuhr concluded that we cannot trust him either.[121] *Time* magazine reviewed *The Machiavellians* with Sidney Hook's *Hero in History* (1943) in a review titled "Is Democracy Possible?" It unified the men by noting their Marxist heritage and how, in the wake of the Soviet fiasco, both wondered whether democracy could ever exist.[122] Although Burnham in *The Machiavellians* presented the theory that true democracy was impossible, Hook believed it could be achieved, but only with difficulty.

Chapter 6

Samuel Francis, George Orwell, the Bureaucratic Elite, and Power

The Managerial Revolution and *The Machiavellians* promote a worldview that distrusts the bureaucracy, government, and the ruling elite. *The Managerial Revolution* predicts a future ruled by a managerial and bureaucratic elite. *The Machiavellians* insists that the elites only work to perpetuate their power and privilege, making them the enemies of democracy. Burnham further popularized the disproportionate (some would say excessive) power of the bureaucracy in a 1959 piece for *Human Events* (the conservative magazine that was one of Ronald Reagan's favorites). In a piece titled "The Bureaucracy: The Fourth Branch of Government," Burnham argues that the bureaucracy is an independent force that wields its own power and even usurps other branches of government: "*In a process well known to modern Washington, the official, who may be the Secretary or Assistant Secretary of one of the major departments becomes the dupe or tool or front of the permanent civil servants whom he is assigned to direct.*"[1] Burnham provides the example of the faceless "permanent officers" of the Public Health Services.[2] These people advocated for the expansion of government health-care services to promote their own power and special interests. They may not be ideological socialists, but they usually vote liberal. And it is not just health care in which nonelected officials wield power. Agriculture, education, social insurance, housing, and even the military have members whose entire livelihood is invested in the state.[3] The distrustful Machiavellian maintains that they naturally oppose any policy that shrinks the state because that would mean cutting their own throat.

Burnham contends that the bureaucracy does not just shape domestic policy. Through groups like the Central Intelligence Agency (CIA), the bureaucracy even directs foreign policy. The State Department and the Foreign Service are loaded with people whose "independent power" is so great, they are designated "Indians" because they exist outside the bounds of any federal oversight. Burnham insists that even some foreign policy decisions were made by the "permanent bureaucracy rather than the President and his supposedly policy-making appointees."[4] The military bureaucracy in particular has expanded in power and influence because of the large sums of money invested in the institution. For support, Burnham cites C. Wright Mills's work *The Power Elite* (Mills drew from *The Managerial Revolution*).

Burnham, of course, did not invent the idea of a powerful and privileged bureaucracy. As already noted, the ex-Marxist was influenced by Trotsky. Before him, Max Weber highlighted the importance of the bureaucracy, particularly describing its impersonal features. What Burnham did do for his American audience—particularly conservatives—in *The Managerial Revolution*, *The Machiavellians*, and subsequent writings was to conceive of managerialism and bureaucracy as powerful political forces, ones that needed to be thwarted to reclaim democracy. They were the enemies of the people who needed to be resisted.

This philosophy has shaped a certain part of the American electorate. For them, this fight is against "the deep state," an unelected group of clandestine bureaucrats that exercise too much power. In his book *The Deep State: The Fall of the Constitution and the Rise of a Shadow Government* (2016), the former Congressional staffer Mike Lofgren echoes Burnham by describing a powerful and subtle second level of government: "Yes, there is another government concealed beneath the one that is visible at either end of Pennsylvania Avenue, a hybrid entity of public and private institutions ruling the country . . . only intermittently controlled by the visible state whose leaders we nominally choose."[5] It is not a conspiracy theory, Lofgren insists, because it is all based on experience.[6] He writes that "invisible threads of money" connect the Deep State to areas outside of Washington, DC, like Wall Street and Silicon Valley.[7] Lofgren compares these people to Milovan Djilas's "new class," a group that the Yugoslavian dissident claimed had hijacked communist regimes and were concerned only with perpetuating their status;

they were a privileged bureaucracy.[8] What Lofgren does not mention is that Djilas borrowed from Burnham and Trotsky.[9]

Samuel Francis used Burnham's ideas to express a related worldview three decades ago. Considering himself Burnham's heir, Francis extolled Burnham's analysis of the managerial elite and provided a conduit between Burnham and parts of the American right.[10] He advised Pat Buchanan, who contended that the paleoconservative Francis actually surpassed Burnham as a theoretician of power.[11] Francis wrote a syndicated column for the *Washington Times* for several years in the early 1990s until his dismissal for making racist comments. He maintained that there were "natural differences between the races," although he denied that this makes one race superior to another.[12] Francis went on to write for a host of conservative journals and magazines. This does not mean that Francis (again like the registered Independent Burnham and to some degree Trump) supported the Republican Party; he chided Republicans who—despite their words—did little to reduce abortion, curb illegal immigration, or shrink the size of government. In essence, Ronald Reagan was an insufficient conservative Republican for Burnham's leading disciple who was not persuaded by the Great Communicator's words.

Insight from *The Managerial Revolution* and *The Machiavellians* pervades Francis's writings. For example, when analyzing American culture, he describes an underlying power struggle: "Culture . . . necessarily concerns power, and the conflicts of the last several years over the National Endowment for the Arts, rap music, obscenity, and multiculturalism are really a struggle for cultural power. The issue is simple: Who gets to define the norms by which the American people will live?"[13] Francis uses figures like Robert Mapplethorpe, Sista Souljah, and movie mogul Lew Wasserman to show how liberal elites exercise cultural power. He suggests that the conservative "religious Right" offered pathetic resistance by resorting to feeble doctrines such as "family values." Francis pessimistically asserts that a cultural war rages and insists that conservatives are losing because they did not understand the nature of power.

Burnham's expositor Francis declares that contemporary American politics is really the struggle for power between two classes: the elites and the nonelite masses, or between the dominant "exploiters" and "Middle Americans." He argues that transnational elites promote hypertaxation and globalization to crush Middle Americans and their values. Their locus of power can be found in the bureaucracy that "oversees the formulation and execution of foreign policy."[14] They collaborate with democratically elected politicians across the political spectrum to advance their interests. Francis demands war against "the establishment" in the name of democracy.[15]

Francis advocates for "Eurocentric cultural order."[16] Influenced by Burnham, Francis saw the United States as part of a broader European or Western civilization. He believed that its traditions should be defended and continued. Proclaiming concerns that President Trump would advance two decades later, Francis lambasts both Democratic and Republican "establishment" politicians, such as Bill Clinton, George H. W. Bush, and Bob Dole for their collaboration with globalist elites. Francis deplored the tendency of many elites to diminish the significance of nations and civilizations. He interpreted wars in Iraq as attempts to establish a new global world order, one that worked against the interests of the United States.

Like his mentor Burnham, the paleoconservative Francis uses concepts advanced by Marx's disciples in his effort to understand the world. In a section of his writings titled "The Cultural Hegemony of the Managerial Regime," Francis quotes the Marxist power-theorist Antonio Gramsci who used "cultural hegemony" to explain how the ruling classes exercise power.[17] Whereas Gramsci argued that the bourgeoisie use the media, intelligentsia, educational institutions, and religion to promote their interests, Francis argues that the elite managerial class—with the help of modern technology—uses the same means to wrest control from the bourgeoisie. Francis contends that "cultural hegemony allows the managerial elite to manipulate 'consent' on a mass level."[18] This group also uses the bureaucracy to protect and promote their interests through the "managerial bureaucracy."[19]

Parts of Francis's worldview—like Burnham's—were influenced by Marxism. It is just bereft of economic reductionism. Early in *The Communist Manifesto*, Marx proclaims: "Freeman and slave, patrician and plebeian, lord and serf, guild-master and journeyman, in a word, oppressor and oppressed, stood in constant opposition to one another, carried on an uninterrupted, now hidden, now open fight."[20] For Marx, all subgroups were joining one of the two competing economic classes, and this dualist interpretation of society—with two groups vying for power and supremacy—characterizes Francis's social analysis. In "From Household to Nation," Francis insists: "The significant polarization within American society is between the elites increasingly unified as a ruling class that relies on the national state as its principal instrument of power, and Middle America itself, which lacks the technocratic and managerial skills that yield control of the machinery of power."[21]

Other subgroups like the religious and the secular, White and Black, and national and global were falling into one of the two opposing camps.[22] Consistent with Marx and Burnham in *The Managerial Revolution*, Francis argues that the state is merely a tool for the powerful to exercise power and advance their interests.

George Orwell is another elite and power theorist inspired by Burnham who has influenced contemporary conservatives. According to William Steinhoff, a biographer, "His [Orwell's] reaction to Burnham's arguments was intense; it is marked by the paradox of love and hate, acceptance and rejection."[23] Orwell first mentioned Burnham publicly in a January 1944 article titled "As I Please" for *Tribune* newspaper. Writing that he had read a friendly review of Burnham's *The Managerial Revolution*, Orwell agreed with Burnham that the world was dividing into power blocs, and collectivism was not necessarily any more democratic than any other system of government. For Orwell, Burnham failed by believing that Nazi Germany was invincible. Burnham naively assumed that Nazi Germany and the Soviet Union could not fight each other because they were essentially the same. Orwell attributed Burnham's errors to "wish-thinking": "Hating both Britain and the U.S.S.R., Burnham (and many other American intellectuals of similar outlook) wanted to see both of these countries conquered, and was also unable to admit that there *was* an essential difference between Russia and Germany. But the basic error of this school of thought is its contempt for the common man."[24] On this point, Orwell misunderstood the arguments in *The Managerial Revolution*. Although Burnham did question in 1940 whether Britain could survive a Nazi onslaught, he was merely trying to describe what was happening in the world and to predict where it was going.

Burnham replied to Orwell's criticisms by stating that it was clear that Orwell had never read *The Managerial Revolution*.[25] Acknowledging that he had not foreseen the war between the Soviet Union and Germany, Burnham claimed he never said that either side was invincible. Nor did he write that totalitarianism was "unavoidable."[26] Rather, its advent was just "probable."[27] Sensitive to references to his failed predictions, Burnham criticized the democratic-socialist Orwell for not recognizing the difference between the two concepts. Regarding his "hating" of Britain and the USSR, Burnham replied that he hated no one. And if he did, he would not waste a powerful emotion on an "abstraction," such as a nation.[28] The author of *The Managerial Revolution* said he just had "convinced opinions" about the Stalinist regime, especially its lack of regard for the most noble human ideals, such as truth and freedom.[29]

CHAPTER 6

Orwell's regard for Burnham seems to have risen shortly after this exchange. In an "As I Please" article published in February 1945, Orwell predicted that the war against Germany would end soon. Japan would follow because it could not withstand the combined might of the United States and Britain. The world was "splitting up into the two or three huge super-states forecast in James Burnham's *Managerial Revolution*. One cannot draw their exact boundaries as yet, but one can see more or less what areas they will comprise."[30] Orwell predicted that the remaining super-states would become entrenched in permanent war. Psychological and economic clashes would characterize this war, not bombs and violence.[31]

Orwell reviewed *The Managerial Society* and *The Machiavellians* in 1946 for a periodical called *Polemic*. His "Second Thoughts on James Burnham" describes Burnham's philosophy as follows: "Every great social movement, every war, every revolution, every political programme, however edifying and Utopian, really has behind it the ambitions of some sectional group which is out to grab power for itself. Power can never be restrained by any ethical or religious code, but only by other power."[32] The future author of *1984* contends that Burnham was intoxicated with power and worshipped those who had power. This led the power-worshipper to misinterpret reality: "Power worship blurs political judgement because it leads, almost unavoidably, to the belief that present trends will continue. Whoever is winning at the moment will always seem to be invincible. If the Japanese have conquered south Asia, then they will keep south Asia forever, if the Germans have captured Tobruk, they will infallibly capture Cairo; if the Russians are in Berlin, it will not be long before they are in London: and so on."[33] Orwell asserts that this explained why Burnham could not imagine a world without Hitler or Stalin in power, a world without collectivism. As a new ruling elite emerged, the Machiavellian could find little fault with it. This power-worshipping was actually a "mental disease," Orwell suggests.[34] He correctly identifies themes that permeated Burnham's writings his entire life: apocalyptic visions, nations clashing against nations, and social classes rising and falling; everything occurs in a "melodramatic way."[35]

Despite these criticisms, Orwell still drew from Burnham in *1984*. John Atkins, a biographer, maintained that "Orwell discovered this conception of the political future in James Burnham's *The Managerial Revolution*. Although he was as critical of much in this book he found it the most fruitful of all modern books of political speculation."[36] Like Burnham, Orwell presented a dystopian vision for the future. In *1984*, he describes a postindustrial collectivist society that is neither capitalist nor socialist. The society is run by bland managers who delude the people. Orwell immortalized Burnham's distinction between "formal" words and their real meaning when he wrote: "WAR IS PEACE, FREEDOM IS SLAVERY, IGNORANCE IS STRENGTH."[37] In their desire to maintain power, the sly rulers manipulate the masses with words.

Who would these new rulers be? As Orwell predicts in *1984*, "The new aristocracy was made up for the most part of bureaucrats, scientists, technicians, trade-union organizers, publicity experts, sociologists, teachers, journalists, and professional politicians."[38] Although less greedy than preceding ruling classes, they would be hungrier for power.[39] It was assumed, Orwell suggests, that if the capitalists were expropriated, socialism would follow.[40] And the capitalists had been eliminated; private property had vanished.[41] Everything was collectivized, but economic inequality and hierarchy remained.[42] Further revealing Burnham's influence, *1984*'s tripartite division of the world centered around postindustrial regions representing the United States and Britain; Continental Europe and Russia; and China, Japan, Korea, and Southeast Asia.

Arguably, the climax of *1984* comes when O'Brien reveals the "truth" to Winston: "The Party seeks power entirely for its own sake. We are not interested in the good of others; we are interested solely in power. Not wealth or luxury or long life or happiness: only power, pure power."[43] *The Machiavellians* impressed upon Orwell the ruling elite's intoxication with power, for power's sake.[44]

Chapter 7

Using Power against Communism

The themes of power and struggle were central in Burnham's next three books: *The Struggle for the World* (1947), *The Coming Defeat of Communism* (1950), and *Containment or Liberation* (1953). This trilogy was the foundation of Burnham's geopolitical strategy. These works were also partly responsible for America's Cold War success. One writer called Burnham the "intellectual architect" of America's Cold War victory.[1] Another deemed him "Reagan's Geopolitical Genius."[2] George Nash, a historian of conservatism, wrote, "More than any other single person, Burnham supplied the conservative intellectual movement with the theoretical formulation for victory in the cold war."[3] A host of figures shaped US foreign policy during the Cold War, but Burnham has a crucial place among these writers.

During World War II, Burnham joined the Office of Strategic Services (OSS) where he specialized in analyzing geopolitical issues.[4] He wrote three important pieces during this time, partly in preparation for the Yalta conference.[5] Each drew attention to Stalin's grand designs. The first, titled the "The Sixth Turn of the Communist Screw," was published in *Partisan Review* in the summer of 1944. It describes fluctuations in Soviet policy that moved not from left to right like a pendulum, but rather in a spiral path like a screw. With each turn, the power of the Soviet's ruling managerial elite expanded. The current phase—what

Burnham called the Tehran Phase—saw Soviet power encroach into Europe, leading to the "de facto Stalinist domination of the Continent."[6] This turn produced a clash in Greece between the Communist-directed Elam and the British.[7] Burnham was already imagining a divided Europe.

Where could the next turn lead? Dangerous omens whirled in Asia, where the Soviets had earlier concluded a neutrality treaty with Japan. Burnham mused, what if Stalin did not want a total defeat of Japan? What if he sought to utilize Japan to expand Soviet influence into China? In the essay's final paragraph, Burnham asks: "What then will the communist policy in the United States be? It can all be—perhaps has all been—mapped in advance. The 7th, the new leftist period, will have its made-to-order propaganda, slogans and tactics. And woe then to the war-mongers! We Want Our Boys Home Again! Don't Let Our Daddies Die in the Jungles!"[8] The future anticommunist hardliner anticipated clashes between Americans and communists in the East. He feared Soviet propaganda would weaken American resolve.

His second piece, titled "Stalin and the Junkers," appeared in *The Commonweal*, a Catholic journal (Burnham's brother Phillip was an editor for the journal). Published in September 1944 as Soviet troops marched West, Burnham maintains that Stalin and his collaborators knew that war is a military *and* political enterprise; as the Soviet army advanced, so did communism. Burnham contends that Stalin was already preparing for a Soviet-controlled Eastern Europe: "Eurasia must be made, under Soviet leadership, an impregnable fortress."[9] To help accomplish this, the native Georgian shrewdly obtained support from some important former Prussian nobles, the Junkers. Stalin convinced this group that they should support a communist-led Free Germany Committee because the Junkers were enemies of Hitler, too. For them, anything had to be better than the Nazi regime. Collaboration served the interests of both sides (some Junkers would become leaders in the communist German Democratic Republic). Burnham swore that the future of Eastern Europe—and possibly even the whole world—depended on the fate of this Free Germany Committee. Who controlled it could control the world.[10]

By early 1945, Allied victory over Germany was virtually assured. Burnham used the occasion to suggest (possibly tongue-in-cheek) in a *Partisan Review* article that attitudes toward the general secretary of the Communist Party needed to be revised. His "Lenin's Heir" piece should not be interpreted so much as a hagiography of Stalin as a rejection of Trotsky's version of Stalin, and by extension, Trotsky himself. Trotsky

84 CHAPTER 7

argued that Stalin betrayed the Bolshevik Revolution. Burnham argued that from a Marxist perspective, Stalin should be considered a man who fulfilled the 1917 revolution.[11] Stalin, not Trotsky, was the perfect Bolshevik.[12]

Trotsky's biography, written at the end of his life and published posthumously, painted a portrait of Stalin as a man bereft of redeeming features, not just personally, but critically for any Marxist, historically. Portrayed as crude, ignorant, and lacking any sort of imagination, Trotsky insisted that his fellow Bolshevik rose because of his unscrupulous behavior. In "Lenin's Heir," Burnham opines that the post–World War II era required a fresh look at the Soviet *generalissimo*. Stalin must be regarded as a great military leader. Despite inferior resources, he initiated action. His assumption of power in the USSR showed he was a master political strategist, too. According to Burnham, Stalin's crushing of political opponents—not all at once, but over an extended period—further attested to his genius.[13] Free from external restraints and traditional customs, Burnham suggests that Stalin was Nietzsche's *ubermensch*. Parts of this work may have been hyperbolic. Burnham was often sardonic.[14]

Nonetheless, the article paints a portrait of Stalin as a man who should not be underestimated, particularly diplomatically. The piece's most significant part was Burnham's analysis of Stalin's geopolitical vision: domination of Eurasia. A specialist on nationalism, Stalin has brilliantly made communism patriotic: "Free Poland, Free China, ELAS, Maquis, Partisans, Chou En lai, Browder, Tito, Thorez, Toledano, Togliatti."[15] Burnham writes of Stalin's grand design: "So does Soviet power emanating from the integrally totalitarian center, proceed outward by Absorption (the Baltics, Bessarabia, Bukovina, East Poland), Domination (Finland, the Balkans, Mongolia, North China and tomorrow Germany), Orienting Influence (Italy, France, Turkey, Iran and South China."[16] Beginning a theme that would soon dominate his writings, Burnham even suggests that the boundaries could extend to the United States. He associates this with "Appeasement."[17]

Just as the term "Cold War"—war between the United States and Stalin's communist empire—was entering the American lexicon in 1947, Burnham analyzed the communist mind and its relation to art and film with a review of Sergei Eisenstein's works on Ivan the Terrible, or part I given that Stalin had banned part II.[18] Relatedly, in 1946, the Zhdanov Doctrine emerged. Named after Stalin's henchman, Andrei Zhdanov, it sought to purify Soviet film, art, and writings from foreign or imperialist influence. Many writers and artists were censored. Burnham used the occasion to write that communism's moral shortcomings were not the problem because if it were just that, communism would easily dissolve when confronted with the good. But like Satan—the onetime angel—communism craftily deceived people by appearing to be good.[19] Like Satan, it seduced people into thinking it was good, partly because it was related to the good: "Its chains for the human spirit have been twisted from the most splendid of man's feelings and hopes—his cry for justice, his sense of brotherhood, his longing for freedom."[20] Burnham contends that these powerful ideals will always move men. And they are good. The former Marxist admits that he agreed with communists that art is the highest expression of good; the artist must be esteemed because he or she shapes human souls. Communism, however, distorts everything by making the artist a propagandist for communism.[21] Communism prevents artists from being what they need to be: a truth teller. The artist becomes enslaved instead of being the free agent he or she was meant to be.[22]

"The Sixth Turn of the Communist Screw," "Stalin and the Junkers," "Lenin's Heir," and the review of Eisenstein's works reveal Burnham's disdain with communism. Like most Americans during World War II, while never extolling the virtues of communism, Burnham at least accepted the existence of the Soviet Union. His *Managerial Revolution* even predicted its persistence. This evaporated at the end of war. For the next thirty years, Burnham would apply his ideas about power to the international arena by proclaiming that a power struggle raged between the United States and the Soviet Empire. The fate of humanity rested on the outcome. The United States had to use power, or it would be used to destroy her.[23]

And the United States must help liberate the people of Eastern Europe. This audacious notion was partly inspired by Victor Kravchenko's *I Chose Freedom* (1946), a book Burnham called one of the most absorbing that he had ever read about the Soviet Union.[24] The Ukrainian author served as a captain in the Soviet army during World War II and came to the United States to help administer Lend-Lease aid. He defected soon after. *I Chose Freedom* provides dramatic firsthand accounts of Soviet atrocities. It condemns naive US foreign policymakers who sympathized with Stalin. What could be done? Kravchenko demands liberation: "The next step toward world security lies not in a world organization—though that must come—but in the liberation of the Russian masses from their tyrants.... The liberation of Russia from its totalitarian yoke, I may be told, is a matter that concerns only the Russians. Those who think so are profoundly wrong. In many ways the safety of all civilization and the chance for enduring peace depend on that liberation."[25] This idea became the hallmark of Burnham's writings, and it made him one of the most important geopolitical writers in the second half of the twentieth century. His World War II writings alerted readers to Soviet expansion. His post-1945 writings were bolder: they argued for liberation.

In the aftermath of World War II, Burnham's attitudes toward freedom and democracy continued to evolve. Whereas in *The Managerial Revolution* he questioned the nature and future of these concepts, and in *The Machiavellians* he denied the possibility of true democracy whatsoever, the horrors of Nazism and its unequivocal defeat showed Burnham that some political values were genuine. Democracy was good. It could win. It must win. And now, for the new Cold Warrior, democracy began to be defined by what actually existed in the United States. At least here—in contrast to the Soviet Union—totalitarianism was thwarted by different branches of the government holding power. And people could voice their displeasure without fearing deportation. Freedom and democracy became more than just words for Burnham. They had to be preserved, fought for, and maybe even spread.

These ideas provide the foundation for Burnham's *The Struggle for the World* (1947). A postwar analysis of foreign affairs in the burgeoning Cold War era, the book opens by announcing that the Third World War began in April 1944 when Greek soldiers, under the direction of Moscow, mutinied against the British Empire.[26] Two years later, the clashes became more extreme in the Greek Civil War. This new war pitted the United States against another totalitarian system, except this one was communist. Burnham insists that the United States had to participate. The rest of the book explains how and why.

Like *The Managerial Revolution*, *The Struggle for the World* begins with "The Problem." Burnham argues that the United States was still an immature, provincial nation.[27] For the past two centuries, she has focused her energies on expanding westward and clearing the wilderness that curbed her growth.[28] Now, says Burnham, the United States needs to recognize her adulthood by shouldering the responsibilities that came with it. Her young men must stand up. They might be tempted to return home from the battlefields of World War II to a life of peace and quiet; young men are naturally provincial. But Burnham insists that they have to continue to fight.[29]

Burnham bristles at America's leaders. He argues that they consistently vacillated: "The United States forces Argentina into the United Nations, then takes the lead against Argentina by publishing the Blue Book on Peron; the public is compelled to accept Tito, then the effort is made to help [Yugoslavian General Draža] Mihailović at his trial and thereby injure Tito; in China there is a flip-flop every few months."[30] The United States accepted Soviet occupied Poland, and then aided the anticommunist Polish resistance. This could not continue.

To protect freedom and democracy, resolute American leaders must emerge. They needed to recognize that totalitarian leaders inherently differed from democratic ones. Burnham insists, "These totalitarian movements, with their steel discipline, their monolithic structure, their cement of terror, their rigid and total ideology, their pervasion of every aspect of the lives of their members, are of a species totally different from what we are accustomed to think of as 'political parties.'"[31] Western leaders tragically allowed communist parties to participate in democratic politics, seemingly unaware that the goal of communists was to destroy democratic politics.[32]

Continuing the Machiavellian distrust of words, Burnham insists that when it came to rhetorical battles, the United States was losing. Despite the fact that the Soviets were weaker throughout World War II, the USSR gained more at the conferences. Burnham suggests that meeting and bargaining with communists would prove to be as effective as dealing with Hitler in Munich in 1938. The world must be examined how it really is, not how we wish it to be. The Machiavellian blames this naivete on the US tradition of "democratic-idealism" preached by Thomas Jefferson.[33] Burnham advocates a realistic view of international relations; abstract morality should not guide foreign policy. He contends that the real nature of geopolitics could never be understood in a civics class or by studying the Constitution—those were meaningless words.[34] In reality, Burnham writes, we live in turbulent times characterized by communist desires for world conquest.

The author seeks to educate his reader about the true nature of communism because one must know the enemy to successfully confront him. Continuing more ideas from *The Machiavellians*, *The Struggle for the World* affirms that the supreme objective of communism is power.[35] The communist desire to eliminate private property stemmed from their desire to limit everyone else's power. Although communists preach liberation, they seek social totalitarianism when they monopolize power (e.g., all private property).[36] Burnham argues that once they achieve power, terror is employed to maintain power. This could not just be reduced to Stalin. Invoking a debate that still rages, Burnham maintains that there was no essential difference between Lenin and Stalin. Terror had been part Bolshevism experience even before 1917.[37] Stalin merely continued what Lenin started. Using terror to acquire power was inherent in the communist experience.

Burnham asserts in *The Struggle for the World* that no group uses more means to acquire power than communists. One example is a "united front," when communists cooperate with noncommunists by joining noncommunist organizations like committees, societies, newspapers, magazines, and leagues to promote communism. The noncommunist may be aware of communist activity but ignores it because the communist helps them advance a cause: "The non-communist sees a certain task to be done—an arrested Negro to be defended, Chinese children to feed, trade unions to organize, colonial independence to further."[38] The noncommunist eagerly works with everyone willing to advance his or her cause. The communist sees things differently: he or she just wants to spread communism. The "united front" also provides the communists with new opportunities to weaken noncommunist institutions and exploit them for their own purposes, such as when funds raised for Spanish loyalists instead go to the Soviet secret police. Collaboration with communists is never benign.

In *The Struggle for the World*, Burnham tells the reader that communists do not participate in national politics and government to improve the condition of the nation. Communists want to destroy every nation and all political parties so they can rule over them. An example occurred in the Soviet-controlled sector of Germany (East and West Germany had not yet been declared), where separate socialist and communist parties existed. Under the guise of "unity," the parties came together to form the Socialist Unity Party.[39] Next, socialists were either exiled from the party or were executed. What emerged from the wake of the merger was the German Communist Party, which monopolized all power. In communist fashion, this was progress and the next stage of social development.[40] Therefore, it was good.

Practices like these could be applied to the United States. Burnham believed that communists did not try to solve political problems in the United States; they sought to exacerbate them by employing the divide-and-conquer strategy. He contends, "Within the United States, the communists arouse and exploit every decisive possibility. Labor against capital, big business against little business, C.I.O. against A.F. of

L., farmers against business, Negros against Whites, Christians against Jews, Protestants against Catholics, landlords against tenants, foreign against native born, South against North, unemployed against employed: wherever there is a rift in national life, the communist tactic is to deepen and tear that rift."[41] Burnham acknowledges that many of these rifts would occur even without communism, but communists did not try to solve the problems, they exploited them for their own political advantage. They exaggerated class conflict and other conflicts between groups.[42] Those who worked with the communists might not recognize that the communist goal was not to amend the United States, but rather to smash it because the communists knew that the United States was the greatest obstacle to the communist world empire.[43] Weakening and demoralizing the United States would enable the communists to win the struggle, possibly even before a shot was fired.[44]

Resembling a religion for Burnham, he asserts in *The Struggle for the World* that the communist movement gains followers because of the myths it espoused, such as the belief of a kingdom of heaven on Earth.[45] It provided hope for the downtrodden, a utopia where all men are free and equal, a world free of exploitation, hunger, and war. The moral dreamer would gain certainty about the imminent coming of this world, albeit after bloodshed. Burnham theorizes that communism soothed Western man's despair that emerged in the post-Renaissance era as secularism and liberal democracy failed to provide security. The former sympathizer says that communist myths were believed more frequently outside the Soviet Union than within it. Although American journalists and French poets might believe communist myths, workers living within the Soviet Union knew that they were slaves.[46]

In *The Struggle for the World*, Burnham takes time to explore the question: is a Soviet world empire desirable? Like a good Machiavellian, everything should be examined, not passively accepted, even the possibility of a communist empire. Burnham writes that Americans working for the Communist Party believed that it was desirable.[47] And in some respects, this seemed rational. After all, a communist empire would end nations, therefore wars between them, and subsequently the need to use the atomic bomb.[48] But the cons of the Soviet Empire outweighed everything else. First, communism seemed to lead to a lower standard of living.[49] Possibly influenced by some of the responses by economists to *The Managerial Revolution*, Burnham states that certain matters could not be centrally planned for the economy to run efficiently.[50] According to Communist propaganda, its society had no unemployment and enjoyed complete job security. The anticommunist reminds the reader that prisoners have no unemployment and complete job security, too.[51]

Communism denied economic freedom, too. Of course, Burnham notes that capitalism also sometimes failed in this respect, but at least the deficient American economic system allowed workers the freedom to select or reject their job, or even start their own business.[52] Burnham asserts that under communism, these rights vanish.

More generally, communism subordinates the cherished Western ideal of the individual.[53] Burnham argues that Christianity had made individualism central to the Western tradition by emphasizing individual morality, responsibility, guilt, and personal immortality. Individual freedoms and liberties—which are best promoted by democracy—have continued these ideas in a more secular form. But communism eradicates all sacred traditions. Everything becomes subordinated to the party, the state, the revolution, and even the historical process; these transcend the individual.[54] Insisting that the collectivizing economic process in the USSR that took the lives of millions of people was inherent in communism, Burnham writes that collectivization applied what communists preach: the subordination of the individual to the collective good.

The author contends that even truth gets subordinated to the advancement of communism. In traditional Western thought, truth came from the eternal mind of God. In the more secular Western tradition that emerged after the Renaissance, truth came through the scientific method. Communism viewed truth differently. Truth only becomes truth when it advances class struggle and the interests of the communist party.[55] Scientific truth becomes scientific truth only if it conforms to Marxism.[56] The same is true of statistics. And history. The dialectical method determines all truth.

Burnham ends the chapter "Is a Communist World Empire Desirable?" in typical Burnham fashion. The final paragraph is pithy and direct: although there may be some advantages to communism, the costs are too high.

Part II of *The Struggle for the World* is titled "What Ought to Be Done," part III is titled "What Could Be Done," and part IV is titled "What Will Be Done." All are obvious plays on the title of Lenin's work *What Is to Be Done*. Communists extolled Lenin's work, and it even shaped some contemporary left-wing thought. Rejecting an evolutionary road to socialism preached by Marxists such as Eduard Bernstein, *What Is to Be Done* is a call to action.

Burnham demands action, too. He tries to abolish the notion that peace had to be the goal of foreign policy in "What Ought to Be Done." The international realist had condemned pacificism as a Marxist and a Machiavellian. Now, he denounces pacificism as a Cold Warrior. Burnham insists that those who preached peace were naïve because no nation can have peace as a primary goal. This would mean suicide.[57] That does not mean that war was required. Nations must simply be prepared to wage war, at all times, at all costs. Their existence depended on it. If a group stops defending its institutions, it will collapse, either from internal decay or external invasion. France came dangerously close to this scenario when in the years between the two world wars she theorized that it was better to lose a war than fight one.[58] Burnham argues that pacifists, despite their pretensions, were not moral, at least in the Cold War context. By calling on their own nations to disarm when communism sought to conquer, they endangered the lives of their people. This was not a moral act.[59]

Given the Soviet desire for world conquest, Burnham maintains that the individual had only three moral options regarding communism: (1) They can be apathetic and completely remove themselves from politics and its "moral significance."[60] In this example, they will be overrun by communists, but these will have no moral consequences because their morality bears no relation to political events. (2) They can believe that communism provides the best answers for world problems. In this example, they should try to ensure communist victory as quickly and painlessly as possible. (3) They can do everything possible to prevent the spread of communism, by whatever means necessary.[61] For the rest of his work, Burnham speaks only to those interested in the third option. These people had consciousness of the raging struggle. Burnham rejected passivity. Something had to be done.

For the Machiavellian, realistic attitudes are a prerequisite for morality. Acting morally means seeing the world as it really is, and then acting accordingly. Naiveite about world affairs only leads to communist conquest, hardly a moral phenomenon. During the emerging Cold War era Burnham's moral person was an anticommunist hardliner.

For those who did recognize the morality of struggle, Burnham demands an offensive strategy. The Soviets sought world conquest, and a defensive strategy would not suffice: "A defensive strategy can never win; all it can do is prolong loss: defensive strategy, because it is negative, is never enough. The defensive policy stated in the previous chapter would be able to halt and even reverse for a time communist Eurasian advance. It would make more difficult the communists' path toward their final goal and would delay their arrival. Communist victory, however, still would be the end result."[62] The United States had to adopt an offensive strategy against an opponent bent on world domination. Burnham insists that "power must be there, with the known readiness to use it, whether in the indirect form of paralyzing economic sanctions or in the direct explosion of bomb."[63] Communists proceed irrespective of the human cost in the hope of achieving a world empire. The United States must respond with power. Military strength was critical because it demonstrated power.[64]

Propaganda provides another way for the United States to exercise power. Burnham argues that a fundamental difference existed between Soviet and potential American propaganda: American propaganda could actually be true.[65] Instead of discerning between eastern and western conceptions of democracy, the United States should expose to the world the totalitarian system that existed on the other side of the Iron Curtain. The propaganda should penetrate Soviet borders and let the captured citizens know that the United States is willing to condemn their oppressors.[66]

Only what Burnham called an "American empire" could prevent more communist conquest. He did not mean a world in which the United States placed foreign nations under her yoke. Burnham's empire was a soft empire, one in which the United States provided leadership and guidance in the struggle against communism.[67] It resembles what actually existed in the Cold War era. He writes: "By world empire I mean a state, not necessarily world-wide in a literal extent but world dominating in political power, set up at least in part through coercion (quite probably including war, but certainly threat of war), and in which one group of peoples (its nucleus being one of the existing nations) would hold more than its equal share of power."[68] Burnham counters isolationist arguments by arguing that the United States was already involved in parts of the world; a soft American empire existed in Europe, Japan, and the Philippines. Moreover, empires by themselves are not necessarily antidemocratic. Burnham asks, were not two of the most famous democracies in history, ancient Athens and nineteenth-century England, also imperialist, with subjects?[69] Empires do not have to have to be totalitarian; they can be compatible with democracy. A loss of some independence does not mean a loss of freedom for the population.[70]

Burnham rejects the idea that the United States should use power to promote democracy everywhere:

> It would be fatally wrong for the United States to adopt officially the feeling of many of its citizens that all nations ought to model their political institutions after the United States pattern. Others may not like the pattern and may still be neither barbarians nor menaces to world security. . . . If the United States wants to be first among nations, it will not succeed most easily by insisting that all other nations humble themselves before the Bald Eagle. On the contrary, it will do best if it demonstrates that other nations, through friendship with the United States, increase and guard their political dignity and honor.[71]

Nations need not follow the American political model to be part of this grand empire. The United States must understand the local languages and traditions of the world's nations because this breeds respect for the dominant power.[72]

Some Burnham biographers like Christopher Hitchens and Binoy Kampmark have cited Burnham as an early neoconservative, at least geopolitically.[73] And later neoconservatives did appropriate parts of Burnham's thought. But Burnham's passage above suggests that he would not have agreed with some neoconservative assumptions. The Cold War hardliner does advocate an aggressive foreign policy that undermined communism and liberated Eastern Europeans; he does believe that democracy could prevail there. In *The Struggle for the World*, Burnham calls for a "democratic world order." This, however, must be understood in the context of the Cold War: Burnham sought an empire or world order of existing democratic countries that agitated communism. This was a strategic empire based on relationships designed to combat communism in the late 1940s, not a prescription to improve the future world. The mature Burnham was not an idealogue or a universalist. As chapters 10 and 11 reveal, Burnham questioned whether parts of the non-Western world were even capable of Western-style democracy.

His anticommunism was not ideological, but practical. Communists sought to enslave humanity. Power had to be used against communists not because they were godless or even totalitarian, but because they sought to expand their totalitarian system around the world. Burnham believed that the United States had to react against Soviet aggression by using power to defend herself. Burnham was an "America Firster."

CHAPTER 7

Unlike pre- and post-Cold War "America Firsters," his prioritizing the United States meant US engagement with the world. The haunting specter of communism required this. Isolationism would not suffice because one of the ways to prevent war—to prevent Soviet encroachment—was achieved through an American-centered empire that confronted communism.[74] Anything else would lead to the destruction of the United States. How could any patriot support this?

War was not the best option for Burnham, at least not now. He ordered a robust American empire because it made the Soviets fear war; if the Soviets believed they could not win a war, they would not start a war.[75] An engaged, vigilant American empire limited Soviet initiative, throwing a cog into their grand design.[76] External pressure would weaken the whole structure: "The walls of their strategic Eurasian fortress, so apparently firm now as much because of the absence of pressure without as from strength within, would begin to crumble."[77] External pressure could bust the Soviet system. This was what an American empire could provide.

It was not a reverence for Americana that inspired any of this because Burnham thought American culture lacked depth. He asks: "Who, listening to a few hours to the American radio, could repress a shudder if he thought that the price of survival would be the Americanization of the world?"[78] He recognizes American geopolitical strength, but culturally he was a Europhile. For example, Burnham believed that European art was the only art worth studying.[79] He just preferred an American empire to a communist one, and in his mind, only one could prevail.

Burnham relates his ideas about civilization and empire with Arnold Toynbee's. Toynbee, a fellow alumnus of Balliol College, penned one of the seminal works of twentieth-century history, *A Study of History* (1934-1961). Running to a staggering 3.5 million words, the work is twelve volumes and took decades to complete. It compares more than two dozen civilizations, most of which were extinct. Toynbee insists that civilizations may not die from murder, but from suicide. And unlike Oswald Spengler who viewed civilizations as organic phenomena—they all lived, then died—Toynbee believes that while all civilizations struggled, descent was not inevitable. He writes that successful civilizations thrive under the dynamic leadership of elite, creative minorities, during periods of crisis. As long as these great figures exist, a civilization can meet any challenge. This demand for an elite leadership was music to Burnham's ears. For him, the Cold War was the crisis that determined whether the United States would live or die. Resolute individuals must arise.

The Struggle for the World is pessimistic. If judged by the evidence, Burnham reasons that it seems unlikely that the United States would adopt a consistent, long-term strategy aimed at defeating communism.[80] Rather, the United States will continue to practice a policy of "vacillation." American politicians who preferred winning elections over defeating communism were the main culprits. Instead of projecting strength against communism, they look at every geopolitical issue individually, seeking to maximize the issue for political advantage.[81] Eras of "toughness, appeasement, isolationism, internationalism and chauvinism" characterize US foreign policy.[82] According to Burnham, this is the worst of all strategies because everything adds up to nothing, effectively making it no policy whatsoever.[83] Demoralizing followers and disheartening friends, the battle was lost before it had begun.[84]

Burnham ends the book in the darkest way possible: with a vivid description of nuclear war. In a chapter titled "The Outcome," Burnham asks the reader to imagine two scenarios: the first in which the Soviet Union had an atomic arsenal. Given the American policy of containment, and the Soviet policy of world conquest, if nuclear war broke out, the USSR would probably launch first.[85] The United States will survive the initial attack. However, because the American social structure is more dependent on industry, the damage inflicted by a Soviet atomic bomb could not be matched with US retaliation. The pessimist writes that American vacillation would enable the Soviets to quickly neutralize non-Western countries and Western Europe.[86] Thriving communist agents within the United States would engage in "material and psychological sabotage."[87] For all of these reasons, American defeat was certain.[88]

It did not have to be this way. Burnham presents a more optimistic alternative by demanding an American monopoly on atomic weapons. The nature of the war—and hence the fate of the world—hinged on whether the Soviets had nuclear power.[89] Denying the Soviets these weapons would change everything, he believed. Under this theoretical scenario, a first strike by the United States would devastate the Soviet Union. Burnham argues: "The strategic plan must be, it would seem, to strike an immediate, paralyzing blow with atomic weapons at the Caucasian oil fields, Moscow, and a dozen or more of the chief Soviet and Soviet-controlled cities and industrial concentrations."[90] Coupled with an adequate subsequent foreign policy, the war would be over.[91] The world would see that the United States had the will and means to stop communism.

This scenario was premised on what Burnham describes as a "positive" foreign policy after America's first strike, one in which the United

States did not vacillate. Instead, the United States would relentlessly use political means to eliminate communism, such as directly thwarting communist activists.[92] The hardliner theorizes that if the United States vacillated after the successful first strike—if she showed any weakness—all that was gained by the successful first strike would be lost. Communists might lose some cities in the Soviet Empire, but they would continue to politically maneuver against the United States.[93] Exploiting racial and social divisions, the communists will simply wear down the United States.[94] If a "positive" political strategy did not follow a first strike, communism would persist. International opinion would turn against the United States. It would be seen as a brutal murderer.[95]

The critic of US foreign policy in some respects anticipated America's biggest Cold War debacle by a generation by writing that when the battle eventually occurred, the United States may not fully use her strength. Americans would be too sickened and conscience-ridden by what would seem to them a never-ending senseless slaughter, leading nowhere.[96] Burnham predicts: "The military leadership would be disoriented by the inability of their plans based on technical superiority to effect a decision. . . . From the standpoint of the United States, the entire world would have turned into an ambush and a desert. In the long night, nerves would finally crack, the sentries would fire their last shots into the darkness, and it would all be over."[97] This path could best be avoided by immediately using power, maybe even nuclear power.[98]

The apocalyptic thinker feared that war between communists and the West could begin at any time, even before this book had been published.[99] The future of Western civilization hung in the balance. As Toynbee suggested, great civilizations can survive difficult times. The United States had a choice. And she had to choose wisely.

Daniel Kelly downplayed the significance of *The Struggle for the World* by distinguishing between "what it predicted and what actually happened."[100] The biographer notes that Burnham's apocalyptic visions never materialized. And this is true. But the book was not just prophecy; it was intended to shape policy: Burnham wanted to raise awareness of communism's threat during a critical era in history. Active US participation in the Cold War was not inevitable just two years after more than four hundred thousand Americans had perished in World War II.[101] Many Americans including important politicians, such Robert A. Taft, favored isolationism, believing entry into European affairs would lead to a less prosperous United States. And possibly to another war. Why should Americans die for Europeans? Burnham argues in *The Struggle for the World* that Americans must be willing to die because communists did not merely threaten Europeans. They desired global conquest.

Many of the themes propounded in the book were not original.[102] In 1945–1946, other books, speeches, memorandum, letters, long telegrams, and articles were crafted that desired some sort of American response to communism. But from a historical perspective, *The Struggle for the World* may be the first important geopolitical book of the Cold War era. It was the richest analysis of Soviet communism—and none demanded US involvement more dramatically. It did shape opinion, both inside and outside the beltway.

The Struggle for the World appeared the same week President Truman announced that the United States would support Greek and Turkish forces against communism. Truman's press secretary, Charlie Ross, said he recommended that Truman read the book.[103] Insisting that US security depended on thwarting the spread of totalitarian regimes, Truman pledged support for any nation resisting communist aggression. Unlike Franklin D. Roosevelt and his vice president predecessor, Henry Wallace, Truman resisted cooperating with the Soviet Union. He pledged economic assistance to war-torn Europe. The United Kingdom, France, and West Germany received most of the aid. As the United States rejected isolationism, Burnham did something rare for him: he approved.

According to the *Christian Century*, a strong parallel existed between Burnham's and Truman's ideas. An editorial reads: "There is reason to fear it more than a coincidence that the Truman Doctrine was announced and the Burnham book published in the same week. It is certainly no coincidence at all that Mr. Burnham is now, on the radio and otherwise, one of the most vehement champions of the Truman policy."[104] The article continues that Burnham's and Truman's aims were indistinguishable because both wish to contain and weaken the Soviet Union. Would Truman literally follow all of Burnham's ideas? The editorial suggests that Americans should hope not. It would probably lead to another world war.

Publishing magnate Henry Luce helped spread Burnham's ideas. *Life* magazine popularized *The Struggle for the World* by producing a thirteen-page condensed version. Its title read: "Struggle for the World: Western Civilization Is Doomed by Communism, Says Controversial New Book, Unless U.S. Stops Vacillating, Bids for World Empire."[105] Luce's *Time* magazine argued in its summary, "Only one defense of Burnham's book can be made: it is—appallingly—true."[106] With the help of this public attention, *The Struggle for the World* appeared on the *New York Times* best seller list.[107]

The book resonated with a significant former classmate. George Kennan was two years ahead of Burnham at Princeton, and like Burnham, Kennan was an elitist who opposed unbridled popular democracy.[108] Kennan and Burnham both recognized some America capitalist deficiencies, but both still favored the American system, particularly because of the freedom of thought it protected.[109] The details of their personal and intellectual relationship are murky. The two men worked for the Office of Policy Coordination in the late 1940s under the direction of Frank Wisner. Kennan's "long telegram" appeared a year before *The Struggle for the World*. Burnham certainly read the memorandum that outlined the diplomat's views on Soviet designs. He continued some of the subjects it propounded, such as the importance of educating Americans about the Soviet threat. In his essay, Kennan writes: "We must see that our public is educated to the realities of the Russian situation. I cannot over-emphasize [the] importance of this."[110] The telegram also contains details about Soviet propaganda efforts, their desire to disrupt the "internal harmony of our society," and the impossibility of peaceful coexistence.

Kennan lauded *The Struggle for the World*, writing that it "contains as masterly an analysis of the world communist movement as I have ever seen."[111] He sent two copies to Charles "Chip" Bohlen, requesting that one be sent to John Paton Davies in March 1947.[112] Kennan's initially anonymous "The Sources of Soviet Conduct" was published several months after *The Struggle for the World*. One of the differences between Kennan's "long telegram" of 1946 and his "Sources of Soviet Conduct" of 1947 is the emphasis the latter places on the Soviet quest for power. Kennan's seven-thousand-word essay uses the word *power* about seventy times. Most paragraphs make multiple references to the concept, usually in the context of describing the Soviet desires. Kennan's anonymous article appeared in July 1947, although according to John Lewis Gaddis, Kennan wrote most of it between January and early March (*The Struggle for the World* appeared in mid-March).[113] The future ambassador's conceptions of the Soviet Union may have developed independently of Burnham's. Nonetheless, both men agreed that the Soviet state inherently expands. They agreed that the United States had to act. But they differed over the appropriate course of action, specifically over how aggressive and confrontational US foreign policy needed to be. This divide would erupt publicly in several years.

George Orwell reviewed *The Struggle for the World* and called the book "a product of the atomic bomb."[114] He summarizes Burnham's book as follows: soon the world would be composed of two superpowers with atomic weapons, each ready to annihilate the other. The Soviet Union had the geographical advantage because it controlled the Eurasian heartland. The two superpowers are ruled by unscrupulous men who seek only power. What can be done? Burnham scoffs at pacifism. Instead, the United States should recognize its own strength and be willing to use it. An American empire must emerge. Orwell writes that that although Burnham may be called a warmonger, he had "intellectual courage."[115] If Burnham correctly depicts the situation, his course of action would probably be correct. The English author maintains, however, "Burnham, as usual, sees everything in the darkest colours and allows us only five years, or at the most ten."[116] He overestimates the political deftness of Soviet leaders because according to Orwell, they often bumbled, too. The review contends that Burnham's "realist" position meant that he underestimated the historical role played by sheer force. Burnham believed that because something *was* happening, nothing else *could* happen.[117] Therefore, because Germany was winning the war, she had to win the war. Continuing arguments he made in "Second Thoughts of James Burnham," Orwell asserts that the author of *The Struggle for the World* was too obsessed with power. For Burnham, communism was *big*, so although it was evil, it still deserved some admiration.[118] But Burnham exaggerates; he always thought in terms of "monsters and cataclysms."[119] The future author of *1984* concludes that history is never as melodramatic as the apocalyptic Cold Warrior suggested.

Other reviews of *The Struggle for the World* would have done little to dissuade Burnham about the naiveté of the American public. Arthur Schlesinger Jr. describes Burnham's apocalyptic thinking in a book review for *The Nation*. He compared *The Struggle for the World* to Tom Paine's *Common Sense* because it was clear, passionate, and dramatic. Schlesinger concedes that Burnham accurately notes the Soviet desire for global conquest, but that did not mean they were on the verge of accomplishing it. Schlesinger maintains that Burnham could more easily take extreme positions from afar, but those working in government like George Marshall had to deal with a more complex reality. Burnham's black-and-white vision cannot work in real life. Schlesinger asserts, "Even for a writer with Burnham's talent for the apocalyptic, *The Struggle for the World* is quite a mouthful."[120] The Harvard historian worried that the book's ideas might lead to a reckless foreign policy, one in which the United States may "fight first, then reconstruct afterward."[121] Schlesinger concludes that we should be thankful that Burnham was not secretary of state.

Schlesinger's *The Vital Center: The Politics of Freedom* (1949) replies to Burnham's ideas directly. Schlesinger agrees with Burnham that a new era in US foreign policy must emerge. They also agree that the United States must adopt a position of global leadership because the nation had matured; she must leave naïve adolescence behind. Both recognize the United States' natural isolationist tendencies. Both favor the reconstruction of Western Europe through aid programs, such as the Marshall Plan. Schlesinger, however, rejects Burnham's hyperaggressive foreign policy by arguing that "today a policy of Western intimidation, with the flourish of guided missiles and atomic bombs, would ... allow the Communist regime to hide its totalitarian purposes behind a cloak of self-defense."[122] Nothing would do more to bring Soviet people together in defense of their government than war with the West. Schlesinger believes that containment avoids the extremes of intimidation and appeasement.[123] Disagreeing with Democrats like Henry Wallace who merely wanted to diffuse the Cold War through cooperation, Schlesinger advocates a general military buildup in Western Europe, but only as a means to deter Soviet attack.[124] He suggests that "internal contradictions" would eventually bring down the Soviet Union.[125] Schlesinger wanted to win the Cold War. He just preferred playing a waiting game.

By the late 1940s, Burnham's aggressive anticommunist reputation was rising in France. *The Managerial Revolution* had initially earned him some notoriety there after it was reviewed by Raymond Aron.[126] Like Orwell, Aron was captivated by the book, although he questioned Burnham's predictions.[127] Writing about *The Managerial Revolution* in 1943, Aron disagrees with Burnham that capitalism was moribund and that planned economies ruled the future.[128] After World War II, the anticommunist philosophers became friends.[129] In his review of *The Struggle for the World*—a book that was immediately translated into French in 1947—Aron supports Burnham's basic view that two irreconcilable superpowers ruled the world. He questions, however, whether American hegemony was the best possible future outcome.[130] This would be a common theme among French anticommunist intellectuals.

In 1948, a brief dialogue between Burnham and Andre Malraux was published under the title *The Case for De Gaulle*. Also a former leftist, Malraux was appointed Charles De Gaulle's minister of information after World War II. Agreeing that the world was in a state of crisis,

Burnham and Malraux worried that the Third Force—a self-proclaimed middle way between Gaullism and communism—could not successfully thwart the challenges of the age. In this exchange, Burnham tells Malraux that he sought a strong, economically prosperous France that would work with the United States against communism. Burnham worries that Frenchmen were too concerned with "American imperialism" when it was the Soviets who sought to enslave them.[131] The American Cold Warrior says France should fear the United States' reluctance for the responsibility of world leadership, not her imperialist ambitions.[132] Burnham notes that Europe and the United States needed each other in the struggle against communism. To strengthen Europe, he advocates a European Confederation that would consist of common currency, banking, credit, transport, and electric power.[133] Malraux replies that Frenchmen would resist such a course if it strengthened Germany. He favors a European confederation that would be led by France.[134] Consisted with Gaullism, Malraux, while opposing communism, preferred a more independent course.

Right around the time this dialogue appeared, Burnham published an academic article titled "What Is the Purpose of the United Nations?" It begins with his typical criticism of verbiage; humans ascribe far more power to words than they actually have. Historians will say that a certain treaty ended a certain war, but that is not really true because words do not end wars.[135] Burnham writes that contracts and treaties describe only what the minds had already agreed upon. This explains why the League of Nations—a body that emphasized words and treaties—could not stop World War II. Nations pursue their own interests and will agree to certain words when it benefits them. France loved the League of Nations because it was in her self-interest to limit German armaments.[136] The United States saw little advantage in joining the League, so it refused.

Burnham argues that the newly formed United Nations was useless because it provides cover for the communists.[137] Continuing Trotsky's assumption that international governing bodies are just pawns on a chessboard and that the real work goes on behind the scenes, Burnham maintains that the United Nations becomes a "smokescreen, behind which world communism can proceed with a minimum of hindrance in carrying out its own communist policy."[138] This argument turns Trotsky's idea that the League of Nations promotes the interests of the imperialist nations on its head. Now, the international governing body protects the communists, such as their efforts to advance in Germany and the Far East.[139] Burnham insists that the goal of diplomats should not be to reach agreement with Soviet foreign minister Andrei Gromyko, but instead should prevent him from destroying democracies.[140]

The critic of the international diplomacy was called to testify before Congress in February 1948, ostensibly over the issue of legislation designed to thwart the Communist Party in the United States. It gave Burnham another platform to express his anticommunism. He stated that "communism is a world movement, which operates within all nations, and already holds full power over a vast area comprising the former Russian Empire together with the territories and peoples conquered since 1939."[141] He demanded that the United States take the proper steps to curb its influence. Continuing themes from *The Struggle for the World*, Burnham testified that these measures should include the following:

1. Education: The American people must be educated about the nature and threat of communism. Consciousness must be raised.
2. Exposure: Too often, communists dupe the public by appearing as liberals, progressives, and even patriots and humanitarians. Masks must be stripped from their faces. At the same time, Burnham recognized the difference between honest liberals and communists. The government needed to make this distinction, too, because falsely accusing liberals benefited the communists.
3. Illegalization: The communist party must be banned. Its stated goal was to overthrow the government of the United States using violence and terror. What about constitutional protections? Burnham argues that these guarantees had never been applied in an absolute sense. And a democratic government should never interpret its laws in such a way that democracy becomes impossible. For the Machiavellian hardliner, sometimes democracy had to be limited so it could survive. The committee members (including Richard Nixon) were impressed. One even stated that he wished Burnham was a member of their committee.[142]

Burnham's testimony followed on the heels of a famous actor who testified before Congress about the involvement of communists in Hollywood. Communists had extended their influence into parts of the film industry, including the Screen Actors Guild. Stating that he abhorred communism and its tactics, this self-described New Deal liberal disagreed with Burnham over the need for banning the Communist

Party. He stated: "As a citizen I would hesitate, or not like, to see any political party outlawed on the basis of its political ideology. We have spent a hundred and seventy years in this country on the basis that democracy is strong enough to stand up and fight against the inroads of any ideology."[143] His views about communism and its tactics never changed, but his political ideology would, partly thanks to Burnham. His name was Ronald Reagan.

CHAPTER 8

A Strategy for Liberation

In 1948–1949, Burnham took his family on a cross-country vacation filled with camping, fishing, hiking, and, of course, writing.[1] The trip softened him. Visiting the Midwest, Northwest, and Southwest, Burnham experienced Americana at its finest. Describing the trip to Sidney Hook as exceeding his expectations, he was particularly impressed with the people—whom he still called "the provincial masses"—he met along the way.[2] Usually condescending toward Americans, Burnham finally came to see them more deeply, more intimately. He realized that the average American did understand world affairs; Americans grasped the true nature and reality of communism. He states, "I have come to feel during the past six months that in this country today, the masses . . . are in advance of their leaders."[3] Americans were not naïve. They did not want war, but they were not afraid of it either. They did not know if war would come, but if it did, they knew that they had to win. There was no alternative. Burnham experienced some patriotism, and the optimistic Burnham even made a brief appearance.

His next book reflects this optimism. Titled *The Coming Defeat of Communism* (1950), Burnham calls it a continuation of *The Struggle for the World*.[4] The book's epigraph is a proverb that Lenin used: "Who says A, must say B," meaning that once a first step is taken, the next one must follow.[5] Burnham suggests that talking about defeating communism was insufficient. A guide for anticommunists, *The Coming Defeat of Communism* demanded action.

Burnham begins the book by stating that many books and articles had been written describing the Soviet threat. All Americans had heard the idea that the fate of humanity was at stake, but government leaders did not seem to recognize the crisis because their policies did not correspond with their words. And those brave citizens who sought to oust communist representatives from public life were accused of "hysteria."[6] Since World War II, the United States could boast only of thwarting Stalin in Berlin. Communists could boast about conquering China. Always keeping score, the hardliner asks, who was winning the Cold War? He answers that anyone who believed that trends favored the Americans were deceiving themselves.[7]

Burnham does describe some American successes in the early Cold War, or at least as much as he was able to express positive evaluations of American foreign policy. Compliments and flattery never came easily for him. They were usually coupled with criticisms. For example, in *The Coming Defeat of Communism*, he calls the Berlin Airlift a "dazzling technical and human achievement" and a "technical success."[8] Burnham, however, prefers a more aggressive response. First, the United States should have sent an armed convoy to Berlin. Yes, this would have been risky because a general war could have followed, but Burnham argued that the Soviets would not have resisted.[9] Second, the intervention of Greece in 1947 was not bad because without US assistance, Greece would have fallen to the communists. The United States, however, gained nothing in Greece; it only avoided an important loss. The strategy in Greece was purely defensive and because a defensive policy is never adequate, Greece could not be called a victory. Third, Burnham concedes that the Marshall Plan did improve the European economy and helped thwart communist advancement in the region. That did not mean he believed it was well-intentioned because he wrote that no one wants a poor trade partner who is unable to buy one's goods. American policymakers should not be interpreted as humanitarian. Moreover, the Marshall Plan was also defensive and inadequate.[10] All seeming Cold War successes were not really successes for Burnham; they were "negative successes." If the United States wanted to win the Cold War, policymakers had to escape this treadmill.[11]

In *The Coming Defeat of Communism*, Burnham eagerly proclaims American failures in the early Cold War. First, Western policy against the Soviet Union was not formally unified. One day, policymakers accurately noted the Soviet desire for world conquest, but the next they would announce that the Soviets were "sincere" in wanting peace. One day, American leaders condemned persecution in Czechoslovakia; the next, trade was promoted with Czechoslovakia, something that could only strengthen the communist regime.[12] Second, Burnham argues that US foreign policy was too narrow.[13] The Cold War was not just a geopolitical or ideological struggle. It was a political, economic, ideological, sociological, and military conflict. Each of these fields related to the others, so they all must be fought simultaneously. Retreating or compromising on one meant retreating or compromising on all. Third, he continues to lambast containment because a defensive policy can never win.[14] Finally and relatedly, he notes the United States had no real objective. Condemning the Soviet torture of priests in Poland while simultaneously allowing communism to fester there was pointless.[15]

The international realist criticized conferences, too. Burnham believed that "vague abstractions" like peace, international law, friendship, and cooperation were meaningless.[16] It seemed that whenever conferences were held (e.g., Yalta, Potsdam, Tehran), the Soviets always got the better end of the bargain. Compromises and trade-offs occurred during the conferences; the United States would fulfill their end of the bargain, then the Soviets would renege.[17] Examples included Soviet promises of democracy and religious toleration. The problem, he believed, was that US representatives naively assumed that they and the Soviets, although differing in means and ends, could still reach some common ground. Burnham contends in *The Coming Defeat of Communism* that no common ground existed between the superpowers. Communists only want world domination, and no cooperation could occur with an opponent bent on your destruction. Regardless, conferences only reflected the power that had already been achieved by one side. Burnham maintains: "Important historical problems are settled by wars, and by semi- or non-military clash of economic, political social and ideological forces. The conferences reflect and articulate the real power equilibrium that has been reached by other means."[18] The Cold War must be fought and won. Maybe then conferences could be held.

These ideas were partly aimed at famed American journalist and foreign policy strategist Walter Lippman. In 1947, about six months after *The Struggle for the World* appeared, Lippman published a sixty-two-page work titled *The Cold War*. George Kennan's containment policy bore the brunt of the journalist's criticisms.[19] Lippman wanted to restrain Soviet power and influence too, he just questioned the applicability of containment. For example, he did not believe that US policymakers could use the free market to fight against a planned economy because that would require a constant allocation of economic resources to different parts of the world, something the free market could not handle.[20] Moreover, containment could lead the United States to fight wars in which it was geographically disadvantaged, such as on the Eurasian continent.[21] And contra Kennan, Lippman downplayed the relevance of Bolshevik ideology when attempting to explain Soviet expansion. He focused on the Soviet army; stopping the spread of communism meant stopping the Red Army.[22] Lippmann believed that negotiating with communists could prove fruitful because rival powers had reached settlements before. Diplomacy does not mean converting opponents or ending rivalries.[23] Diplomacy can, however, stop aggression.[24]

Lippman also believed that Western and Central Europe should play a role in curbing Soviet expansion. So did Burnham. He believed that the United States and Europe were natural allies in the Cold War.[25] America and Europe remained part of Western civilization, even as World War I and World War II divided them. Their similarities transcend any past political differences. Despite the destruction that World War II had wrought across the continent, Europe still surpassed Asia and India in science, technology, and industry.[26] Burnham suggests that Europe might be too weak and tired after centuries of war, tyranny, and revolution.[27] Communists persisted in Western Europe, with complete freedom. The United States must convince Europe that her own fate depended on her ability to defeat communism. Europeans must be willing—under the leadership of the United States—to push back communism, to bust through the Berlin Wall, to bring all of Europe back together again.[28]

In chapter 8, titled "The Vulnerability of the Communist Empire," Burnham asserts that before an enemy can be defeated, its strengths and weaknesses must be recognized.[29] Contrary to conventional wisdom, the Soviet Union was weak: "The Communist empire is weaker, potentially weaker at any rate, than the non-communist public now generally believes."[30] Despite professed successes of New Economic Policies and Five-Year Plans, Burnham insists that the Soviet economy was poor and backward. And they lacked general technological expertise. This was demonstrated during World War II when Soviet soldiers lacked the basic technological skills—whether it be electrical or mechanical—that the US soldiers possessed. Signs of economic discontent existed too, particularly within the satellite nations where famines occurred. The Soviets eliminated the usual ebb and flow in business cycles by keeping their system in a state of permanent crisis.[31]

Burnham reasons that this weakness would mitigate the chances of an attack against the United States soon. But such an attack could not be discounted. The United States must be prepared. The Soviets might preach peace, yet they deceived, proven by how they invested and glorified the Red Army.[32] In the meantime, the United States should consider aggressive measures—a first strike in fact could be "preventative."[33] By this Burnham did not mean that it would prevent war, but a first strike meant a better chance of preventing defeat. Only power deterred the Soviets. Working with the Soviets, on the other hand, increased the chances of defeat because, "experience uniformly proves that communists are always emboldened to further aggression by friendship, conciliation or appeasement."[34] The United States must always be ready to use military force.[35]

Burnham calls part III of his work, "The Plan." Its first subtitle is "The Turn to the Offensive." He contends that the first step in fighting the Cold War was to recognize the raging struggle. It was not a future event; it was happening now. We had grown accustomed to wars beginning with declarations and then proceeding as military clashes. The hardliner says that those days were over: "This means that both direct military preparation and its attendant economic measures should be advanced continuously, day by day."[36] He maintains that there would be no "D-Day"—no specific date that military engagement with the enemy would begin. It already had. Greece and Turkey were examples.

Parts of *The Coming Defeat of Communism* are the fruit of the first James Burnham who optimistically believed democracy could prevail if the United States properly used its force and power. Burnham argues that the United States had been too passive against communism and that this could be corrected with a "few hundred bombs in the right spots."[37] He even suggests the United States should launch an immediate, preemptive attack: "Why should not the United States launch an all-out armed attack at once, and get the whole business over with? . . . In the United States, the idea of striking the first blow is morally repellent to most people. I believe that this moral attitude arises out of intellectual confusion."[38] Burnham proclaims that if a first strike would save lives and create a more humane world, "then to strike such a blow, far from being morally wrong, is morally obligatory."[39] He contends that it was no different than striking Hitler when he remilitarized the Rhineland in 1936. Such a seemingly aggressive measure would actually have been defensive, and morally correct.[40]

Burnham sometimes demonstrated a more nuanced view of the Cold War, one that did not see the conflict as a black-and-white struggle that had to be fought using black-or-white means (war or pacificism). He believed that violence alone could not bring peace to the world because although great historical problems are never solved without some force, force alone solves nothing.[41] Burnham also recommended nonmilitary means—what he called "political war"—to weaken communism. Force did not always have to be military force: "Political-subversive war against communism now, rather than immediate all-out armed attack, thus not only assures victory, but assures the victory will be worth winning."[42] The masses around the world must be educated about the nature of communism, and this would not be achieved by dropping bombs.

One form of political warfare was propaganda. In chapter 11 of *The Coming Defeat of Communism*, titled "The Propaganda Attack," the hardliner argues that propaganda must be used against communism because the communists employed propaganda to advance their cause. And propaganda has always been part of life.[43] Burnham asserts that the advent of new technologies and literacy has just changed the way it was transmitted.[44] Small propaganda was a waste of time. Everything must be big. And the means should vary. Short-wave radio that promoted the Voice of America provided the most obvious example, but the means to spread propaganda were almost limitless: books, magazines, newspapers, pamphlets, posters, maps, charts, movies, plays, stickers, and matchbox covers were just some of the examples Burnham gave.[45] Propaganda can be supported by the government or by private individuals. Average Americans could send magazines they read overseas, on their own, without support or consent of the government. Who were the targets? Burnham says everyone, even communist leaders.[46] Lenin's former disciple advocated propaganda that agitated the communist ruling classes, not the capitalist ones.

In *The Coming Defeat of Communism*, Burnham notes that propaganda must be both for and against something. The architects of the French Revolution, he says, were obviously against privilege and despotism. They were for liberty, equality, and fraternity. Applied to the Cold War, US propaganda obviously opposed Soviet conquest and the subsequent enslavement of humanity. Burnham describes America's principles as follows: "We believe individual human beings to be of an infinitely higher moral worth than any secular end or goal. We believe in an open, not a closed society, in the right of men and nations to be different—within the limits, at any rate, that are imposed by that very right; and in their freedom to explore varied routes to earthly and eternal salvation."[47] Westerners should not feel inferior when using propaganda. And they should trust its ability to persuade.[48]

His ideas about political warfare and propaganda were not original. By 1950, the Central Intelligence Agency (CIA) had already begun using political warfare methods. In April 1948, Kennan wrote a secret memo tilted "The Inauguration of Organized Political Warfare."[49] It was influenced by *The Struggle for the World*. Like Burnham's 1947 book, the memo began with "The Problem." Kennan defines political warfare as the attempt to achieve a nation's objectives, short of war.[50] This included covert and overt operations. Psychological, economic, and political means could all be employed. The Foreign Service officer specifically recommends provoking resistance in satellite states by using propaganda. Consistent with Burnham, Kennan even recommends liberation in this memo (his "long telegram" and "Sources of Soviet Conduct" make no mention of liberation). He calls for a "Liberation Committee" whose purpose would be "to form centers of national hope and revive a sense of purpose among political refugees from the Soviet World; to provide an inspiration for continuing popular resistance within the countries of the Soviet World; and to provide a potential nucleus for the all-out liberation movements in the event of war."[51] For Kennan, the Kremlin employed political warfare against the United States, and the United States must do the same against communists.

Burnham agreed with all of this. Defeating communism while avoiding total war was possible. With proper strategy, the United States could create conditions that would lead to popular revolts and subsequently to the breakup of the Soviet Union: "The possibility of defeating communism without total war depends, on the last analysis, upon sufficient internal breakup of the Soviet Empire by revolutions of one kind or another—by political upsets which, whatever their social content and by whomever made, would at least crack the hold of the monolithic Kremlin machine."[52] These revolts, of course, would not occur without some sort of external pressure. That was where hard and soft power came in.

The Coming Defeat of Communism argues that an aggressive US foreign policy should foster revolts in satellite states.[53] These states provided fertile soil for opposition movements because the Soviets had yet to, and probably never would, fully absorb the masses into the party bureaucracy.

The ex-Marxist intimates that contradictions existed between the Soviet ruling class and the masses that they ruled over in satellite states. Popular revolts could ignite if opposition leaders in these areas were properly utilized; the people needed leadership. Lenin's former admirer employed Leninist means: "[The masses] will revolt only if they acquire a leadership, and through that leadership some measure of organization."[54] The unled masses cannot revolt on their own, but with the proper leadership, they can bring down communism.[55] Exiles and even US representatives should be used to foment strikes, sit-downs, and uprisings in satellite states.[56]

Another precondition for the breakup up of the Soviet Union would be a division among the Communist Party elite. Burnham speculates that any division among the party elite would be advantageous for communist opponents because it was a "law of politics" that internal revolution required a divided elite.[57] Revolts must also be led by party members. The anticommunist declares: "The leadership in the first stages (except for what can be supplied externally) can only come from *within* the Party itself, by a division in the Party. This fact is the master key to the overthrow—or even the serious weakening—of the Soviet regime from within."[58] Tito and Soviet defectors proved that Soviet leaders were not a monolithic bloc. The anticommunist maintains that purges also showed that some Soviet leaders resisted the regime. Divisions were inevitable. The death of Stalin and economic crises would all provoke division within party leadership. The United States had to foster these divisions.[59] Communists promoted divisions in the United States; the United States must reply in kind.

Burnham argues that a division of the ruling elite would occur when the Soviets felt insecure.[60] These insecurities must be exacerbated because fear prompts divisions. Despite their strong rhetoric, some Soviet leaders were plagued by doubt.[61] They worried that the lofty ideals they preached could never be reached. The United States should exacerbate those fears with displays of strength and confidence. This could be demonstrated rhetorically, diplomatically, and militarily.

Burnham also recognizes the leadership role that the Catholic Church would play in ending communism in these satellite states. Communists had persecuted religious leaders since the early days of the Bolshevik Revolution. After World War II, religious leaders in Eastern Europe were arrested and sent to Soviet internment camps. The Soviets knew that the Catholic Church was a potent oppositional force. So did Burnham. He maintains that the Church may lack military might, but the Cold War was not only about armaments. The Church had other vast resources, like a faith that offered an alternative to communist faith and two thousand years of fighting against its enemies. The atheist asserts in *The Coming Defeat of Communism* that the Catholic Church offered powerful leadership and "Resistance" (Burnham always capitalized the word) in satellite states.[62] These Catholic communities offered practical resistance to communism in the form of underground masses, celebration of Saint's Days, and the protection of priests.[63] They should not be underestimated when confronting the Soviet behemoth.

The Coming Defeat of Communism reveals Burnham's profound disdain for American businessmen. He spends a chapter criticizing them, arguing that if the future of the United States lay in the hands of her capitalists, she was doomed because they remained a reactionary class. He criticizes business owners for their lack of knowledge of anything outside of business. Art, philosophy, politics, and social affairs provided some examples. This meant that other than the profits they reaped, they offered little for the struggle against communism because they were too ignorant, greedy, and cowardly.[64] The former Marxist continues that the overall benefit of American corporations for society was slight, if not malignant, because they had an antagonizing effect on the rest of society.[65] This, Burnham contends, was used by communists to recruit new members. In the struggle against communism, the United States could not rely on its capitalists.

The optimistic Burnham who believed that democracy could prevail appears in the final chapter of the book, titled "The Inevitability of Communist Defeat." Reversing some of his earlier positions, Burnham writes that the communist advance had been slowed more than he expected when he wrote *The Struggle for the World* in 1947.[66] Maintaining that the Soviets did have the geographic advantage, Burnham theorizes that strategic position by itself did not mean victory.[67] The United States could offset this with the methods Burnham demands: intelligence, human power, and force. The United States needed more determined men and women who synthesized force and will in the struggle against communism.

The optimist predicts in *The Coming Defeat of Communism* that these individuals would emerge. Western civilization was aging, but the United States was not old. It was not ready to quit. She would show will. He describes a letter he received from a Czechoslovakian who had obtained a copy of *The Struggle for the World*. The man pleaded with Burnham: Americans must believe in the inevitable victory of democracy because if they did not, democracy could not prevail.[68]

Burnham concludes the book with a thinly veiled Hegelian-Marxist reference: "The defeat of communism, probable on the facts, is also *inevitable*, because there are enough determined men in the world—and their number daily grows—who have so resolved. The knowledge and intelligence, which enter into a synthesis of politics, are still needed in order to make that defeat as fruitful as possible a victory, as sparing as possible of blood and treasure. But the issue is no longer in doubt. Doubt is vanquished by the act of will that makes the decision. The future becomes the servant, not the master."[69] For Hegel, two concepts existed that relied on each other for their existence: master and slave. They must struggle against one another because each viewed the other as a threat. Each side must exert its will to survive. One must conquer, thus becoming the master.

The Coming Defeat of Communism turns Marxism-Leninism on its head: instead of rationalizing the inevitable victory of the proletariat, Burnham rationalizes the inevitable victory of democracy. Instead of calling the bourgeois class and their false ideas impediments to peace and progress, he says this of Marxists. Instead of trying to raise class consciousness against the evils of capitalism, he does so against communism. Instead of using propaganda to foment revolts against capitalism, he urges propaganda to foment revolts against communism. Instead of demanding that an elite leadership guide the masses against capitalism, he demands that elites in Eastern Europe inspire the masses against communism. Marx had argued that war raged in society (whether people recognized it or not) between the bourgeoisie and the workers. Burnham now argues that war raged between the Soviets and Americans, whether or not Americans wanted to acknowledge it. Instead of trying to provoke divides in American society in an effort to destroy her, he wanted to divide Soviet leadership in an effort to bust the Soviet system.

The Coming Defeat of Communism may be the most prescient book of the early Cold War era. Burnham does not just describe communism's weakness or predict its defeat. He delineates the ways it would falter. First, he predicts that a divide in Soviet leadership that would precede the fall of communism.[70] Second, he describes how Catholic Church opposition would undermine communism.[71] Third, he foretells the crucial role that satellite states would play in provoking the collapse of the Soviet Union. Finally, Burnham describes the role that American use of power—both and hard and soft—would play in contributing to its collapse.[72]

Burnham's Cold War polemic found its target audience, both at home and abroad. For example, the book struck a chord with Ewert

Freiherr von Dellingshausen, a member of West Germany's Department of All-German Affairs.[73] With help from the CIA, this group provided covert support for rollback groups in the hopes of achieving reunification. It intended to be a guiding light for those on the other side of the Iron Curtain.[74] And its leading members believed that psychological warfare was critical. Von Dellingshausen asserted the importance of "coordinating all tactical measures of psychological warfare" with potential dissidents in East Germany.[75] The agency used balloons to smuggle anticommunist propaganda across the Iron Curtain.[76]

According to a scholarly review of *The Coming Defeat of Communism*, "This polemic, like Mr. Burnham's earlier works, is being much discussed and is exceedingly influential."[77] Historian John P. Diggins wrote that by the time of the Korean War in 1950, Burnham's writings "had considerable influence in the State Department, the Pentagon, and the Central Intelligence Agency, especially among those officials who wanted to oppose the policy of containment with a new strategy of liberation-rollback."[78] Burnham was now one of America's leading Cold Warriors.

The *New York Times* promoted Burnham and his new book. Its first review describes the author as "the leading exponent of the Don't-just-stand-there-*do*-something school at the moment."[79] In a second review, James Reston contends that Burnham's view of the Cold War was too simplistic because Tito showed that different forms of communism existed, so one aggressive policy could not suffice. Fearing Burnham's prescriptions could lead to war, the journalist reminds the reader of Burnham's failed predictions in *The Managerial Revolution* and his past support for some communist policies during the 1930s as a Trotskyite.[80] The next week Burnham was interviewed by a *New York Times* journalist, Harvey Breit: "Tall, slim, 44 years old, a good Midwesterner as well as a Princeton and Oxford man, Mr. Burnham is gifted with a persuasively logical mind that makes even his most questionable opinions seem obvious and inevitable."[81] Burnham contends that the main point of his book was to convince the reader that if the United States adopted a consistent, forceful policy against the Soviet Union, the communist empire could not survive. The Soviet Union was weak and could not withstand American moral, political, and military force. Negotiating with communists was pointless because you could not compromise with someone who wanted to conquer you. When reminded that many of his past predictions had failed to materialize, Burnham retorts that many of his predictions had come true. He compares himself to a baseball player who did not bat a thousand but was still a pretty good player.

Burnham's aggressive approach seemed to be an alternative to Kennan's containment policy. Geopolitically, Kennan too fashioned himself an international realist. He recognized that the United States would have to use power to thwart communism. The two men differed in how the United States should use its power, with Burnham arguing for aggressive rollback and Kennan favoring containment.[82] The *Washington Post* compared the two writers in a piece called "Burnham versus Kennan."[83] It began by noting that Washington, DC, was divided into two camps: Burnhamites and Kennanists. The former's views in *The Coming Defeat of Communism* were "current staples of conversation at Washington salons and dinner tables and in the offices of the Pentagon."[84] Burnham declares that to defeat communism, the United States must employ the same offensive tactics that the communists employed. The article lauds Burnham's "incisive logic" and wonders what type of world would emerge out of the ashes of communism in Eastern Europe.

The Coming Defeat of Communism may have helped inspire National Security Council Report 68 (NSC-68). According to its primary author, Paul Nitze, the drafting of the document began in mid-February 1950, right after Burnham's book appeared.[85] NSC-68 held that the fundamental goal of the Kremlin "is to retain and solidify their absolute power, first in the Soviet Union and second in the areas now under their control. In the minds of the Soviet leaders, however, achievement of this design requires the dynamic extension of their authority and the ultimate elimination of any effective opposition to their authority."[86] Guided by a "fanatical faith, antithetical to our own," Soviet leaders viewed the United States as their foremost obstacle to world conquest.[87] The council requested a significant increase in military spending, recommended strengthening the American nuclear arsenal, and recommended aid to any country facing Soviet encroachment. Another American goal should be to "place the maximum strain on the Soviet structure of power and particularly on the relationships between Moscow and the satellite countries."[88]

Several months after NSC-68 was created, North Korea invaded South Korea. The United States sent military forces to protect the South Korea. The Cold War, as Burnham had predicted, turned violent. And the United States was not passive. The *New York Times* reported that "like the war that ended in 1945, this also is a war of liberation."[89] Burnham had to have approved of the means and the ends.

John Foster Dulles published *War or Peace* in April 1950. The future secretary of state certainly read Burnham's works. In his award-winning

CHAPTER 8

biography of Dulles, Townsend Hoopes emphasizes the significance of Burnham's *Containment or Liberation* by stating that it reinforced "arguments of those who already saw inadequacy in a purely defensive American response."[90] It provided inspiration for "liberation-rollback" against what seemed to be a "house of cards."[91] Like *The Managerial Revolution* and *The Struggle for the World*, Dulles's *War or Peace* begins with "The Problem." In contrast, *The Struggle for the World* ends with "What Will Be Done," whereas *War or Peace* concludes with "What Needs to Be Done." Dulles contends that war was probable "unless by positive and well-directed efforts we fend it off."[92] But he refutes Burnham by arguing that, under certain circumstances, conferences and agreements could succeed in promoting peace and weakening the USSR. Dulles cites the 1949 conference with the Soviets in Paris at which the Soviets and Americans reached an agreement to lift the Soviet blockade of Berlin. Dulles defends the agreements by insisting that Americans did not sacrifice honor or interests.[93] For the diplomat, negotiations could yield victories.

Dulles also continues Burnham's habit of "keeping score," and he came to the same conclusion: the United States was losing the Cold War. In a chapter titled "The Five Year Score," Dulles argues that that the Soviets had suffered some losses in Berlin and Yugoslavia, where Tito began pursuing an independent course from Stalin. And more often than not, the United Nations thwarted the Soviets. But these needed to be measured against communist gains in Eastern Europe, Central Europe, and Asia. Communist parties were making inroads in Africa and Latin America, too. On the whole, Dulles maintains, the Soviet were winning the Cold War. Their plusses outnumbered their minuses by a large margin.[94] For Dulles, and Burnham, more needed to be done.

Chapter 9

Thought and Action

Burnham took a leave from New York University in 1948 so he could spend more time raising awareness of the communist threat.[1] He was now free to direct all of his intellectual energies toward fighting communism. In the late 1940s and early 1950s, few Americans spent more time and energy—and came up with more creative ways to undermine communism—than Burnham. The Burnhams even moved from New York to Washington, DC, where Burnham would have more contact with policymakers.

At this point in his intellectual career, Burnham can be described as a right-wing Leninist. Like the Russian revolutionary, he now dedicated his entire professional career to the cause. He wanted to be a man of thought *and* action—someone whose ideas corresponded to the real world. Marxists laud this as praxis. And like Lenin (the greatest champion of praxis in Marxist history), patience was not a virtue; both men demanded immediate action. The fate of the world hung in the balance.

Burnham became a Central Intelligence Agency (CIA) operative. He joined the Office of Policy Coordination (OPC), a wing of the CIA dedicated to more covert operations.[2] Much of Burnham's tenure remains shrouded in classified documents. He refused to talk about his time at the agency.[3] What is known comes from the few declassified documents that exist and records Burnham kept himself. The main beneficiaries of Burnham's ideas were other OPC agents.

Usually working from home, Burnham never traveled to the OPC's offices.[4] And as in his Marxist days, he had a pseudonym: Kenneth E. Hambley. He procured funding to finance anticommunist publications, including money to translate and publish *The Coming Defeat of Communism* in foreign languages.[5] Through the OPC, "Kenneth Hambley" used the proceeds of this book to help fund a Russian-language anti-Soviet newspaper called *Passev*.[6] Hundreds of copies were covertly distributed to Soviet military personnel in what was now East Germany.[7] "Hambley" was reimbursed by the OPC.[8] These were part of Burnham's clandestine political warfare activities.

Burnham's mind conjured up myriad ways to thwart communism abroad. For example, 1950 was a Catholic jubilee year. Burnham wanted to use the occasion to exploit the Soviet persecution of Catholic priests by setting up an exhibit in Rome that demonstrated communist persecution of religion. Recommending that the museum be dramatic and accessible, he wrote that specific exhibits could include examples of communist anti-Catholic writing, anti-Catholic cartoons, and revealing statistics about the fate of churches and priests in the Soviet Union. This should be accompanied with lectures and "horror pictures."[9]

Soviet propagandists worked diligently to create a cult of Stalin, particularly among the youth.[10] Burnham responded by recommending that Americans covertly use the anniversary of Lenin's death to undermine the Stalinist regime. This could best be achieved by popularizing Lenin's "Last Will and Testament," which scolded Stalin and attempted to limit his influence. Anticommunist propaganda should emphasize that although Lenin crushed dissenters, there were at least some semblances of inner party democracy during his era.[11] Burnham maintained that unlike Hitler in Nazi Germany, the leader of the Soviet Union was not loved. He was just feared. US propaganda should counter the notion that Stalin was strong by highlighting his follies. Burnham even wanted to plant a rumor of imminent revolts on Stalin's birthday.[12]

The anticommunist insisted that the most effective political cartoons used standardized figures, such as Uncle Sam. He wanted standard versions of Stalin, the Soviet secret agent, the commissar, and Red Army generals. Once standardized, these images should never change because variation weakens propaganda.[13]

The Cold Warrior recommended less benign ways to sabotage communism; when it came to defending America's security, the ends justified the means. Machiavelli insists in *Discourses* that "when it is absolutely a question of the safety of one's country, there must be no question of just or unjust, of merciful or cruel, of praiseworthy or disgraceful; instead, setting aside every scruple, one must follow to the utmost any plan that will save her life and keep her liberty."[14] In 1953, Burnham assisted Kermit Roosevelt in planning the overthrow of the prime minister of Iran, Muhammad Mossadegh, whom the CIA believed was too pro-Soviet.[15] According to another story, while at the OPC, Burnham suggested kidnapping a Soviet spy, who would then be pumped full of "truth serum" in an effort to catch other Soviet spies.[16] Because the Federal Bureau of Investigation (FBI) forbade such practices, Burnham and his team would have to do the job secretly.[17] For better or worse, the funds necessary could not obtained.[18]

Burnham spent more time recommending soft power. In October 1949, the People's Republic of China was proclaimed. Two months later, Burnham was asked about the possibility of using political warfare there.[19] He said it had to complement and correlate with an overall policy. If there is no offensive plan, then there can be no offensive political warfare. This meant that if the United States did not adopt an offensive military and political strategy in China, the offensive political or psychological warfare was pointless. Writing in "Psychological Warfare in China," Burnham argues that "from the point of view—above all—of psychological warfare, what sense can it make to attack the Chinese communists by PW methods while at the same time the Chinese government is recognized and traded with?"[20] If, however, the US policy was to prevent Chinese communists from expanding power, then a different form of political warfare must follow.[21]

Psychological war was one prong of political warfare. Burnham believed that it allowed the United States to strike at the heart of the Soviet Empire without resorting to open war. War was always a possible option for Burnham, but not the best one. While at the CIA, he wrote a piece called "Psychological Warfare or Else." It insists that psychological warfare was the only alternative to the atomic bomb.[22] Burnham likens the Soviet Union to a city run by gangsters; they seek to bring the entire world under their control. Their home base is Moscow, so US psychological war efforts must focus there. The best way to weaken the regime was to provoke internal splits within the party in Moscow.[23] This should be the goal of psychological warfare.

The professor-turned-CIA agent insisted that US psychological warfare was as old as the American republic. The Declaration of Independence and

Gettysburg Address were early examples.[24] Woodrow Wilson's Fourteen Points must be understood as psychological warfare that undermined the enemy. The United States had robust means of communication, which meant she was amply equipped to engage in psychological. The telephone, telegraph, radio, electronics, printing, and reproduction devices constituted an array of psychological warfare instruments.

In "Psychological Warfare or Else," Burnham maintains that traditionally, the United States had waited until after the war started to employ psychological warfare, but the best psychological warfare occurred before the battle began.[25] He asserts that Hitler used psychological warfare to take the Ruhr, the Saar, and Austria. He never had to fire a shot. The State Department had ably used some psychological warfare, including the Voice of America, books, magazines, and sponsoring trips to America by foreign nationals.[26] Burnham contends that the Department of Defense needed to follow suit because wars were not always decided on the battlefield.

Many of Burnham's days at the CIA were consumed with coordinating the Congress for Cultural Freedom (CCF). Secretly financed by the CIA (how many of the participants knew or cared about this is unknown), the CCF was a direct response to the Soviet-sponsored Scientific and Cultural Conference for World Peace. This event was held in New York in 1949 and was arranged by the National Council of the Arts, Sciences and Professions, a communist organization. The program for the Soviet conference stated that the threat of nuclear war imperiled the democratic rights of all Americans.[27] Academics and intellectuals could not feel safe in the "ivory tower."[28] Peace and cooperation between the superpowers had to be promoted through "mutual understanding."[29] The Soviet side maintained that you did not blow up your neighbor just because you did not like the way he treated his wife.[30] Organizers of the event gathered under the pretense that they were on the side of peace, the United States on the side of war. Prominent participants and sponsors included W. E. B. Du Bois, Albert Einstein, Charlie Chaplin, Paul Robeson, Henry Wallace, and a host of other scientists, academics, musicians, and journalists.[31]

Burnham played an important role in the responding American conference, which was held in June 1950 in West Berlin. The *New York Times* called it "the first major offensive against Soviet propagandists."[32] Inaugural attendees and sponsors included Bertrand Russell, John Dewey, Hugh-Trevor Roper, Benedetto Croce, A. J. Ayer, Sidney Hook, and Arthur Schlesinger. The congress's location of West Berlin demonstrated the United States' commitment to freedom given that Berlin was the center of the Cold War. A raucous affair, its attendants agreed that no middle ground could exist between freedom and Soviet communism. Arthur Koestler opened the event with a presentation that Burnham must have approved of: Soviet use of the words "peace" and "democracy" meant nothing.[33]

Burnham presented a paper titled "Rhetoric and Peace." Irked by communist pretenses of pacificism, the speech maintains that seemingly the "good man" was for peace and his opponents were "reactionaries."[34] Burnham continues that history plays a trick on those easily duped by such language: "After all, is it not the Voice of the Lord of Katyn and Kolyma which, from Bucharest, speaks to the world under the Cominform banner, 'For a Lasting Peace, For Peoples' Democracy'? Is it not the government of three hundred divisions that launches the movement of the Partisans of Peace? We have allowed ourselves to be trapped and jailed by our words—this leftist bait which has proved our poison."[35] Burnham states that communists had bound liberals with their own slogans because the progressive man of the noncommunist left is guilt-ridden when he compares himself with the bolder communist.[36] Inferiority and even some envy follows.

Never one for nuanced speech, the apocalyptic writer created an uproar when he said flatly: "Moreover, I must add, in order to be fully honest, that I am not, under any and all circumstances against atomic bombs. I am against those bombs now stored or to be stored later in Siberia or in the Caucasus, designated for the destruction of Paris, London, Brussels, Rome, New York and Chicago . . . and of Western Civilization, generally. But I am for those bombs made in Los Alamos, Hanford, and Oak Ridge, and guarded I not know where in the Rockies or American desert."[37] And how could Western Europeans disagree? Burnham suggests that it was the existence of these bombs (and their potential usage) that prevented Western Europeans from becoming slaves in the Soviet Empire. But what about Black people in the United States that communists used as evidence when demeaning US democracy? Burnham retorts that at least they were not sent to slave camps when demanding more freedom.[38]

The intransigent anticommunist desperately tried to convince his listeners that the United States could not be passive: Americans had to be willing to use force against communism. Burnham routinely lectured at the Naval War College, the National War College, the Air War College, and the Johns Hopkins School for Advanced International

Studies. For example, in September 1951, he spoke to the Naval War College on the topic of the philosophy of communism.[39] Burnham warns his audience that communist thought was powerful and should not be underestimated. He describes basic Marxist concepts, such as the dialectic and the unity of opposites. Distinguishing between socialists and communists, Burnham proclaims that whereas the former sought to reform society, communists wanted to regenerate it by provoking conflict between the bourgeoisie and proletariat. For communists, this class struggle would lead to revolution and subsequently a "dictatorship of the proletariat"—a transitionary period between capitalism and communism—that in reality was just a dictatorship of the Communist Party.[40] This acquisition of power was the real goal of the party:

> The problem of the Revolution, therefore, is to prepare, achieve, defend, and expand the Communist monopoly of power. Until the monopoly is complete (that is to say, unchallenged and unchallengeable on a world scale), this is, was, and will continue to be the goal of Communism. If this is understood—that the practical, the strategic goal is the world monopoly of Communist power—then everything essential can be understood through this. And if there is any doubt or confusion on this point, then nothing is understood, and I repeat and emphasize NOTHING, no matter how much formal studying has been done in connection with Communism—NOTHING is understood until this is understood.[41]

Only when this fact was recognized could the United States successfully confront the behemoth.

Burnham's *Containment or Liberation* (1953) was the third part of his anticommunist trilogy. Continuing themes from *The Struggle of the World* and *The Coming Defeat of Communism*, the book argues that containment was not aggressive enough. The bully on the block does not feel threatened by containment.[42] It lacked purpose because it could respond only to Soviet aggression.[43] Carl von Clausewitz would not have approved, as the German military strategist stated, "An absolute defense completely contradicts the conception of war."[44] Defensive measures may be necessary, but they must always be part of an offensive strategy that weakens the opponent.[45]

Using Berlin as an example, Burnham insists in *Containment or Liberation* that containment had achieved nothing: boundaries were clearly drawn, yet Soviets consistently applied pressure against Westerners by blockading sectors, shooting at planes, raiding houses, kidnapping citizens, and sending their gangs roaming through the streets.[46] Rather than replying in kind, Western powers just protested. The author asks: Why can't the West shoot at Soviet planes or kidnap a communist? Why must communists always sleep secure?

The proponent of liberation maintains that containment had not been working. The line held in Europe, but Europe was not the Cold War's only stage. Burnham relates Soviet and Chinese communism, insisting that Mao's victory had expanded the Soviet sphere.[47] And communists had strongholds into Indochina and India. Sure, they were modest, but Mao's communist takeover of China started with small takeovers of the country.[48] The West was also losing standing in the Middle East, providing more potential openings for communism.

Burnham wrote that the only area of the world that had grown substantially stronger during the era of containment was the United States. He did approve of the expanding US defense budget, calling it "a factor of the greatest world significance."[49] Unfortunately, the rest of Western Europe had not kept pace. He asserts in *Containment or Liberation* that the Soviet-supported Polish army was larger than any Western European army.[50] This weakness provided the Soviets with confidence, allowing them to feel secure in their control of the satellite states.[51] In theory, the North Atlantic Treaty Organization (NATO) showed Western European strength. In reality, Burnham argues, it was unorganized and dominated by squabbles.

Even as the center of the Cold War shifted from Europe to Asia during the Korean War, Europe was always on Burnham's mind. He maintains in *Containment or Liberation* that the United States must work with Western Europe to thwart communism because Europe was part of the United States' "destiny" and "fate."[52] Europeans favored containment because they did not want to be conquered, but they also did not want war. For Burnham, that was not sufficient. Making some of the same arguments he had made about the United States in *The Struggle for the World*, Burnham says Europe must act like an adult internationally.[53] She cannot hide. American policymakers should make Europe understand that "neutralism" was not in her best interest.[54]

Burnham notes that the heart of communism did not exist in Western Europe, however. The United States needed an Eastern European strategy that focused on liberating satellite states from the Kremlin. Attacking the periphery of the Soviet Empire, such as in Korea, had little impact: "By this Korean action, the enemy has bled American resources, pinned down a sizeable American force in a strategically pointless location, and diverted his opponent from the targets that count."[55] An Asian emphasis would not win the Cold War because the heart of communism did not exist in Korea, an area Burnham compares to fingers.[56] Focusing on Asia allowed the communists to consolidate control of the "heartland" unfettered. Maintaining that the Soviet Union was weaker than general opinion recognized, Burnham argues that liberation could be achieved only by weakening the heartland.

The proponent of liberation demands that the American government use more forms of political warfare, or "methods of struggle other than those of formal military warfare, insofar as these methods are guided by a strategic objective."[57] Burnham contends that Soviet communism conquered China primarily by using political warfare; the Soviets sent instructors and organizers into China.[58] Soviet political warfare was designed to actually defeat the enemy.[59] American political warfare, in contrast, remained inchoate. Americans did invest large sums of money in psychological warfare, also known as propaganda. However, whereas the goal of Soviet propaganda was to defeat the enemy, Burnham laments that the primary goal of American propaganda was to ensure that the United States was loved. He calls this "a profound characteristic of American culture."[60] Burnham maintains that we want Western Europeans to love us for our high standard of living, Eastern Europeans to love us because we will never invade them, and Muslims to love us for our efforts to promote pilgrimages to Mecca through our "magic carpet" program in 1952.[61] But what most Americans failed to understand, Burnham moans, was that "in their ardent youth, Americans have not yet learned the tragic lesson that the most powerful cannot be loved—hated, envied, feared, obeyed, respected, even honored perhaps, but not loved."[62] Political warfare and defeating communism should motivate Americans, not a need to be loved.

The book also fired a shot at George Kennan. Burnham's mastery of words and cleverness as a writer reveal themselves here. He could be underhanded. Burnham writes that psychologists say that emotions reveal the real person. Then what does this tell us about Kennan? The hardliner grants that Kennan is anticommunist from a rational perspective, yet his writings did not reveal a heart-felt disdain for communism. His analyses were always "pale" and "abstract."[63] Kennan's most emotional statements found in his *American Diplomacy, 1900–1950* (1951) were not directed at the Soviets, but rather against those strong anticommunists who preached against moderation, patience, and tolerance.[64] For Burnham, Kennan did not loathe communists, but extreme anticommunists; he could never really win the Cold War. *Containment or Liberation* argues that Kennan's "realist" foreign policy of containment was appeasement.[65] Just as appeasement accepted the existence of Nazism, proponents of containment saw communism as a "legitimate child of human civilization, and therefore [they] wish to bring the Soviet Empire within the family of nations."[66] Burnham placed Secretary of State Dean Acheson in the camp of appeasers, too.[67]

Burnham's criticism of Kennan was unjust because the diplomat never saw communism as legitimate. He hated communism, believing it was a guise for Russian expansionist predilections. Kennan held that containment provided a way not just to check communism, but to end it. He believed that with proper external pressure, the USSR would wilt. Kennan suggests in "Sources of Soviet Conduct" that American force in the form of containment would "promote tendencies which must eventually find their outlet in either the break-up or the gradual mellowing of Soviet power."[68] In 1948, he called the liberation of Eastern Europe a "long term objective."[69] Although his means softened over the years, Kennan's ends mirrored Burnham. Like Schlesinger, he just preferred playing a waiting game.

Burnham could not wait. The root issue that divided the two Cold Warriors was the same that divided Lenin and some of his fellow Marxists: impatience. Lenin lambasted his comrades such as Lev Kamenev and Grigory Zinoviev who denied that Russia was ripe for revolution in 1917. Burnham did the same to his fellow Cold Warriors who sought patience with the Soviet Union. He always believed that the present moment required action. Lenin wrote on the eve of the 1917 Russian Revolution: "The situation is critical in the extreme. In fact it is now clear that to delay the uprising would be fatal.... We must not wait! We may lose everything!"[70] America's most impatient anticommunist could not have said it better.

What is liberation and how is it achieved? Burnham quotes in *Containment or Liberation* a Hungarian exile who says, "Liberation for us, and for all peoples who wish to live in dignity and enjoy equality of rights, must consist in the restoration of national independence."[71] Liberation sought to free the subjects of Eastern Europe and recognize their individual rights. Words alone would not suffice: "Liberation cannot be a Sunday doctrine, but must inform and guide day by day, routine behavior, as well as the great and special actions."[72] Specific ways to achieve this included recognizing the Polish and other "free" governments in exile.[73] Communist China should not be recognized.

And Burnham wanted captive nations to have their own armies, supported by the West.[74] He demanded a free university in Europe, too.[75] These were all forms of political warfare that would undermine communism in Eastern Europe:

> What could more enhearten the subject peoples or more dismay their rulers than news of a representative of free Poland sitting in the councils of NATO; free regiments marching under the flags of Rumania, Esthonia, Russia; a free Ukrainian unit capturing a hill in Korea or wiping out one of Ho Chi Minh's detachments in Indochina; a class of a thousand young East Europeans graduating from their free university with degrees in administration, agriculture, and engineering; twenty thousand East European, Chinese, and Russian exiles combining military training with agriculture in North Africa; a NATO destroyer manned by Baltic seamen; free spokesmen of all the captive nations received with honor in Whitehall, the Quai d'Orsay, and the Department of State.[76]

Burnham maintains that the aggressive foreign policy of liberation had another advantage over containment: it did not require the United States to flip-flop. Under containment, one day, American forces were at peace. When communists encroached, they resorted to war. Then, when the communists retreated, "peace" ensued. Then war may follow. No such discontinuity existed under a policy of liberation as the same basic principles always held. Under containment, Americans only sometimes were for freedom. Under liberation, Americans always fought for freedom.[77] And this put the Soviets on the defensive.[78]

Parts of *Containment or Liberation* were reprinted in magazines. For example, several chapters appeared in the conservative journal *American Mercury*. Other parts of a chapter were published in *This Week Magazine*, a supplement that was included in many Sunday newspapers. One article title asked, "Can America Liberate the World?"[79] Mainly featuring content from the last chapter of the book, this piece includes Burnham's usual criticism of containment, which he argues could be only a temporary measure. If adopted as a long-term policy, it could never work. In fact, it was already cracking, evidenced by the loss of China, troubles in Indochina, and flareups in the Middle East.[80] A section subtitled "Goal Is Freedom" maintains that the United States must adopt a goal of liberation for all people living under communist governments. This means national, social, and individual liberation. People must be free from slave camps and secret police. They should be free to worship

God (if they choose) and to cultivate their own land. Burnham insists that the United States could win the Cold War if she aggressively sought liberation. He proclaims: "Through such a policy, carried out in action as well as in words, those who believe in liberation are convinced that we can release the energies of all the subject peoples of the Soviet Empire, and thereby weaken and finally shatter its imperial structure."[81] Specific means included "all-sided political warfare" and military action where necessary.

The book contains some possible objections to the policy of liberation, including the following: (1) Our allies may oppose it. (2) It would involve the United States in a crusade. (3) It was none of the United States' business how Eastern Europe was run. Burnham asserts the general veracity of the first objection, particularly among Western Europeans. They seemingly benefited from containment, something Burnham blames on the American lack of resolve. If Western Europeans saw real American resolve to liberate the people of Eastern Europe, they would be more willing to support the cause because it would be easier to reject a half-heartedly carried out policy. If the United States demonstrated force and will, Western Europe would subsequently follow.

And what is wrong with a crusade, Burnham asks?[82] Yes, it was intellectually fashionable to oppose crusades because they seemed dangerous and futile. He reasons that the struggle against communism and the liberation of eight hundred million people deserved to become a crusade. Communism already viewed its mission as a crusade—a crusade to eradicate capitalism and usher in a new era of history. This crusade pitted two antagonistic, irreconcilable forces against each other. Communists maintained this was all historical necessity. And communists did not compromise. They advanced. Burnham argues that if the United States wanted to win, she must interpret the struggle as a crusade. Americans must be willing to declare that their system of political freedom and representative government is better than "tyranny" and the "sovereignty of the secret police."[83] He proclaims that moral equivalency will not win this crusade.

And, of course, Burnham contends, it is America's business what happens in Eastern Europe. US security is at stake. Just because bombs are not currently being dropped does not mean we are safe.

Containment or Liberation was widely read, although it was less popular than his first two anticommunist polemics. Arthur Schlesinger panned it in *The New Republic*, calling it an "absurd book by an absurd man."[84] Kennan later stated that the book was "a well-written and persuasive book aimed largely against myself and the doctrine of containment."[85] Right around the time the book appeared, confirmation hearings for Kennan's replacement as ambassador to the USSR were underway. Chip Bohlen was asked by Senator Bourke Hickenlooper (R-IA) whether he had read the book. The nominee replied that he had not, although he had read articles written by Burnham. The senator suggested that the future ambassador to the Soviet Union read the book.[86] CIA director Allen Dulles requested and received a copy of the book upon hearing that it attacked CIA analyst Sherman Kent. The director told Kent not to worry.[87]

When the book arguing for the liberation of Eastern Europe appeared in early 1953, some Americans were feeling more threatened by communism's subversive elements at home than its expansion abroad. The Soviet detonation of the atomic bomb, espionage cases, and the Korean War stimulated domestic fears in the United States between 1949 and 1953. Like World War II, this era changed much, both in the United States and in Burnham's mind. When this period began, Burnham collaborated with anticommunist liberals and leftists. At the Congress for Cultural Freedom, he worked with Daniel Bell, Diana Trilling, and Schlesinger. At *Partisan Review*, he collaborated with leftists such as Mary McCarthy, Dwight Macdonald, and Philip Rahv. But like his collaborations with Marxists, Burnham's association with these people would end in rather dramatic fashion. The rise of Joseph McCarthy was the spark that led to a conflagration between Burnham and his onetime friends.

Burnham loved McCarthy's goals of exposing communists.[88] The means? Burnham tried to walk a fine line by taking a moderate stance. In a piece titled "Editor Meets Senator," Burnham generally supported the committee's investigations while critiquing McCarthy's reasoning when determining what made someone a communist; he suggested that some of McCarthy's targets had not been proven guilty.[89] That was not sufficient for liberals, most of whom deemed McCarthy a demagogue. Schlesinger insisted that the American Committee of Cultural Freedom (the ACCF, an independent affiliate of the CCF that Burnham helped create) formally condemn him.[90] Burnham hesitated. He even questioned Schlesinger's anticommunist commitment.[91] Burnham called himself "anti-anti-McCarthyite," maintaining that those who were obsessed with McCarthy were not his team; in fact, they contributed to a "united front" with communists, something that only abetted communism.[92] When Daniel Bell and Irving Kristol introduced a resolution condemning McCarthy and communism, Burnham rejected it, insisting that although he was not pro-McCarthy, the senator from Wisconsin should be treated fairly.[93]

Burnham had to know this would not suffice and his refusal to fully condemn the senator ostracized him. A preface for Medgar Evans's *The Secret Fight for the A-Bomb*—a book that held American scientists accountable for giving the Soviets atomic secrets—further associated Burnham with McCarthyites.[94] Prominent American scientists demanded that he resign from *Partisan Review*'s executive committee, or they would disassociate from it.[95] Readers wondered why a "McCarthyite" like Burnham remained on the advisory board.[96] Thirteen years after submitting a formal letter of resignation from the worker's party, Burnham did the same from *Partisan Review*. Friendships were spurned again. Contending that his name on the advisory board meant little, Burnham lamented that the one-time anticommunist bastion seemed to be lowering its standards.[97] The anti-anti-McCarthyite wrote that McCarthyism may have been the central issue for *Partisan Review*, but it was not for him. He did not consider himself pro- or anti-McCarthy; he believed that McCarthy should be lauded for what he had uncovered, just as he should be condemned for his false accusations. Burnham insisted that "McCarthyism" was an invention of "communist tacticians" and that "Eastern seaboard" intellectuals had taken the communist bait and ran with it, promoting the idea that McCarthyism, not communism, was America's biggest threat.[98] *Partisan Review* had fallen for the trick.

This ended his association not just with *Partisan Review* but also with liberals. He resigned from the ACCF shortly after.[99] His tenure with the CIA ended in 1953, as some of its members considered him too pro-McCarthy.[100] Philip Rahv wrote that by refusing to condemn McCarthy, Burnham had committed professional "suicide."[101] A *National Review* editor later maintained that Burnham never harbored any bitterness over the loss of friendships and prestige among liberals.[102] Burnham, however, dedicated most of the rest of his professional career to haranguing liberals.

The Web of Subversion (1954) seeks to justify Burnham's anti-anti-McCarthyite positions. Based mostly on Congressional testimony, it analyzes communist espionage in the United States, something Burnham argues was vastly underestimated. In some respects, his attitude toward communism mirrors some contemporary attitudes about racism: communists were everywhere. And they had to be outed. The more latent form was particularly disconcerting: "Our concern," the anticommunist tells his readers, "is not with open, professed Communists, but only with *the underground*—the illegal apparatus and the hidden, secret Communist agents and collaborators."[103] The book suggests that the latent communism was scariest because it escaped detection. Burnham insists that "during the 1930s and 1940s, an invisible web was spun over Washington. Its interlaced threads were extended to nearly every executive department and agency, to the military establishment of the White House itself, and to many of the committees of Congress.... In reality one should say there are several interlacing webs, interlocked networks. They are part of the underground."[104] Conspirators occupied different positions, and their functions and motives varied. Communism should never be underestimated.[105]

Burnham opines that some seemingly good, decent people, unwittingly promoted communism. Although they may not be overtly communist, they still fostered a communist system by working with communists. He asks: What about these obscure American citizens who made up part of the communist web?[106] Do they realize they are promoting evil? Burnham contends: "It is possible that some of them, individually, have not understood these truths. If so, this ignorance mitigates [not eliminates] their legal and no doubt moral guilt."[107] The anticommunist watchman insists that communist sympathies can occur in the most mundane activities, such as mailing a letter for a friend, unaware that the letter spreads communist propaganda.[108]

The Web of Subversion provides another example of the Burnham who saw the world more darkly. He maintains that "there is some reason to doubt that so many lambs in our flock are totally white."[109] For the Marxist Burnham, the world writhed in sin because of the corrupt nature of capitalism. *The Managerial Revolution* and *The Machiavellians* describe how a small group of duplicitous, clandestine elites ruled (or will rule) the world. Burnham had found a reason to interpret the Cold War era just as ghastly: communists, or those who unwittingly abetted communism, dominated American society. An invisible web connects them all.

Burnham describes the extent of communist activity, such as the existence of "cells," or groups of communists that had infiltrated American institutions. One example was the Ware Cell, centered around Harold Ware, a member of the Department of Agriculture.[110] Other important members of this cell were John Abt and Nathan Witt, also members of the Department of Agriculture, Victor Perlo of the Treasury Department, attorney Lee Pressman, and Alger Hiss.[111] Hiss's infamous odyssey began in 1948 when Whittaker Chambers accused the former State Department member of being a Soviet spy. Hiss denied the charges in front of the House Un-American Activities Committee and even denied knowing Chambers. Evidence to the contrary was presented, and Hiss was found guilty of perjury (the statute of limitations on treason had passed) in a celebrated trial.

According to the *Web of Subversion*, the public record showed that communists had infiltrated virtually every conceivable public institution: the administrative staff at the White House; the Departments of State, Treasury, Army, Navy, Defense, Justice, Agriculture, Labor, and Commerce; six Congressional committees; the Bureau of Ordinance; the Signal Corps; the Office of Strategic Services; the National Labor Relations Board the Works Progress Administration; the War Production Board; the Foreign Economic Association; the Exchange Commission; and the Bureau of Census were just part of a litany of examples Burnham used to show how wide and deep the web of subversion extended.[112] President Roosevelt kept Hiss by his side at Yalta, Burnham reminds the reader.[113] And those collaborating communist agents moved seamlessly from one agency to another, slowly climbing the ladder and subsequently influencing US policy. Burnham suggests that given its prominent role in shaping US foreign policy, communist infiltration of the State Department was particularly disconcerting. How deeply the web of subversion had entangled the State Department would never be known, but communist influence was undeniable.

Even the highest office in the land had been penetrated by communists. Burnham again reminds the reader that Alger Hiss had been Roosevelt's assistant at Yalta. Owen Lattimore, another suspected communist agent, was Roosevelt's personal envoy to Chiang Kai-shek, and "Mrs. Roosevelt's hospitality has extended still further toward the left."[114] Examples include Harry Hopkins and David Niles. Americans should be aware, and afraid.

This did not even include "fellow travelers, sympathizers and mere dupes" who wittingly or unwittingly promoted communism.[115] And that was just in the government. Communist activity permeated all levels of society, including the most important American institutions. Burnham insists, "Thickly or tenuously the web has extended into most social institutions: trade unions, churches, the educational system, the press, the movies, the theater, radio and TV, foundations, book publishing, pacificist organizations, civil rights and other reform groups."[116] Communists were everywhere.

How deeply had these fundamental institutions of US politics and life been stained by communists? Burnham suspects that we would never know because many communists were not publicly identified, but they were quietly allowed to resign to avoid scandal and public embarrassment.[117] And to what extent had America's armed forces—the institution designed to protect our freedom—been ensnared? Again, he contends, "we cannot give a precise quantitative answer."[118] Burnham's emphasis about the unknowability of the number of communists provided fertile soil for the idea that it was widespread. Because we did not know, it could be 1 percent, 10 percent, or 50 percent, or it could even be true that the vast majority of people have been inflicted with this evil. We just did not know. All the more reason to remain vigilant. In *The Web of Subversion*, Burnham calls communism a "chameleon."[119] More common than most people realized, it took many different forms; it could be difficult to see and define.

The idea that invisible malignant agents exert powerful influence over this visible world remains an enduring legacy of the medieval and early modern eras, when people believed that concealed Satan and his subtle minions sought dominion over the world.[120] The powerful Satan did not announce his arrival, nor was he immediately perceived. But for some of the learned, his influence was nearly ubiquitous. The hiddenness is significant because the believer can attribute a vast array of phenomena to the evil. The more hidden the evil becomes (whether it be Satan's minions, communism, or racism), the easier it becomes to assert its influence. If the evil were visible, it could be refuted by simply stating that no one saw it, and therefore, it could not have existed when and where it allegedly struck. Making the evil latent allows one to maximize its influence.

How much damage had the evil communists done? Burnham claims that this was difficult to delineate (again, meaning it could be great). He notes that communists existed at every level of government. And the US government had made mistakes in its policies toward communists. For Burnham, examples abounded: the Soviets received nuclear secrets. Alger Hiss's position meant he had access to all classified information. And US foreign policy toward China had failed since China fell to the communists, something Burnham blames on communist influence or the "web of subversion."[121] Analysis of US policy in Yugoslavia led to the same conclusion: during World War II, there were two anti-Nazi groups, a procommunist one led by Tito and an anticommunist group led by Mihailović. The United States had backed Tito, facilitating the spread of communism in the Balkans.[122] Burnham insinuates that by connecting the dots, you could see how communist infiltration had damaged America and the world.

The Web of Subversion reads like one of the politically charged and ideologically driven articles that are the norm in American media today. It relies on guilt by association. The work is based on truths, but it was filled with half-truths and suggestions that could never really be proven or disproven, such as the assertion that communist subversion led to the victory of communism in China. This made it seductive, allowing the believer to rationalize the worst possible scenario. After all, it could not be disproven that communist agents had played a critical role in shaping US foreign policy. Given this, it was not irrational to believe that they did. Soon after its release, a condensed conversion was published by the John Birch Society.[123]

The book received mixed reviews. Arthur Schlesinger exploited the book's weaknesses by arguing that the author was "fundamentally uncritical."[124] Schlesinger conceded that there had been "systematic Soviet espionage activity within the United States government."[125] It was a legitimate problem. Burnham failed, however, because he did not discriminate among the various accusations; he accepted them all at face value. For Burnham, if person x said person y was a communist, it must be true. Certainly, sometimes it was true, but often, the evidence was weak. Schlesinger contended that the accusations against men like John K. Fairbanks and John Vincent Carter were less credible. Moreover, Schlesinger argued, the anticommunist failed to prove any significant influence of the communists. Yes, communists had served in all departments, but Burnham did not prove that they significantly influenced policy. Finally, the reviewer noted that Burnham asserted communist influence without seeking to explain it with other, more rational, alternatives. For example, yes, there were communists in the State Department, and yes, the United States chose the procommunists over the anticommunists in Yugoslavia. But Burnham failed to acknowledge that the English had supported Tito months before the Americans did and had urged the United States to do the same. Did that mean Churchill was caught in some web of communist espionage, too?

Irving Kristol was moderately impressed, stating that the work "presents a terse and lucid summary of what has been discovered by various investigating committees about Communist espionage networks in the United States government."[126] But like Schlesinger, he describes some of the book's flaws, writing that Burnham was "strong on first causes, weak on contingent ones."[127] Kristol believed that Burnham sometimes overstated his case. For example, Burnham wrote that American communist party boss Earl Browder bragged that thirteen thousand US soldiers were party members. It was too bad that Burnham had not provided details about how these men had shaped policy, maybe because it was negligible. The same held true for Burnham's contention that McCarthy discovered a secret communist cell at Fort Monmouth. Unfortunately, the author gave no evidence for the claim, leading Kristol to speculate that Burnham "has deduced it from—if one may say so—underground premises."[128] Kristol audaciously challenged Burnham's use of logic.

During the first half of the 1950s, Burnham also wrote for *The Freeman*, a conservative libertarian journal that in many ways was a precursor to the *National Review*, both in style and substance. He continued flailing at anyone who he believed assisted the communist cause. Some of his notable targets were Chip Bohlen, Owen Lattimore, and John Paton Davies. In a piece titled, "Was Bohlen a Blunder?," he criticizes President Eisenhower's nomination for ambassador to the Soviet Union for making concessions to the Soviets at Yalta.[129] Burnham also implicates Lattimore and Davies as two of many "dupes" at the Institute of Pacific Relations who unwittingly promoted communism by blocking Western attempts to thwart Communist conquest of China.[130]

Burnham was not a perfect fit at *The Freeman*. Unlike most of the contributors, he was not a laissez-faire capitalist. But he generally espoused social libertarianism, at least valuing individual freedom in the abstract. His most memorable piece, titled "No Firecrackers Allowed," begins in Burnham's characteristic sardonic style: "Last Fourth of July was a good day for meditation in our locality. The hot holiday quiet was unbroken by snap of firecracker, boom of daybomb, or whish of rocket. The torpedoes and cap pistols were silent. In the evening there were no pinwheels, Roman candles, or even hand-waved sparklers to contend with the late-settling summer darkness."[131] A few states resisted laws against fireworks, but Burnham surmises these outlaws would soon surrender to the forces of "Progress." Thankfully, Burnham maintains, this meant fewer children would lose fingers and eyes. And fewer babies—prone to mistake firecrackers for Tootsie Rolls—would develop stomach aches. Of course, with nothing else to do on the national holiday, more kids would demand evening drives, an equally dangerous endeavor. Burnham notes sarcastically that we know that when government restricts our freedom, it is always for our good. He remains wistful for his youth, a time when hearing the morning's first firecrackers created the same excitement as opening Christmas presents.

But this piece also has a serious side. It tells the reader that freedom is not always lost overnight in dramatic fashion. Liberty can erode gradually. Our freedom to travel had been restricted because of passports. Even before we received our paychecks, taxes are taken out. Some workers are forced to join unions. Again, the government tells us it is for our own good, but what if we disagree? Burnham concludes that the issue is not necessarily the deprivations of liberty—some of which were necessary—but instead how easily the citizens acquiesce. For the next Fourth of July, he pledged to supply some bootleg liquor, a copy of *The Federalist Papers*, and loud fireworks, just to remind people of what the Fourth of July was all about.[132] These antistatist ideas would suit Burnham well during the final phase of his writing career.

CHAPTER 10

National Review, *Congress and the American Tradition*, and *Suicide of the West*

During his tenure at the Central Intelligence Agency in the early 1950s, James Burnham met a charismatic recent Yale graduate named William F. Buckley. Twenty years Burnham's junior, Buckley was also raised in a wealthy Catholic family. Although Burnham had abandoned Catholicism as a young adult, Buckley practiced and preached his faith. Both were relatively aristocratic in outlook; they questioned the innate abilities of the masses. And both men liked to argue for the mere sake of arguing. Buckley needed sparring partners, too, although he attacked more gently and humorously than Burnham.

In 1955, Burnham helped cofound with Buckley the conservative magazine *National Review* (*NR*). *NR* became the most important conservative journal of the second half of the twentieth century. Its publisher's statement from the first issue in November 1955 explains that the magazine opposed "Big Brother government," any attempts at social engineering, and the conformity of the intellectuals. Diplomatically, the magazine called communism "satanic utopianism."[1] Coexistence with the USSR was neither possible, desirable, nor honorable; victory had to be achieved. The magazine harvested writers from *The Freeman*. A June 1954 edition of *The Freeman* included articles from future *NR* columnists Buckley, Burnham, Max Eastman, and Russel Kirk. Along with Burnham, inaugural editors Willmoore Kendall and Willi Schlamm had been former leftists. The magazine accommodated various conservative voices, and intellectual disagreements between editors were encouraged.[2] Buckley later called Burnham *NR*'s "dominant intellectual influence."[3]

Burnham's columns usually denounced liberals, communists, and other pundits. He continued to spread themes he had preached in his three anticommunist works: war raged. It could not be wished away. Maybe Americans did not want to fight the Cold War, but the Cold War had to be fought. And won. And it *could* be won. The Soviet Union was weak. The United States just needed a consistent, aggressive foreign policy aimed at its destruction. When combined, America's best weapons were force and will. *NR* gave the Cold Warrior a megaphone that he used to promote these ideas to American conservatives for the next twenty-three years in hundreds of columns and various blurbs.

The magazine's appearance was fortuitous because the months after its founding were critical in Cold War history, allowing the magazine and Burnham to showcase their strong anticommunist voices. The impetus was Nikita Khrushchev's "secret speech" in February 1956. Never intended to be publicized, Khrushchev detailed the crimes of Joseph Stalin. The speech was a bombshell because no longer could evidence about Stalin's brutality be dismissed as an imperialist invention; it had now been corroborated. Riots ensued in Stalin's native Georgia. The speech confirmed to anticommunists like Burnham what they already believed: that there was no essential difference between Hitler and Stalin, or the systems they ruled over. Communism equaled Nazism.

Burnham responded by resurrecting the issue of Lenin and his responsibility for the Soviet catastrophe. Khrushchev exalted Lenin in his speech, insisting that the Bolshevik used violence only when necessary. Dismissing Marxists and other leftists who assumed that everything would have been different in the first socialist society had Lenin lived, Burnham maintains in an *NR* article that Lenin condemned "imperialists" and "class enemies" more forcefully than Stalin.[4] And Lenin's penchant for blood was greater than Stalin's, before, during, and even after the Revolution. What about Trotsky? His former American disciple flatly muses that maybe his body could be held in a mausoleum too, except it had been cremated after his assassination—by his comrades. Violence and terror were endemic in the communist experience.

Khrushchev's speech also sparked significant revolts against Soviet influence in Eastern Europe. In Poland, anticommunist protests were crushed with the help of dozens of Soviet tanks. *NR*'s senior editor dryly notes: "And as they rolled over Polish bodies the Communist tanks flattened also the soft rhetoric of our George Kennans and Stewart Alsops, our experts and smug journalists, who have been telling us how the Soviet regime has come to be accepted by its subjects, how (in Kennan's servile words) 'there is a finality, for better or worse, about what has occurred in Eastern Europe.'"[5] Burnham retorts that helpless Poles clasping hands when confronted by tanks—emboldened by the soldiers who joined them—spoke the truth about the Soviet empire, not America's "correspondents and diplomats."[6]

Encouraged by the spirit of criticism, what began as an attempt to voice concerns became a full-fledged revolution in Hungary where Imre Nagy established a more liberal regime. Fearing change, particularly the Hungarian desire to leave the Warsaw Pact, Khrushchev responded again with tanks. Roughly thirty thousand Hungarians were killed. Nagy was executed and a new pro-Soviet government was established. The crushing of the revolt marked a crucial moment in the history of communism. The French and Italian Communist Parties fractured while the British Communist Party lost two-thirds of its members.[7]

The lack of an immediate US response devastated Burnham. Rollback could have begun. Buckley said he had never seen Burnham so angry.[8] The United States formally practiced containment or inaction, so hopes for the liberation of Eastern Europe were lost. Burnham argues in a blurb that it appeared to European nations that Americans had helped incite revolts, yet failed to support them when they materialized.[9] Two weeks later he wrote: "The rulers of the Soviet Union appear to have proved what the world has long suspected: that they can perpetuate no aggression so bold, or brutality so base, as to cause the United States to take a stand."[10] He later insisted that no better opportunity for liberation had existed because all of Eastern Europe stirred with discontent as the post-Stalin regime was still raw.[11] The Hungarians showed their hatred for the Soviet regime and the United States idled. From this point onward, Burnham wrote, everyone knew that the United States would not materially support anyone trying to free themselves from the Soviet yoke.

A lack of Western response in the Middle East irked the hardliner, too. Several months before the Hungarian Revolution, Egyptian President Gamal Nasser nationalized the British-owned and operated Suez Canal, angering most of the West. "The decline of Western prestige has never been more starkly pointed than by Gamal Abdel Nasser's seizure of the Suez Canal Company," Burnham begins one piece.[12] Contending that Nasser "hijacked" the canal from its rightful owners, Burnham asserts that the British were not expelled from India and Egypt with force. Rather, she (and the United States) suffered from a "moral collapse—a defect of will."[13] And there were practical consequences because the canal was part of the chain that linked the West (not the "Soviet dominated Heartland") to the oil-rich Middle East.[14] Without Western guards at the canal, communists could also have more access to Asia and Africa.

When it came to Israel's position in the region, Burnham was not a Zionist. He recognized the tendency of Israel to expand, and how it used the Western media to promote its interests. He just favored Israel when it blocked Soviet encroachment, as it did in his mind in 1956. In 1955 Egypt purchased large sums of arms from the Soviets (via Czechoslovakia), leading Burnham to declare, "Today the Communists arrive openly, bearing arms and gifts—and ideas."[15] Burnham was concerned with geopolitical significance of the sale. Invoking the geographer Halford Mackinder, Burnham stressed the strategic importance of the Near East since it is a "Land Bridge" between Eurasia and Africa.[16]

The sale of Soviet arms to Egypt and the Suez crisis helped provoke Israel to attack Egypt on October 29, 1956. Two days later, the British and French joined them. However, the Soviets ominously hinted that they would assist Egypt. Fearing a broader Soviet-US conflict, the Eisenhower administration pressured the Israeli, French, and British governments to remove their troops while the UN condemned the attack. Burnham felt this was another show of Western weakness. He bemoaned in "Abstractions Kill the West," that the condemnation sacrificed "our allies, our strategic interests, and the inner imperatives of our civilization."[17] Burnham wondered how the UN, with American support, could criticize France and Britain while condoning Nasser, "a willing tool of Communist imperialism."[18] Burnham shows what he believed was the irony of Eisenhower's policies in Hungary and the Middle East: instead of applying force and pressure against the Soviets in Hungary, the administration chose to do so against France and Britain in the Middle East as they fought against Soviet infiltration.[19]

Burnham never saw American and Western involvement in foreign parts of the world as forms of imperialism because they countered Soviet imperialism. He asserted that those who did were duped by communist propaganda. Burnham believed that the United States and Europe must act—preferably in concert—to confront communism, wherever it tried to spread. He had little concern for UN legalities. For the Machiavellian, the ends always justified the means because in the geopolitical arena, only power restrained power.

During *NR*'s first full year, Burnham championed ideas that he preached as a Marxist and as a Machiavellian. In the critical Cold War year of 1956, he demanded action. Eastern Europe and the Middle East had become tests of Western will. Inexorable historical trends that shaped the world may no longer favor our civilization. Power must be demonstrated in some form, or it would be used to erase the now-contracting West. He would soon tackle this subject more fully in a book.

After a year of working with fellow *NR* editors, Burnham helped provoke a crisis that nearly led to his resignation. It began when he suggested that the United States work with Soviet leadership to remove communist troops from satellite territories—what Burnham called the objective. Western powers would leave West Germany too; she could then be unified and completely disarmed. Central and Eastern Europe would be neutralized.[20] Why would the Soviets accept this? Burnham contended that the move would permit the Soviets to concentrate on fixing their turbulent home front. In Leninist terms, it meant taking one step backward so two could be taken foreword.[21]

The proposal earned the indignation of most *NR* editors, including Buckley. They deemed it unrealistic and in violation of one of Burnham's own cardinal principles: never negotiate with communists. Burnham's most notable critic was Willi Schlamm, arguably the original number-two man at *NR*, after Buckley. Genuine animosity existed between Burnham and Schlamm. According to former *NR* staffer Daniel Kelly, Schlamm threatened to quit the magazine if Burnham's proposal was published. Burnham told Buckley that he needed to assert more "authority" and that he should not coddle Schlamm's "neuroses." Personal tensions between Burnham and Schlamm simmered. Burnham offered to resign, but Buckley would not allow it. The frustrated Schlamm left the magazine a year later, never to return.[22] Burnham exerted power. He became the de facto number-two man at *NR*.

Burnham's *NR* articles usually interpreted the Cold War in an unconventional manner; he never trusted the pundits, or the communists. For example, *Sputnik* did not impress Burnham. In its wake, as Westerners lauded Soviet science and technology, Burnham penned a piece titled "Disinformation Bureaus" that described how "Red psychosis" promoted a tendency to believe anything positive about the Soviet Union.[23] Everyone believes, he wrote in the article, that the Russian standard of living had risen since tsarist days, despite a lack of evidence for this contention. Or, if the Soviets had lots of bombers and warships, then they must have a great air force and navy. Or, because they had advanced mechanized agriculture, they must produce lots of food. Or, the Soviets were ahead of the United States scientifically and technologically, so they must lead in the fields of mechanics and engineering. According to Burnham, the Soviets told us that *Sputnik I* weighed 184 pounds and that *Sputnik II* weighed 1,120 pounds. But why do we believe them? Insisting that the Soviets were masters of disinformation, he contended that they had special schools aimed at teaching dissimulation (as did the United States). They taught that the best way to persuade intelligent people to believe a falsehood is not to tell them something untrue, but rather to present them with independent items, allowing them to deduce the falsehood on their own.[24] This was how communists manipulated Westerners.

Burnham proclaimed that communists were liars. In fact, it was their revolutionary duty to lie.[25] In an article titled "Words of East and West," the senior *NR* editor asserts that Westerners assume that the nature of discourse is to communicate information and truth. Any errors in communication are accidental. But this is a Western phenomenon, not a universal one. Burnham insists that Japanese politeness has nothing to do with how they really feel about you. For many Africans, the line between reality and illusion, science and magic, past and future is vastly different than that of Westerners. A Muslim's religious faith may differ dramatically from the words he or she expresses to define it. For Burnham, this means that when communist nations like China say that rice production had doubled, it should be questioned. When the Soviets say they have fired a 7.1-ton satellite, it might not be the truth. If Khrushchev continues to preach disarmament to reduce tensions, we needed to resist the natural inclination to believe him. For the Soviets, words were merely more weapons in the Cold War. Burnham reminds the reader that Sun Tzu wrote that "all warfare is based on deception."[26]

Burnham also reviewed books for *NR*, such as Henry Kissinger's *Nuclear Weapons and Foreign Policy* (1957). He acknowledges that the book's arguments were formidable. What most interested the reviewer, however, was the liberal reaction to the book: liberals loved it. The work was sponsored by the Council on Foreign Relations, a "bristling fortress of the Liberal Establishment."[27] Even J. Robert Oppenheimer praised the book. All of this despite the fact it was a "massive retaliatory assault on the foundations of Liberal foreign policy."[28] On issues such as coexistence, disarmament, the banning of nuclear weapons, and Soviet sincerity, Burnham declares that Henry Kissinger "shatters the logical supports of the Liberal façade."[29] Then why then did liberals extoll the book? Burnham posits some theories: maybe it was because Kissinger did not assault individuals by name; he described arguments made by Dean Acheson and other liberal publicists, but he never criticizes them. Or maybe it is because Kissinger, nor his bibliography, cite any "Liberal-anathematized writer."[30] Such citations would seem necessary because, as Burnham contends, "a good part of the cogent analysis of, say Soviet intentions and methods is not altogether a fresh discovery by Mr. Kissinger."[31] Burnham was feeling shunned by liberals.

And to some degree he was. John Kenneth Galbraith provides one example. He was an archetype liberal who Burnham roasted.[32] Galbraith tried to malign Burnham by ignoring him. Galbraith's classic work *The New Industrial State* (1967) makes references to "the managerial class," "the managerial revolution," and "managerial capitalism," but credit was not given to Burnham in the first edition. The omission was so glaring that Galbraith subsequently wrote Burnham to acknowledge his influence and apologize, stating that "we liberals have ignored your contribution."[33] He promised that Burnham's name would appear in future editions. And it did, in a footnote. The note cites Burnham for popularizing the term "managerial revolution" and continues by stating that "partly, perhaps, because he was a strong and on occasion eccentric conservative, and change in economics is usually led by liberals, Burnham's contribution has not had the recognition it merited."[34] Galbraith would later send a follow-up letter apologizing for calling Burnham "eccentric."

Burnham's favorite target was America's most famous diplomat, and maybe the field's most important writer. Shortly after reviewing Kissinger's book, Burnham briefly reviewed Kennan's *The Decision to Intervene* (1958), a work that described US involvement in the Russian Revolution.[35] Burnham extolls the contents and historical analysis of this book, recommending that Kennan spend more time writing diplomatic history and less time complicating it by lecturing in England. In late 1957, Kennan delivered six lectures at Oxford that analyzed US-Soviet relations called the Reith Lectures. Burnham would have been vexed by Kennan's description of Soviet economic and technological advances, suggestions that non-Western nations could have normal relations with the USSR, his fears of a nuclear arms race, and his questioning the utility of a stronger, US-led North Atlantic Treaty Organization.[36] Many of Burnham's Cold War writings were tacitly aimed at Kennan, especially the latter's thoughts on an arms race.

Kennan received and at least occasionally read *NR*. In December 1958, an article appeared in the *National Review Bulletin* (an *NR* supplement edited by Burnham) that declared that the former ambassador to the Soviet Union wanted to eliminate America's atomic weaponry.[37] A perplexed Kennan wrote a letter to the editor, insisting that he had never made such statements.[38] He contended that he found *NR* "lively, well-edited and rarely dull."[39] But Kennan noted significant differences between himself and the editors. For example, he did not believe that the United States needed to engage in an "all-out war" against Russia as soon as possible. Containment's architect deemed this view "catastrophic."[40]

In 1959, Burnham temporarily turned his attention toward domestic affairs when he penned *Congress and the American Tradition*. The book was partly an attempt to defend McCarthy and his investigations, and partly a demand that Congress assert its authority. Deeply pessimistic, the work feared that Congress might soon be vanquished by a Caesar-like executive.[41] Burnham wanted to justify the predictions made in *The Managerial Revolution*: power was becoming more centralized through the bureaucracy. And he sought to apply his ideas presented in *The Machiavellians*: for democracy to succeed, central authority must be curbed. Congress had to assert power.

Burnham writes that the Founding Fathers were not "ideologues" like the leaders of the French Revolution because they recognized that people were not completely good or rational.[42] America's founders liked ideas, but they did not worship "Reason,"[43] and they respected tradition.[44] For example, the author notes that John Dickinson of Delaware wrote: "Experience must be our only guide. Reason may mislead us."[45] The founders sought to create a government that was neither too strong nor too weak. It had to collect taxes and defeat foreign enemies, yet too strong a government would limit justice and liberty.[46]

The anti-idealogue theorizes in *Congress and the American Tradition* that whatever type of political system existed, power naturally concentrates in the sovereign.[47] America's founders tried to thwart this with different branches of government; ambition must counteract ambition. This worked for more than one hundred years because in the nineteenth-century Congress curbed the power of the presidency. Burnham contends that America's great political leaders during this time were members of congress and senators, such Henry Clay, Daniel Webster, John C. Calhoun, and John Quincy Adams. He notes that Adams preferred the position of congressman to president because, as Adams wrote in 1830, Congress degraded no one, not even the president.[48] In 1832, Calhoun resigned the vice presidency to become a senator. That was how it was supposed to be.

The system began to falter in the twentieth century when imbalance emerged. In the book, Burnham claims that Woodrow Wilson began the shift from congressional government to presidential government.[49] Franklin D. Roosevelt perpetuated the trend, bathing alone in America's celestial light while Congress slumbered in the shadows. The process continued with Harry Truman. He did not even get congressional support for his war in 1950, reasoning in his memoirs that a president must act without congressional authorization if Congress stalled.[50] Burnham notes that Nixon resigned from the Senate in 1952 to become vice president, a reversal of Calhoun.

This centralization meant more power for the bureaucracy, what Burnham calls the "fourth branch of government."[51] He suggests that government agencies exercised "extraordinary authority" over national life.[52] In theory, these agencies were arms of Congress because Congress created them and could abolish them. In practice, these agencies developed their own political life. They expand, and then Congress loses the ability to supervise them. They became independent and sovereign: "The bureaucracy, like the Carolingian Mayors of the palace in eighth century France, not merely wields its own share of the sovereign power but begins to challenge the older branches for supremacy."[53] Burnham argues that their arrogance grows, evidenced by the fact that in meetings between bureaucrats and members of congress, the former were more likely to be tardy than the latter.[54]

Congress and the American Tradition insists that liberals fostered Caesarism because of their faith in reason and government. They believe that when guided by reasonable men, government promotes reform and progress.[55] For Burnham, conservatives have more realistic attitudes toward human nature because they recognize that people are not always governed by reason. Conservatives favor a mixture of elements—some aristocratic, some democratic—in their efforts to balance power.[56] Conservatives will usually favor Congress over the president.[57] And they are more prone to take the Constitution—a document that restricts the power of the executive—literally. All of this leads to the diffusion of power.

Congressional investigations were one way for Congress to assert its authority.[58] Contrary to the liberal argument (during the McCarthy era) that congressional committees were dangerous, the anti-anti-McCarthyite states that they were required to preserve the republic. He declares that congressional investigations were normal. There had been 30 by 1814 and more than 330 and by 1928. The pace had quickened during the 1940s and 1950s. And Burnham insists in *Congress and the American Tradition* that virtually nothing had escaped the grasp of congressional investigation committees: wars, banks, riots, scandals, mining, agricultural, railroads, lobbying, real estate, the post office, and oil were some examples.[59] Modern congressional committees were in fact quite benign; Benjamin Wade, chair of the Committee on the Conduct of the Civil War, was allegedly eager to use a sawed-off shotgun that he kept under his desk.[60] Burnham believed that the purpose of investigation was critical for democracy, specifically their goal to inform the public: "Through public investigations Congress informs the citizens about the nation's problems at the same time that it is informing itself."[61] Liberal critics of investigation committees have to recognize that a democratic form of government cannot exist without the power to investigate.[62] Even Woodrow Wilson—hardly a defender of Congress—wrote about the importance of Congress as an oversight committee that reported its findings to the public.[63]

In *Congress and the American Tradition,* Burnham contends that the decline of Congress "takes place within the pattern of the long-term, world-wide historical trends."[64] The rise of liberal ideology in the early twentieth century exemplified this because liberals had assumed most positions of power, both inside and outside of government.[65] Even the Supreme Court under Earl Warren had succumbed to liberalism.[66] Existing political structures linked the managerial elite, the courts and the bureaucracy with a Caesar-like executive.[67] Intermediary institutions such as states were acquiescing.[68] Burnham reminds the reader that he had predicted this "managerial revolution."[69]

The author declares that Congress must remain strong. It must exert power. If present trends continued (and Burnham usually believed they would), Congress would crumble, leaving the United States with a Caesar-like dictatorship in which Congress would become "a legislature in form only."[70] Fearing what Schlesinger would later call an "imperial presidency," Burnham cites Edward Gibbon's description of Augustus: "He destroyed the independence of the senate. The principles of free constitution are irrecoverably lost, when the legislative power is nominated by the executive."[71] Burnham recognizes that humans had free will—although they rarely exercised it properly—so the future was never written in stone. Great leaders willing to resist centralization must emerge. He declares that an active Congress was the only way for liberty and democracy to survive: "If liberty, then Congress, if no Congress, no liberty."[72]

Congress and the American tradition is a product of the second James Burnham, the paleoconservative paragon. Pessimistic about the future of the United States and its democratic system, the work contends that the executive branch had become too active. The best remedy was Congress. Whereas *The Managerial Revolution* assumed that Congress would get subordinated to the managerial and bureaucratic elite, Burnham now champions Congress. It must stay strong. The future of American democracy hinged on this institution.

The book would be the last that he dedicated solely to domestic affairs. Paleoconservative Samuel Francis lamented that Burnham "wasted much of his later career in what turned out to be rather ephemeral anticommunist polemics that had little impact on actual policy after the early 1950's."[73] Francis wished Burnham would have spent more time promoting themes from *The Managerial Revolution, The Machiavellians,* and *Congress and the American Tradition.* But in the post–World War II era, fighting communism was Burnham's *raison d'être.* The United States faced a dangerous international foe that threatened her existence more than a united managerial/bureaucratic elite. The contents of his writings for the next two decades reflect this.

The greatest threat to American democracy for Burnham remained communism. Around the same time as *Congress and the American Tradition* appeared, John Foster Dulles passed away, weeks after resigning his position of secretary of state. Perceived as a man who thwarted communism with religious zeal, Dulles received praise from most of the international community at the end of his life. Burnham was characteristically less impressed. In a piece titled "The Dulles Record: An Appraisal," Burnham writes that Eisenhower's leading diplomat preached liberation but merely practiced containment.[74] At least he really did practice containment, unlike his predecessor, Dean Acheson. The piece claims that Dulles had "deeply believed in blocking further Soviet advance and has striven mightily to uphold his belief in practice. Communism is godless and evil; as such, Mr. Dulles has resisted it from the stern duty imposed by his Calvinist-trained conscience. Communism threatens his country and his civilization; therefore he has resisted as a man of the West and a patriot."[75] These are the kindest words Burnham expressed toward an American Cold Warrior. Burnham still qualified his admiration by bemoaning that Dulles also accepted the negative consequences of containment because he resisted advancing into Soviet territory. He was passive during obvious times of Soviet weakness, such as Stalin's death and the Hungarian Revolution.[76] Consequently, despite success at curbing Soviet advances in Europe, the Soviets had made gains in the Middle East and Africa. Dulles must be judged by this, too, Burnham reasoned. In the late 1950s, the United States was still playing the defensive. More needed to be done.

The 1960 presidential election between John F. Kennedy and Richard Nixon provided an opportunity. Burnham was offered the chance to contribute to the foreign policy plank in the 1960 Republican National Platform. To his credit, he offered specific suggestions: "The purpose of the foreign policy of the United States is to safeguard the national security and advance the national interest. This calls for a peaceful world order based on freedom and justice."[77] For Burnham, peace, freedom, and justice are not inherently good. They are not ends and they do not exist in isolation. Woodrow Wilson's idealism had no place in Burnham's foreign policy. Instead, national interest did. As Burnham reasons, because the communist goal worked against the national interest of the United States, the goal of US foreign policy should be to weaken the communists.[78]

The hardliner continues that the communist world had dedicated itself to the destruction of the United States and the establishment of a communist totalitarian system. Appeasement or a negative foreign policy could not suffice. The United States must work to reduce communist power so that it no longer threatened the United States, and world peace. He writes that the United States should demand the withdrawal of Soviet troops from Eastern Europe, require the liquidation of all Soviet propaganda apparatuses, and call for free elections in Eastern Europe. Once these were confirmed, then and only then would the United States evacuate its overseas bases. Next, both sides could work on mutual disarmament. Until this occurred, the United States had to prepare for World War III. This meant strengthening all aspects of the US armed forces, maintaining existing alliances, obtaining the support of newly developed nations, employing the same psychological propaganda that the communists employed, pledging American support for all free peoples around the world, and continued nuclear testing.[79]

Burnham also wanted to promote more international free trade, especially between the United States and less developed nations. This would not only benefit both sides economically but also would help bring the countries under US sway. Every nation was another potential ally. In the foreign policy plank, he even recommends investing in Africa to promote its economic development.[80]

Kennedy's election provided Burnham another figure to advise (and mostly chastise) from afar. Burnham pleaded with the new administration to focus on Cuba. Removing Castro from power must be America's priority. On the eve of the Bay of Pigs episode in April 1961, he asserts in an *NR* article: "When once the Cuban operation gets really going, with a definite area under anti-Castro control, then it must be carried through with overwhelming power, maximum speed, and total success. Failure would be a catastrophe beyond calculation."[81] Burnham demands US displays of power: "What is crucial is that we should *somewhere*, in *some* theatre or on *some* vital action make a stand of unconditional firmness: that we should strike a blow against the enemy. That blow will reverberate around the world, and will mark, or could mark, the decisive turn."[82] The article presents myriad options: Cuba, the Congo or even Laos. Burnham believed that Cuba was the most plausible option because a strong anti-Castro contingent already existed there. And the new regime was still unstable. The action required US force because a regime built on force must be eliminated using external force.[83]

Predictably, Burnham deemed Kennedy's Bay of Pigs invasion tepid, insisting that the president "lost his nerve" when he canceled a second airstrike.[84] This only made toppling Castro more difficult. Doing so must remain America's top priority, and violence provided the best means: "Our own central power has got to be brought to bear directly, this time: preferably—and it would be more humanely so—in a concentration so massive that prolonged resistance would be out of the question."[85] No alternative existed. Burnham maintains that the unpleasant reality, which so few chose to face openly, although many knew it in their hearts, was that US military action would be required to dislodge the Castro regime.[86]

Burnham's cites *The Economist*'s contention that Kennedy's foreign policy was in "disarray." He maintains that part of the problem was that too much power was given to "eggheads."[87] Rational and intellectual, the eggheads tell us that they know what is best for the rest of us. But they ignore the fact that emotions, passions, habit, and customs play just as an important role in shaping human conduct as rational thought. Arthur Schlesinger was Burnham's perfect egghead. He points out that the Kennedy administration had used the Harvard historian's white paper to guide the Bay of Pigs. According to this document, the Cuban people hated Castro and would revolt against him.[88] Burnham adds sarcastically, "the Cuban people, observing that Professor Schlesinger's boss declined to provide the force that could have smashed Castro's planes and tanks, concluded that it was better to have your head under a yoke than no head at all."[89] Burnham partly faulted the Cuban fiasco on his former Congress for Cultural Freedom ally.

Burnham had hoped the Bay of Pigs would induce some modesty in the young president. The capturing of a U2 spy plane over the USSR on

May 1, 1960, embarrassed the Eisenhower administration. In another *NR* piece, Burnham reasons that the Bay of Pigs was worse because at least the spy plane operation yielded some positive results. This president needed to ensure that his actions matched his lofty rhetoric. For example, Kennedy had reminded an audience that "the complacent, the indulgent and soft societies are to be swept away with debris of history."[90] The hardliner agrees. Nations had fallen without ever firing a shot or having their borders crossed.[91] Yet Kennedy stopped testing nuclear missiles and sought disarmament conferences. The president had acted with confusion toward Cuba and loosened embargos on the Soviet Union. Burnham maintains that instead of speaking eloquently, the young president should temporarily stay silent, reflect on his rhetoric, and then ensure his actions matched his words.[92] The power theorist suggests that the president of the United States take a time-out.

Burnham blamed the president's action in Cuba—and lack of action after the construction of the Berlin Wall—for the Cuban Missile Crisis. Why did Khrushchev put missiles there in the first place? The former Marxist contended that using the Marxist-Leninist paradigm to understand the world, Khrushchev believed the United States was paralyzed because of contradictions inherent in the capitalist system. He was emboldened by Kennedy's weakness. And whereas some Western observers naively viewed Khrushchev as "de-Stalinizing" the USSR, the anticommunist asserts that the attempt to arm Cuba revealed the first secretary's aggressive side. Burnham insists that "the butcher of Ukraine" was probably not a man to be trusted.[93]

According to Burnham, US reluctance to use more hard power in Cuba had geopolitical consequences that would reverberate for years, and probably decades. Almost two years after the Cuban debacle, the Cold War strategist insisted that instability now characterized the world. After World War II, when the United States demonstrated her strength by crushing Germany and Japan, a bipolar world emerged in which conflicts raged only between the superpowers. Everyone now knew that the United States would not use nuclear weapons, under any conditions. Decay seemed to have set in. Americans presumably lacked the requisite will to prevail. Consequently, Charles de Gaulle could easily launch an independent nuclear weapons program, India could annex Goa, and Afro-Asians in the United Nations could assert more power.[94] The breakdown of the bipolar world also means that the Chinese no longer feared the United States or Moscow; they could pursue their own course.⁹⁵ Nations used America's reluctance to use power as a pretext to demonstrate their own power.

President Kennedy was assassinated on Burnham's fifty-eighth birthday. The tragedy provided the apostate Marxist an opportunity to attack the Hegelian–Marxist holist view of reality. Applied to the Kennedy assassination, holism meant "that neither intelligence nor courage nor any techniques, program or policies can make man the self-sufficient master of his fate . . . and that is why John Kennedy's death, or any death, could not be a tragedy for Khrushchev, Mao, or Oswald, but only a passing rearrangement of atoms in the eternal dialectic of matter out of which the universal Communist society, with the beginning of 'truly human history, will inevitably emerge.'"⁹⁶ For Marxist holists, society resembles a giant montage that inevitably progresses toward communism. Individual parts and pieces by themselves are trivial because it is only in relation to the whole that they have any meaning. Kennedy's assassination, for Burnham, was like removing a small speck of paint from the montage. It meant nothing for communists because, for them, everything fundamentally moves toward communism.

Burnham may have denounced holism in this article, but the philosophy remained part of his worldview; he usually saw everything as interconnected. His *Web of Subversion* suggests that American society was linked together by communists who had infiltrated American institutions. Alger Hiss, the Rosenbergs, and Harold Ware were not atypical individuals—they represented a bigger problem. The former Marxist also applied holism to the international arena. Significantly, at this time, Burnham did not distinguish between Soviet and Chinese communism; they composed a giant montage. In his 1960 analysis, he emphasizes their shared Leninist methods and goals of world conquest. Unfortunately, he maintains, American "scholars" and "journalists" were naïve because they trusted Khrushchev's words about peace, cooperation, and disarmament.⁹⁷ And they believed that the alleged Sino-Soviet rift had made communism less threatening because now, internal squabbles hindered its advance.⁹⁸ Burnham says that this was a diversion. He discourages the reader from discerning between different forms of national communism, contending that such a misunderstanding only prevented noncommunists from pursuing the proper course of action.⁹⁹

Burnham's ideas about an aggressive foreign policy influenced one of the most important conservative works of the twentieth century: Barry Goldwater's *Conscience of a Conservative* (1960). Burnham's fingerprints are all over the foreign policy section of the work. The book was ghost-written by Brent Bozell, his colleague at *NR*. *Conscience of a Conservative* attempts to explain the conservative philosophy and make it practical. It contains conservative opinions on myriad issues, such as government regulation, civil rights, taxes, the welfare state, education, and confronting the Soviet behemoth. It appeared on the *New York Times* bestseller list.[100] The book remains relevant to conservatives six decades later.

Domestically, Goldwater insisted that state power inevitably will increase "because of the corrupting influence of power, the natural tendency of men who possess some power to take unto themselves more power. The tendency leads eventually to the acquisition of all power—whether in the hands of one or many makes little difference to the freedom of those left on the outside."[101] For the senator, power was related to freedom. State power, by itself, did not necessarily restrict freedom. Some government actions even increase freedom, such as keeping enemies away and removing obstacles to free trade. But too frequently, especially when those in power are left to their own devices, power becomes concentrated in the hands of the elite, not the people.

The final chapter of *Conscience of a Conservative*, titled "The Soviet Menace," starkly reveals Burnham's influence. It declares:

> Though we are still strong physically, we are in clear and imminent danger of being overwhelmed by alien forces. We are confronted by a revolutionary world movement that possesses not only the will to dominate absolutely every square mile of the globe, but increasingly the capacity to do so: a military power that rivals our own, political warfare, and propaganda skills that are superior to ours, an international fifth column that operates conspiratorially in the heart of our defenses, an ideology that imbues its adherents with a sense of historical mission; and all of these resources controlled by a ruthless despotism that brooks no deviation from the revolutionary course. This threat, moreover, is growing day by day.[102]

Goldwater continued that American political leaders were "appeasing" and "accommodating" the communists. And the United States was not using her power correctly. In *Conscience of a Conservative*, the senator from Arizona insists: "Even in the early 1950s, when America still held unquestioned nuclear superiority, it was clear that we were losing the Cold War. Time and again in my campaign speeches of 1952 I warned my fellow Arizonans that American Foreign Policy has brought us from a position of undisputed power, in seven short years, to the brink of possible disaster. And in the succeeding seven years, that trend, because its cause remains, has continued."[103] The root cause, Goldwater argues, was that the Soviets understood that nature of the conflict while Americans did not. He claims that if an enemy seeks to conquer you, you are at war with the enemy, unless you surrender. While the Soviets were trying to conquer the world, Americans sought to pacify it. This explains why Americans were losing the Cold War. The United States must wage war, or she would perish.[104] These declarations summarized Burnham's Cold War polemics: pessimism, the belief that vacillation characterizes US foreign policy, the futility of dialogue, the skillfulness of Soviet propaganda, American consciousness toward Marxism must be raised, critiques of the concept of peace, the Soviet desire for world conquest, and the idea that communists can be defeated only through aggression.

These words do mean that Goldwater was Burnham's preferred candidate for president. Burnham was less of an ideological purist than many of his *NR* colleagues. He supported the more moderate Nelson Rockefeller over the Arizona senator in Republican primaries. This may be perplexing given Rockefeller's liberal reputation, but this was not based on his foreign policy. The governor's Cold War views were similar to Burnham's: he was a Cold War hawk who sought larger defense budgets, promoted political warfare, and advocated nuclear testing. Like Burnham, he was an economic centrist who was resigned to the New Deal.

Once Goldwater captured the GOP's nomination for president, Burnham made specific suggestions to his campaign. He reminded the senator that it was his duty to safeguard national security. The communists sought to destroy the United States. Therefore, the United States must work to limit the power of communists. Burnham declares in an *NR* article, "This and this only can remove the continuous possibility of general nuclear war, can assure peace and provide the conditions for freedom."[105] The United States must also show its support for captive nations. And it should support a "Freedom Academy" at home and abroad for the training of anticommunist militants.

Burnham believed that the United Nations could not help in the struggle for the world. He continues his criticism of the organization in a pieced titled "What to Do About the UN." Reasoning that all nations pursued their own interests, it asserts that the United Nations, at least diplomatically, was meaningless, regardless of what the "disillusioned junta from the upper echelons of the Establishment" told us.[106] Burnham cites Democrat Cold Warrior Henry "Scoop" Jackson who believed that the United Nations did not provide the best path for peace and justice. According to Burnham, Jackson maintains that "the UN is not a substitute for national policies wisely conceived to uphold our vital interests."[107] It futilely tried to bring peace to a world in which struggle was natural. To weaken it, Burnham argues that the United Nations should not vote on "matters of substance," but only on administrative and procedural measures.[108] This can be achieved by US representatives declaring that they would no longer vote on matters of substance. All subsequent votes would be meaningless. Burnham states that this reform, in turn, would provide the United States—to quote Jackson—"a new mature sense of the burdens of responsible leadership."[109]

The advocate of US leadership addressed what he deemed to be a public revolt against foreign aid. Too often, he maintains, people claimed they were either for or against foreign aid. But that was irrational because foreign aid encompassed so many different areas. Each aspect of foreign aid must be judged individually, based on a cost-benefit analysis.[110] Yet, according to Burnham, this was impossible because no one ever studied the benefits of foreign aid. The president had said he would commit $5 billion in foreign aid to confront communism. But did it really weaken communism? Nobody knew, because no efforts had been made to find out.[111] The general public, however, might not understand aspects of foreign policy. Burnham notes that foreign aid sometimes benefited American businesses because the recipients of the foreign aid often ended up buying American products. He maintains that that $100 million new road in Vietnam benefited the builders of US machines that constructed the road and the owners of the American ships that transported the materials for the road. American engineers, with their special allowances, would all get paid, thanks to foreign aid. Foreign aid would allow for Americans to get rid of their agricultural surplus. And it would also allow the Pentagon to unload older equipment, thus creating a demand for new equipment. This would improve US defenses and benefit its arms manufacturers.[112]

Burnham did not necessarily oppose foreign aid. He believed that foreign aid could be good, as long as it promoted US interests. The internationalist calls some of it an "indispensable instrument of the policy of the United States."[113] Examples included aid to places like Taiwan and South Korea, where US aid was used to bolster defenses. And it allowed the United States to maintain a presence in certain countries. The Soviets had successfully used aid to increase their presence in parts of Africa. However, he questions the way it was administered, something he acknowledges could be "disgraceful."[114] He singles out economic assistance programs that at times bolstered only anti-US interests, such as in Egypt, Brazil, and Bolivia. And sometimes it hindered the receiving country by promoting inflation. Burnham calls the revolt against foreign aid a sort of "neo-isolationism."[115] *NR*'s senior editor maintains that "for every quid there should always be a balancing quo."[116] The United States doled out foreign aid too frequently while demanding nothing that benefited its interests.

In 1964, Burnham pondered the future of Western Civilization in *Suicide of the West: An Essay on the Meaning and Destiny of Liberalism*. The book complements Spengler and Toynbee. Like Spengler, it studies the rise and (potentially) the decline of the West. Like Toynbee, Burnham emphasizes the challenges that confronted Western Civilization. Whereas Spengler saw civilizations as organic units that naturally lived and died, *Suicide of the West* follows Toynbee by asserting that civilizations do not necessarily die naturally—they may commit suicide. The book's primary argument is that liberalism is the ideology of Western suicide because it cannot thwart the West's biggest challenge: communism.

The book reveals the influence of the final thinker that nourished Burnham: Edmund Burke. The young Burnham was a Marxist who believed revolution could regenerate the world. The middle-age Burnham was a Machiavellian who believed that the ruling classes must be resisted for tyranny to be thwarted. The most mature Burnham embraced Burke. Like Machiavelli, Burke was a pragmatic empiricist who eschewed the philosophical method; the English statesman scolded the "professor of metaphysics."[117] Championing prudence, Burke wondered how the same person who would never even tinker with a broken clock would attempt to fix something as complex as society.[118] Burke accepted social change, just gradual social change. He wrote: "All we can do, and that human wisdom can do, is to provide that the change shall proceed by insensible degrees. This has all the benefits which may be in change, without any of the inconveniences of mutation."[119] Burke favored organic change, change that drew from past experiences.

The times must also be considered: Burke held that the French Revolution was fundamentally misguided because it was the product of Enlightenment thinkers and radical politicians. Enlightenment philosophers believed that using reason could improve society. Their political successors, such as Robespierre, applied these ideas by creating wholesale alterations to France, almost overnight. Burke argued that this was too much change too fast. The mature Burnham—writing in tumultuous 1960s and 1970s when the civil rights movement bloomed at home and decolonization (and its legacy) dominated the world abroad—agreed. Like Burke, Burnham accepted change, but he resisted dramatic, quick change led by ambitious individuals. Distrusting change inspired by ideology, *Suicide of the West* suggests that the human mind does not need to constantly meddle in human affairs. Not as rational as believed, sometimes it made things worse.

The book should also be understood as part of a debate between fellow *NR* colleagues Brent Bozell and Frank Meyer over the future of the West. The devoutly Catholic Bozell maintained that the rise of individual freedom in the modern era threatened Western civilization by drawing humankind away from God.[120] He reasoned that restrictions on freedom by government were vital to promote the virtuous life, as expressed by Christianity. Meyer agreed that virtue is important. He differed by contending that humans must have freedom to pursue their own virtue, not one coerced by government.[121] The state cannot be an instrument of virtue, or it becomes authoritarian. Meyer believed Western civilization was declining because freedom and virtue were seen as two separated spheres. He believed that the free individual could and should act virtuously. Western politics and culture unfortunately discouraged this by making people too dependent on each other or the state. Burnham's arguments about the plight of the West revolved around liberalism and its inability to confront Western challenges.

Suicide of the West does not blame liberals for Western decline. The book interprets the ideology as a symptom and argues that liberals cannot slow the civilization's contraction. The book contains insight about the left-hand side of the political spectrum. At the same time, like most politically charged works, the book is illogical at times, and some supposed truths are not as true as the author would have the reader believe. Burnham graciously dedicated the book to "all liberals of good will."[122]

Burnham wanted to define his terms, so he asked, what makes someone liberal? He creates thirty-nine positions that broadly characterized liberals, particularly distinguishing them from everyone else. Examples include the following: all forms of segregation are wrong, everyone has the right to free public education, everyone has the right to express their opinion, progressive and inheritance taxes are fair, society is largely to blame for the failure of individuals, the primary goal of foreign policy should be peace, Joseph McCarthy is the most dangerous man in politics since World War II, nuclear disarmament is good, and congressional investigating committees are dangerous.[123] It was not that conservatives did not believe any of these and that all liberals believed all of them. Rather, liberals would be more likely to agree.

Adopting the scholastic method of Thomas Aquinas, the former philosophy professor posits a liberal argument, and then tries to refute it, such as:

> L2: Human beings are basically rational; reason and science are only proper means for discovering truth and are the sole standards of truth, to which authority, custom, intuition, revelation, etc. must give way.
>
> X2: Human beings are moved by sentiment, passion, intuition and other non-rational impulses at least as much by reason. Any view of man, history and society that neglects the non-rational impulses and their embodiment in custom, prejudice, tradition and authority, or that conceives of a social order in which the non-rational impulses and their embodiments are wholly subject to abstract reason, is an illusion.[124]

Or:

> L14: In social, economic, cultural as well as political affairs, men are of right equal. Social reform should be designed to correct existing inequalities and to equalize the conditions of nature, schooling, residence, employment, recreation and income that produce them.
>
> X14: It is neither possible nor desirable to eliminate all inequalities among human beings. Although it is charitable and prudent to take reasonable measures to temper the extremes of inequality, the obsessive attempt to eliminate inequalities by social reforms and sanctions provokes and can at most only substitute new inequalities for the old.[125]

Burnham insists in *Suicide of the West* that the field of genetics supported his criticisms of liberalism because it reveals that humans have a "permanent sub-stratum" that creates them, distinct from their social environment.[126] He asserts that some people, by their nature, are inferior morally and intellectually.[127] And the pessimist writes that their numbers are increasing in comparison to those with "superior assets."[128]

Burnham expresses doubts about liberal education, arguing that there was no evidence that education based on reason and science could actually solve social ills.[129] He writes that the Athenians were the most educated people of the ancient world. They fell due to internal decay to both the Spartans and Macedonians.[130] Germany may have been the most educated country in the world in the 1920s and 1930s.[131] How did that work out? The Bolshevik Revolution in Russia in 1917 successfully spread mass education, but were the people of Eastern Europe any better off? Burnham notes that Japan adopted Western-style education in the late nineteenth century. What did this lead to? Even in the United States, urban cities tended to be far worse off than their less educated rural counterparts. And the progressively educated cities are worse off in many respects than they were decades ago, before compulsory education arrived.[132]

By emphasizing reparable social conditions, Burnham bemoans that liberals will only reluctantly blame individuals for their criminal behavior. Instead, the onus is placed on some sort of education or institution.[133] This means that the mugger, the poor, and the unemployed "cannot be blamed ... for the faulty institutions into which they were born."[134] The liberal treatment required, then, is not punishment, but simply fixing the social institutions that led to their failures in the first place. For Burnham, this leads to permissive attitudes toward what he called "erring members of the community," especially if they belong to some group that seems "less privileged than the general average."[135] He reasons that if ignorance and faulty institutions explained the homeless, the poor, the mugger, and the jobless, then "the generals, landlords, merchants, bankers and even white segregations ought also, by the same logic, be relieved of their burden of personal guilt."[136] They too are merely unfortunate products of the circumstances into which they were born. Like the mugger, they should not be judged or criticized.

Chiding liberals for having too much faith in humanity, Burnham asserts that they naively believed that all people, when given the choice, would choose peace over war, justice over unfairness. But the author opines that individuals and groups often choose injury and injustice for others and even themselves. Nations like Egypt, Indonesia, and Ghana had chosen despotism over democracy, guns over butter.[137] And for Burnham, the liberal who always opposed segregation was naïve because segregation dominates all societies. Examples include young and old, peasant and warrior, male and female, slave and citizen, believer and unbeliever, rich and poor, egghead and blockhead, chess players and beer drinkers.[138] Burnhams suggests that the division of society into separate spheres was natural and not necessarily bad.

Suicide of the West continues Burnham's attacks on ideology. It argues that ideology attempts to study events by using a preexisting set of ideas, but this precludes the adherent from seeing the bigger, more practical, picture. And ideology cannot be refuted by logical analysis and evidence: "An ideologue—one who thinks ideologically—can't lose. He can't lose because his answer, his interpretation and his attitude have been determined in advance of the particular experience or observation. They are derived from the ideology, and are not subject to the facts. There is no possible argument, observation or experiment that could disprove a firm ideological belief for the very simple reason that an ideologue will not accept any argument, observation or experiment as constituting disproof."[139] Any holes in the ideology can easily be patched up to satisfy the believer. Those working within ideological frameworks must at least sometimes bend reality so it conforms to an ideology. Burnham insists that for the faithful, attitudes can always be adjusted so that no observation can ever undermine ideology.[140] He notes that ideologues divide people into two: those who share my ideology and those who do not. Discussions with "the other kind" are fruitless.[141]

The former Marxist ideologue maintains that humans who favor an ideology do so not because they are convinced rationally that it is true, but rather because it serves a psychological need.[142] The dialectical materialism preached by communists is an extreme example of ideology. Liberalism is another, although it is a softer form of ideology. Burnham calls liberal ideology "not a consciously understood set of rational beliefs, but a bundle of unexamined prejudices and conjoined sentiments."[143] Liberal beliefs are more satisfactory when they are not made fully explicit, but rather lurk in the background, coloring rhetoric.[144] Peace, progress, equality, and democracy warm the heart, but they are in practice quite slippery.[145] Burnham insists that they cannot successfully guide human conduct.

Burnham continues in *Suicide of the West* with an example of two Black men he frequently encountered outside of work. They picked up boxes from stores, a menial task that at least allowed them to feed themselves and their family. He writes that they were friendly and cheerful. The simple operation was organized by "some dim exploiter in the background," who makes small deals with other businesses.[146] The workers earned minimum wage. The mayor of New York wants to raise it, however, in accordance with ideology. The consequence would probably be that the whole business folded, and these men would lose their jobs, prompting them to become "bums and delinquents."[147] For Burnham, society becomes a worse place for everyone involved as the ideology is satisfied.

Liberal attempts to solve the problem of "skid row" provide another example. Burnham notes in *Suicide of the West* that every large city in history has had some sort of end of the line for the poor and destitute.[148] For liberals, it is a macabre situation that requires fixing. For the professed realist, skid row is just part of the "long and wonderfully intricate natural evolution of the city."[149] Self-contained, skid row shields the rest of society from its potential destructiveness. Society after all is "hierarchal and differentiated, not equalized or regimented."[150] Burnham contends that recent liberal attempts to correct the situation in New York City had only made things worse because now, instead of being part of a self-sufficient society, the displaced downtrodden have been "lurching" around the city, bumping into "respectable citizens," and generally making a scene wherever they plod.[151]

Burnham's social philosophy was Burkean. The English statesmen believed that gradations among values and men were natural. In *Reflection on the French Revolution*, he holds that "the levellers therefore only change and pervert the natural order of things; they load the edifice of society, by setting up in the air what the solidarity of the structure requires to be on the ground."[152] The best societies recognize social distinction and duties. Burke did not favor a rigid caste system. He continues by maintaining that wisdom and virtue should be the two qualifications to rule—and these could be found in the common elements of society. He resists, however, social fixing guided by individuals who ignored nature's laws. For Burnham, skid row was a law of nature that could not be fixed.

Burnham argues that these ideologically driven reformers merely tried to assuage their guilt about the fallen world around them.[153] Christianity solved the problem of guilt by recognizing humanity's fallen state.[154] But liberalism has no such pretenses. Consequently, beset by guilt, the liberal becomes consumed with change, what Burnham calls "method rather than results."[155] One attempt at reform follows another. The author compares liberalism to a religion; he contends that the liberal can faithfully go about his day, believing certain myths that give him or her self-assurance. This means showing "loyalty to the correct egalitarian principles, voting for the correct candidates, praising the activists and contributing to their defense funds when they get into trouble, and joining promptly in the outcry against reactionaries who pop up now and then."[156] The liberal spirit is never at rest.[157]

The critic of liberalism shared this skepticism of perpetual reform with Russell Kirk, author of the classic *The Conservative Mind: From Burke* to *Santayana* (1953).[158] Kirk wrote regularly for *NR*, although he rarely mingled with the editors in New York City because he preferred the trappings of agrarian life. Like Burnham, Kirk was a Burkean who questioned laissez-faire capitalism and ideology (the book decries "dupes of ideology").[159] Kirk also saw the darker hues of humanity, and he questioned Enlightenment assumptions about the utility of reason. Championing tradition, Kirk scolded liberal opposition to "permanent things." By this he meant the things that make us human—fixed standards that allow us to judge individuals and societies. In *The Conservative Mind*, Kirk asserts that liberals have little need for any of this as their "lust for change never lacks agents."[160] Kirk believed liberal ideology did not provide tools for understanding and improving the world.

Burnham agrees when he states that the liberal ideology is "not well designed for the stark issue of survival."[161] Many liberals deride Western Civilization, believing it is bereft of redeeming features. And it is certainly not superior, suggesting that it is not worth defending.[162] The author contends in *Suicide of the West* that liberalism prefers the contraction of the West over colonial expansion. Burnham argues that this creates problems in the non-West. In Latin America, for example, liberal ideology enthusiastically wants to eradicate all vestiges of colonial rule, without preparing the requisite structures to replace it. This creates a power vacuum, one probably filled by a dictator or communism.[163]

In his analysis of ideology, Burnham draws from the English political philosopher Michael Oakeshott. His *Rationalism in Politics and Other Essays* (1962) is an idiosyncratic work that nonetheless attracted more attention from conservatives than liberals. In his book, Oakeshott critiques attempts at applying the rationalist method to politics, believing this favored theory over practice. For Oakeshott, human experiences are too diverse to uncover any widely applicable laws or principles, so calls for utopianism should be distrusted. And the human mind—contrary to what it believes—never examines the world in an independent fashion; it is shaped by habit and custom. He specifically condemns the "ideological style of politics," something he called a "confused style."[164]

For Burnham, disarmament remained one of liberalism's biggest flaws. In 1953, the Soviets detonated a hydrogen bomb in northern Kazakhstan, about nine months after the United States did the same in the Pacific. Calls for ending nuclear proliferation followed. The 1955 [Bertrand] Russell-Einstein Manifesto (named after the logician and the physicist who sponsored it) called on world governments and citizens to find peaceful solutions to conflicts. The manifesto stated that to save humanity, people must remember their humanity. It also maintained: "Although an agreement to renounce nuclear weapons as part of a general reduction of armaments would not afford an ultimate solution, it would serve certain important purposes."[165] Marches for disarmament grew in the United States, especially as the Vietnam War escalated.

Burnham writes in *Suicide of the West* that disarmament, in theory, was fine. If everyone renounced their weapons, peace would ensue, and then everyone would win. The problem was that communists had no intention of eliminating their weapons until they had conquered the world. Burnham asserts that communists preached pacificism to the West, shrewdly using propaganda to strengthen their position. He maintains that western liberals misunderstood what the Soviets meant by peace. When Khrushchev preaches the "struggle for peace," he means the fight for the victory of the proletariat and the spread of communism.[166] When this happens, Khrushchev believes, peace will follow. Peace will come only when communism spreads. Burnham argues that for communists, peace existed in North Vietnam and Hungary, but not in the United States or England. Liberals preaching peace naively enabled communism by weakening America's means to fight communism.[167] A world without US arms became a world controlled by communism, hardly a world of peace.

Liberalism's ambivalent attitude toward force and violence provided another example of liberalism's inability to meet Western challenges.[168] Recognizing that not all liberals were pacifists, Burnham noted that Roosevelt, Kennedy, and Johnson all used violence. But because of their intellectual predisposition against violence, they never used it correctly: "They therefore tend to use it [force] ineptly, at the wrong times, and places, against the wrong targets, in the wrong amounts."[169] After all, Burnham insists, force is inherent in society. Everyone knew that if the United States eliminated its military forces and instruments of coercion, it would be overrun immediately. Unfortunately, liberals used just enough force to ensure that the United States was not overrun. Cuba and Vietnam provided examples. Contending that liberals had more say in the Kennedy-Johnson administration than in any previous one, the hardliner argues that, consequently, US use of force had never been so "awkward."[170]

Suicide of the West displays the pessimism of the second James Burnham. He believed that the West was in a period of despair. Hundreds of years of expansion were ending. Cuba and the Middle East provided two recent examples. Communism posed the greatest and most obvious threat to the West because if communists continued to advance at the same rate, they would have conquered the world by the end of the century.[171] The only impediment to communist expansion was the West, but Burnham insists in this book that the West had not shown the ability to reverse communist conquests. It had merely shown the ability to vacillate. Liberals could not defend Western civilization because they could not defeat the communists: they "cannot strike with consistent firmness against communism, either domestically or internationally."[172] Liberals could only defeat conservatives. Although liberals were not communists, the two groups shared too many "axioms" in common, such as secularism, welfarism, and optimism about human nature and its ability to reform.[173] They were even against the same things: McCarthy, Franco, the John Birch Society, colonialism, House Un-American Activities Committee and Herbert Hoover provided just some examples.[174] The author rationalizes that liberals, therefore, could never completely oppose communism. Given that, Burnham reasons, if liberalism prevailed, the West was doomed to fall to communism.

In *Suicide of the West*, Burnham does keep a small measure of optimism—a tiny window open for a ray of light. In the last paragraph of the book, he asserts that the final collapse of the West was not "inevitable."[175] Its contraction could be reversed. If this happens, liberalism will have no more purpose; it will fade away. There are signs of hope—he called his book one of them.

Suicide of the West was Burnham's last original book.[176] And it unifies elements of both James Burnhams. His previous books expressed his domestic and geopolitical fears separately. *The Managerial Revolution* predicted the centralization of American political institutions and economy. The paleoconservative works, *The Machiavellians* and *Congress and the American Tradition*, prescribed ways to resist this trend in order to preserve liberty. *The Struggle for the World*, *The Coming Defeat of Communism*, and *Containment or Liberation* exposed the Soviet threat. They maintained that power had to be used against communists, or they would conquer the world. *Suicide of the West* does all of this. It argues that liberal expansion at home paves the way for authoritarian communist dominance in the West, partly because liberals never properly used force. Unwilling to condemn imperialism, the book recommends Western influence in areas like Cuba, the Middle East, and Eastern Europe—by force if necessary—to save the West.

Some of Burnham's critiques of liberalism are not as logical as the logician would lead the reader to believe. For example, Burnham critiques liberals for their seemingly inconsistent views on race. On one hand, liberals believe race does not really exist—it is a social construct. Yet on the other hand, race was a critical identity for many liberals. Liberals sought not just sympathy for certain races; they desired guilt and culpability. Burnham calls these liberal attitudes toward race "irrational" precisely because of liberal opinions.[177] Why? Because if race does not exist, Burnham reasons, then the race cannot be guilty.[178] Yet when liberals say race does not exist, they mean biologically, not socially. Social perceptions about race are real, as are their social consequences, although they may be misguided. Just because race does not biologically exist does not mean one's perceived race cannot have an impact on another perceived race.

The author's critiques of education are specious, too. Burnham shows no connection between the fall of Athens and its relatively educated citizens. The Athenians also excelled in the arts, poetry, and science more than most anyone else. Does that mean that the fall of Athens undermines these fields in any way? Lots of uneducated civilizations have fallen—Toynbee describes some. Or, yes, the Soviets educated their citizens. And, yes, the Soviet Union was miserable. But again, the logician shows no connections between the two. Conceivably, the Soviet Union would have been even worse if the majority of its citizens remained illiterate during communist rule.

Regarding critiques of reform, Burnham does precisely what he cautions against: he relies on abstract concepts, such as assuaging guilt, instead of focusing on results. Even if one grants that a sense of guilt inspires proponents of change, every attempt at reform must still be judged on its own because sometimes reformers are successful, such as their efforts to improve American urban working and living conditions in the early twentieth century. Skid row may always exist, but some skid rows are more humane than others, such as those that promote the safety of its residents. Reform can be wasteful and make things worse, or it may make things better. Burnham should have studied reform the same way he studied foreign aid, by examining individual cases. The Machiavellian and Burkean approaches constantly analyze the means and the ends. And they avoid extremes on both sides.

Reviews of *Suicide of the West* were predictably divided along ideological lines. Writing for the *New York Review*, leftist Irving Howe panned the book, calling it calling it "as puerile as a Birchite pamphlet."[179] Conservative philosopher and *NR* contributor Gerhart Niemeyer loved it, particularly its critique of "ideological thinking."[180] Henry Kissinger wrote a short review for a German publication. The future secretary of state wrote that the book should be read by Americans and Europeans, arguing that Burnham "proves that the Western world's power has been steadily declining since 1917.... He demonstrates that the cause of this decline is not an external influence nor a lack of material strength, but simply an internal failure—a collapse of the will to survive."[181] Kissinger (a power theorist himself) would soon have the opportunity to exercise that will.

Chapter 11

Vietnam Failure and the Non-Western World

The last fifteen years of James Burnham's writing career were dominated by war in Vietnam. In his analysis of the conflict, the geopolitical strategist usually employed themes that by now had been part of his writings for decades, such as the importance of force, power, and will. These had to be exercised, even if it meant using violence. Leaving the region was not an option because this showed passivity. The fate of Western civilization depended on the United States doing what needed to be done.

As the war escalated in the mid-1960s, public sentiment against it waxed, and so too did calls for withdrawal. Walter Lippman, for example, had opposed US intervention in the region since the days of the Eisenhower administration. Demanding a realist perspective, the journalist did not believe that American interests depended on Vietnam. He sought negations and an honorable American exit because the war seemed unwinnable. Burnham responded to these sentiments by writing: "The alleged impossibility of winning the war seems an article of faith rather than of reason; it is merely asserted without evidence or proof. But it is asserted with so much confidence by the Softs as to affect many of those who want to be Hards. Everyone begins to *assume* that the war could not be won."[1] Burnham wrote that the Vietnam War was a guerrilla or "irregular" war, but democratic forces had defeated communists in irregular battles quite recently. He provided the examples of Greece, Malaya, the Philippines, Guatemala, and Angola. The hardliner insisted that the Vietnam War could be won.

Burnham proclaimed that US national interests *were* at stake in Vietnam because the United States had made it so. Using the analogy of a roulette wheel in Monte Carlo, he insists in a *National Review* article that the spinning wheel has no impact on us, until we placed our chips on it. Once the wheel began to spin with our chips in play, our interests were at stake. And we could not simply stop the wheel to cancel our interests, no matter how foolish our original bet had been. He argues, in the same piece, that "the present conflict in Vietnam has become, by our acts, a major test of our will."[2] Either we pass, or we flunk. And flunking would mean suffering "a staggering defeat with immense, inescapable and cumulative global repercussions precisely because it would prove that our will was weaker."[3] For Burnham, the United States had to demonstrate will in Vietnam.

George Kennan disagreed. His views on Vietnam evolved with the conflict; as involvement escalated, so too did his concern. Considering the war to be a misapplication of containment, the former ambassador testified before the Senate that Southeast Asia was not vital to US interests. He deemed the conflict a Vietnamese civil war. In a 1967 Harvard speech, Kennan declared, "Following the logic of our present policy in Vietnam, it is difficult to conceive to date of an outcome that would be less than disastrous."[4] He sought a gradual withdrawal and an end to the bombing. This was America's best strategic move.

Hans Morgenthau, another geopolitical strategist, also averred that US national interest was served by leaving Vietnam. In *Defense of the National Interest* (1951) he asserts that it is "a moral duty for a nation to always follow in its dealings with other nations but one guiding star, one standard for thought, one rule for action: The National Interest."[5] Power struggles characterized the international arena for Morgenthau, too. But like Kennan and Lipman, Morgenthau fashioned himself a realist opponent of the war. His *A New Foreign Policy for the United States* (1969) seeks to study the basic US foreign policy assumptions that led to the "Vietnam disaster."[6] According to Morgenthau, the United States had remained beholden to past foreign policy principles that no longer served her national interest. For example, Morgenthau argues that anticommunist crusaders failed to recognize that communists were not a monolithic bloc. Soviet, Vietnamese, Yugoslavian, and Chinese communists each pursued their own national interests, not a common one. And they were not all inherently antithetical to the US national interests.

In his review of Morgenthau's book, Burnham questions the author's commitment to the national interest. Although Morgenthau had the reputation as "tough, realistic, no-nonsense, even Machiavellian," Burnham asserts that he was really a liberal.[7] The review contends that the author confused his own (liberal) values with the national interest. This meant confronting Hitler, Franco, and the South Africans while also negotiating with the Soviet Union and leaving Vietnam. Responding to Morgenthau's contention that not all communists threatened the United States, Burnham complains that Morgenthau never tells the reader which communists threaten US interests, which ones do not, and why—except that the Vietnamese do not threaten us.[8] According to Burnham, this argument was based not on national interest, but on the fact that the United States could not win a war against them. Worst of all, this pseudo-Machiavellian had lent his respectable name to "irresponsibility, sentimental pacificism, demagogy, anti-Americanism and disloyalty."[9]

Burnham referred to the Lippman-Kennan-Morgenthau triumvirate in his writings. He agreed with them that the war was not going well. In 1965, Burnham wrote: "Meanwhile the Vietnam vortex has its own dynamics. Day by day it sucks in American men, ships, planes, weapons, supplies and money."[10] He just disagreed on the remedy: Burnham believed more power was needed to win the war because Ho would not be moved by token military measures. The hardliner reasoned, "the stronger the American action, the weaker the communist reply."[11] Characteristic of the first James Burnham, he could only optimistically imagine a future for some semblance of democracy in Southeast Asia if more force was employed, including more violence.

Nuclear weapons were an option. Maintaining that President Johnson's reluctance to use nuclear weapons in Southeast Asia was irrational, Burnham contended that Americans should not feel guilty for having or using them. Given the fact that the United States was currently involved in war in Vietnam, what weapons was it supposed to use? Given that the United States wanted to win the war (if it did not, then why fight?), it must take the required steps to do so. What were the United States' advantages? Burnham believed that they were not superior manpower because Americans were outnumbered in Southeast Asia. Nor was it—nor had it even been—US tactics and strategy. The North during the Civil War as well as the United States in World War I and World War II had not demonstrated a flair for tactical or strategic brilliance. Instead, the United States steamrolled her opponents using "overwhelming firepower to flatten the opposition."[12] George Marshall and Dwight D. Eisenhower waited an extra year to ensure that they had enough firepower to defeat Nazism in Western Europe.[13] Harry S. Truman continued this tradition when he used atomic bombs. So did US soldiers when they wiped out houses from which came enemy fire. To win, Americans had to fight in Vietnam under American terms.[14] This meant using overwhelming hard power, maybe even nuclear weapons.[15] As *National Review*'s second-in-command, Burnham suggested that this would possibly excise the taboo against deploying them, a taboo that worked only against Americans.[16]

Why did Burnham advance such aggressive positions in Vietnam? How could his conception of "national interest" differ from other self-professed realists, such as Kennan, Morgenthau, and Lippman? The Marxist-Leninist-Trotskyite heritage that Burnham never fully abandoned provides an explanation. Unlike Kennan, Morgenthau, and Lippman, Burnham's world was governed by inexorable historical trends that were usually blowing the world somewhere. In the Cold War era, it had to be hurtling toward communism *or* democracy. And the former disciple of V. I. Lenin and Leon Trotsky believed that determined individuals could alter its course. Vietnam had become a test of will. The times required resolute leaders and force. Something had to be done. Passivity and patience never sufficed for Burnham.

Burnham also still used Marxist-Trotskyite holism to understand the world: everything was interrelated. Vietnamese, Soviet, and Chinese communists could not be distinct, just as capitalist nations could not be distinct for Trotsky. In "Permanent Revolution" (1929) Burnham's former Marxist mentor argued against Stalin that independent (nationalist) capitalist economies did not exist; they were all part of a whole.[17] Burnham interpreted communism similarly: Vietnam, the Soviet Union, and China were not distinct, meaning ignoring communism in Southeast Asia and successfully fighting it in Eastern Europe was impossible. A constant struggle must occur everywhere.

American struggles in Vietnam (and the antiwar writings of Kennan, Lippman, and Morgenthau) helped provoke student peace protests, which naturally earned Burnham's ire.[18] As a Marxist, he condemned pacificism by arguing it benefited the imperialist powers that waged war against the working classes. Now, he condemned pacificism by claiming it abetted communism in its war against the free world. He argued that peace was just an abstraction that everyone loved, like Truth, Mother, Home, or Freedom.[19] But again, everything must be contextualized, related to time and place. Burnham maintained that a genuine pacifist opposed all war of all kinds, not by whom and against whom.[20]

Pacificism in the context of Vietnam was not pure; it had become a mode of political and social struggle. Pacifist movements had merged with social movements, so now Congress of Racial Equality (CORE), Student Nonviolent Coordinating Committee (SNCC), and Southern Christian Leadership Conference (SCLC) preached peace. Burnham believed that its advocates had been deceived; they were actually teaching communist propaganda.[21] Liberal pacifists had become "unwitting or heedless dupes."[22] Under the guise of peace, communism advanced. The antipacifist contends that if a liberal merely examined the pamphlets passed out at their protests, he or she would see that.

Burnham insisted that communist propaganda helped foment these protests. He claimed as early as 1960 that communist cadres—inspired by professional French revolutionary and crowd organizer Louis Blanqui—were fomenting anti-war protests.[23] He begins a 1966 piece titled "From Ho, With Love" by quoting a greeting from Ho Chi Minh to the American people on New Year's Eve. Ho wished the American people "peace, prosperity and happiness" while demanding that "American imperialists halt their aggression" so that they could "save American boys from a useless death in an unjust war."[24] Burnham notes how all of this meshed perfectly with the words of the war's domestic opponents. Asserting that this could not be a coincidence, he argues that for Ho and all of Lenin's disciples, revolutionary war is fought on two fronts: military operations on the battlefields and the psychological operations on the enemy's rear. "Psywar operations" were designed to weaken the opponents resolve. Burnham feared it was succeeding.

Even as US foreign policy began shifting its focus to Southeast Asia, Burnham pleaded that Cuba remain on America's radar. He argued that history did not work like television, where everything focused on one point at one time. The hardliner asserted that the most out-of-focus area was Cuba.[25] Unlike South Vietnam, Cuba was actually in enemy hands. And it was not on the other side of the world, but on our doorstep. Given that, why were we investing so much in Vietnam and so little in Cuba? Our only efforts in Cuba included an occasional U2 spy plane, a little help for exiles, and half-hearted economic sanctions. This did not suffice. Burnham maintained that America's reluctance to remove Castro during the Bay of Pigs may have been a "turning point" that started our difficulties in Southeast Asia. He claimed to have been in Southeast Asia at the time of the debacle, and US reluctance to use more hard power shook the nerves of the people there.[26] Toppling Castro in Cuba would show America resolve when it came to defeating the communists.

Burnham's advocacy of American action in places like Cuba and Vietnam should be interpreted as internationalism, not "globalism." He distinguished between the two concepts by maintaining that internationalism was good and natural. Today, we are all internationalists. Technology has made political, cultural, and social isolationism impossible. But this must be distinguished from globalism, which Burnham claimed was based on "abstractions of humanitarian, Liberal, and diluted Marxist ideology."[27] Globalists are "ideological hucksters" who emphasized concepts like "Humanity," "Peace," "Progress," "Equality," and "World Government."[28] They are not guided by social and historical reality, but rather by ideology. According to Burnham, there is no "Humanity" because in real life men are joined by diverse groupings like family, community, club, and party.[29] The United Nations had become a "playground" for globalists, and their new mantra was "disarmament."[30]

The internationalist believed that the United States must use power in the international arena—both hard or soft—or it would be used against her. The United States was a hegemony, after all, whether she liked it or not. Burnham recognized that this was a double-edged sword. On one hand, Americans wanted it all: free travel, free markets to export their goods, the ability to use the dollar anywhere, the opportunity to speak their language everywhere, and procure art from every corner of the globe. But what Americans did not realize was that nothing came free. Being rich and powerful had a price. Americans had duties, or what Burnham called "imperial responsibilities." These included maintaining the health and prosperity not just of her citizens, but of her "allies, associates and clients."[31] Occasionally, the hegemony must kill, without falling into a "paroxysm of guilt."[32] Following World War II, the United States initially succeeded in performing her duties thanks to policies like the Truman Doctrine and the Marshall Plan. Her efforts in the Greek Civil War and Korea were also noble. But, in "Joys and Sorrows of Empire," Burnham complains that she was shirking in Indochina, her latest test, where she had become too consumed with "guilt" and "pious rhetoric."[33] Couldn't the United States renounce her duties, maybe if she promised to limit her privileges? No, she could not. Burnham concludes this article by telling a story from his schoolboy days. The strongest kid on the block did not want to be the champ; he preferred the role of chump. Consequently, he got abused by everyone, even the weakest boy.[34]

The United States could show strength and power by investing in arms, a position that was becoming more controversial as the Vietnam

War escalated. Criticizing disarmament was one of Burnham's favorite intellectual exercises. In one article, Burnham asks, what is wrong with an arms race and nuclear proliferation? "Everyone assumes," he suggests that "having it drilled into them by atomic ideologists for a decade—that it is a dangerous threat to peace (and therefore bad) if additional countries get nuclear weapons. The Treaty of Moscow will tend to inhibit their spread.[35] Therefore, etc. But is it really true that in every case it would be bad if another country became nuclear armed?"[36] Burnham reasons that if a nation like France acquired nuclear weapons, this would deter a Soviet attack on Western Europe.[37] The Soviet appetite for territory was deterred by their opponents' strength, so strengthening the West prevented war.

Moreover, a nuclear arms race would place strain on Soviet society. Burnham maintains, "We can take the most enormous armament building in stride; the Soviet bloc cannot."[38] He reasons in another article that "an 'arms race' is probably our most effective form of political-economic warfare we can conduct against our enemy."[39] It burdens the Soviet economy, thereby weakening the regime. Disarmament we lose; an arms race, we win.

The lifelong proponent of arms could not have foreseen what began to occur during the Vietnam War: the violence became televised. Burnham lamented the fact that some acts of violence were open for all to see, such as the Mỹ Lai massacre. In a *New York Times* article entitled "A War Distorted," he acknowledges moral wrongs were committed at Mỹ Lai, but insists that "what happened in the Mỹ Lai episode is a different matter from what happened and is happening to the Mỹ Lai episode—in myriad news dispatches, the hour upon hour of TV shots and radio-TV commentary, the thousands of articles, speeches, sermons, the scores of books, the meetings, conferences and now the seemingly endless—and relentlessly publicized—session of one, two . . . and how many more trials."[40] He calls it a "a trivial incident within a large and complex whole," a whole included the even greater atrocities committed by the Viet Cong.[41] Moreover, the number of innocent people killed at Mỹ Lai was far fewer than the number of innocent people killed by US bombs in North Vietnam, and this number was even fewer than the number of innocent people killed by US bombs in World War II. Burnham reasons that horrible things happen in war, and they must be contextualized. After all, "Human existence bears no resemblance to the projections of sentimentalists and utopians. But to dwell exclusively on the horrors and obscenities is the road not to vision but to madness. Nor is it necessary that everything be brought at all times into the open for everyone to see. Not every diner need keep always in mind the horrors of the slaughterhouse."[42] The larger picture, the benefits, the ends must be examined, too.

Burnham's beliefs about an arms race and the need to use more power in Vietnam did not mean he was a registered Republican.[43] He preferred political independence. Consistent with his critiques of ideology, he resisted the doctrinaire laissez-faire capitalism promoted by conservatives at *National Review*. Stating that he generally favored the free market against government interventionism, the pragmatic anti-ideologue distinguished between what he called the "real world" and the "theoretical world of von Misean abstractions."[44] He disagreed with most conservative attacks on Medicare, calling them a "routine Pavlovian exercise."[45] His tendency toward favoring trends that existed can be seen in his acceptance of social security and Medicare, something that rankled his colleagues at *National Review*. More so than his fellow editors, Burnham supported the Great Society and resisted attempts to roll back the welfare state.

Burnham demonstrated orthodox conservative (not necessarily Republican) opinions in the 1950s and 1960s when it came to civil rights. The landmark *Brown v. Board of Education* (1954) decision held that racially segregated schools violated the Constitution's Equal Protection Clause. It was denounced in parts of the South. The "Southern Manifesto" (1956)—a document signed by roughly one hundred Southern congressmen and senators—asserted that "states' rights" should supersede judicial authority. Siding with these segregationist arguments, Burnham stated that the issue must be settled locally and politically, and not by the courts. He maintained that the Supreme Court had taken the right away from people to run their own schools.[46] *Brown v. Board* even restricted the freedom of Black people because they no longer had the freedom to attend segregated schools; thus, their power was usurped by the courts, too.[47] Insisting that the Constitution restricted the power of the courts, Burnham pined for the superiority of Congress when it came to creating and enforcing federal laws in the Civil Rights era.[48] The Burkean called Chief Justice Earl Warren "an ideologue" who had turned the Supreme Court into a "political weapon fighting for statist goals."[49]

The Court's decision did inspire more federal action. In 1957, President Eisenhower signed the Civil Rights Act. The final Senate bill removed some enforcement provisions from the original House version. Burnham applauded this. Conceding that Black people's right to vote had been restricted in the South, he condemned the House version as "utopian" and "ideological," in the tradition of Plato, Rousseau, and Marx.[50] Reformers wanted to remake society—with no regard for human nature. And for them, the ends always justified the means.[51] Burnham's attitude toward Black Americans can best be described as paternalistic. A *National Review* editorial titled "Why the South Must Prevail" summarized his views by maintaining that "the problem in the South is not how to get the vote for the Negro, but how to equip the Negro—and a great many Whites—to cast an enlightened and responsible vote."[52] The article continues that the South should not exploit Black people but should work with them to help them achieve cultural equality. It contends that until this was achieved, the White South had a duty to impose its higher civilized standard because "for the time being, it is the advanced race."[53]

Whereas Burnham clamored for immediate action against communism, he did the opposite when he came to equality: he preached patience. Burnham was a Leninist against communism, a Burkean when it came to equality. He demanded consistent direct action against communism, but criticized any domestic social reformer who did the same because Burnham never believed that all people, nations, races, cultures, or civilizations were always equal. For him, a hierarchy of everything and everyone existed. Groups and people could rise and fall, but only slowly. And White America did not reign atop his hierarchy. Europe did. The elitist routinely disparaged the American people and their culture. Of course, because the United States was part of Western Civilization, it was still superior to the non-West (which for Burnham was relevant only in the context of the Cold War). Burnham could be savage when depicting foreign people. Daniel Kelly accurately called him the living embodiment of political incorrectness.[54]

His most unpolitically correct remarks—maybe even racism—were reserved for India. Upon arriving for the first time, Burnham explains in a *National Review* article that "the plane door was Alice's mirror: and on the other side, the inverse wonderland of the West."[55] Calling the whole experience one malicious attack on each of his senses, he describes how India's beggars "arise out of the ground at the approach of a stranger, like the damned before Dante and Virgil in the wildest chasms of hell."[56] The trip made him cherish America's "acholic Irishmen" beggars who merely sinned by using your spare quarter to buy a shot of bad whiskey.[57] He compares leaving India to leaving an August New York sidewalk for an air-conditioned room.[58] Burnham extolls the cleanliness of the airliner's "blonde, bronzed Dutch stewardess," who would help him return home. This at least insinuated a relationship between race and cleanliness.

Burnham could praise non-Westerners. India's harshest critic was giddy over neighboring Ceylon (now Sri Lanka) and its prime minister, John Kotelawala. Burnham stated that the press may call him "pro-Western," but in reality, he was merely anticommunist and he recognized that associations with Western nations were in the best interest of his country.[59] Kotelawala told people the truth: that the communists imposed an imperialism far more wretched than anything favored by Americans. Yes, he collaborated with communist China by selling her rubber, but this was just because no Western country would buy it.[60] And he asked Western powers such as the United States for permission.[61] Burnham liked this. Kotelawala recognized his place among the hierarchy of nations.

The pessimistic proponent of hierarchy analyzed the decolonization movement accordingly. Contending that under no conditions could all of the people of Asia, Latin America, and Africa achieve the same economic status as the West, Burnham wrote, "Most—not all, but most—of these underdeveloped nations of Asia, Africa and Latin America are underdeveloped for good and sufficient reasons—of soil, climate, rainfall, paucity of sources (especially sources of energy), not to speak of the nature of the human groups that inhabit them."[62] He expressed little optimism for Latin America's future because of surging population growth, describing the whole situation in one article as "Malthusian."[63] Policymakers and social reformers must recognize that any program that treats the people of all nations as equal is doomed to fail.[64] Distinctions between groups must be made.[65]

Burnham was familiar with colonized perspectives since he read Frantz Fanon, a writer who analyzed the impact of colonization on colonizer and colonized. Like Burnham, Fanon theorized about violence. The first chapter of *The Wretched of the Earth* is titled "On Violence" and it begins: "National liberation, national reawakening, restoration of the nation to the people or Commonwealth, whatever the name used, whatever the latest expression, decolonization is always a violent event."[66] Consistent with ideas that Burnham presented in *The Machiavellians*, Fanon argues that the ruling classes feign revulsion at violence only to protect their privilege. He demanded that the exploited colonized masses revolt. Burnham believed that Fanon's book offered valuable "insights, often embodied in wonderfully concrete observations or images, that open up compelling perspectives on complicated events; a ruthless stripping of sham and self-delusions."[67] Burnham lauded Fanon's ability to describe the Algerian revolution "psychically as well as politically and strategically."[68]

Fanon demanded immediate change in colonized regions whereas Burnham was skeptical of Africa's future as decolonization gained momentum in the aftermath of World War II. In 1960, for example, more than a dozen African nations gained independence from European colonial rule. Burnham challenged this. He wrote that democracy, in a Western sense, was out of the question there.[69] He believed that African nations could not rule themselves, at least not as well as they could be ruled by Whites, at least not yet. Recognizing that the imperialist system was "abused," he said at the same time, it accomplished much.[70] He called it a "reasonable solution for a transition to civilization."[71] Decolonialization conformed to liberal ideology, but for Burnham, ideology was never a good guide for political policy and action: "Western ideologues and politicians interpret the current African events in terms of their own ideas of 'nationalism' 'self-determinism' 'democracy' and so on. But for most Africans—whatever their origin—these are just ritual words without content."[72] He blamed "ideologues" for trying to compel the world to conform to a preconceived set of ideas.[73] Burnham contended that the idea of a nation presupposed the historical continuity of a people linked by some sort of language, religion, art, law, heroes, and shared experiences of triumphs and failures. Egypt, Ethiopia, and Morocco qualified. Liberia and the Union of South Africa might qualify. The rest of Africa did not. It was organized tribally. How could nationalism succeed on a continent where nations were such artificial constructs?[74]

American policy in Rhodesia particularly disheartened the critic of decolonization. In 1965, the White-run African nation led by Prime Minister Ian Smith announced its independence from Britain. Fearing White minority rule over the African nation, the United Nations, the United States, and Britain deemed it illegal. A standoff ensued. For the first time in its history, the United Nations imposed sanctions. Burnham argued that these actions had only made a difficult situation worse. Highlighting the positive gains made in Rhodesia under White-rule, he wrote that even the *New York Times*—"the purest fountain of un-racism"—published a dispatch that described how the region of "savage tribal warfare, disease, hunger and superstition" had been transformed into "a land of flourishing mining, agricultural and industrial activity."[75] Yes, there was racism in Rhodesia. And Burnham declared that racism was "evil."[76] He speculated that a Black-run Rhodesia would be racist against the Whites who had founded the country.[77] Moreover, by isolating the country, the West risked wrecking everything that had been accomplished under White rule, to the detriment of all.[78] There may be more freedom, democracy, and equality in a majority-ruled Rhodesia—particularly for Blacks—yet that did not make it immediately desirable for Burnham.

He chided Western leaders for demanding majority rule in Africa by arguing that few African governments actually represented the majority of the people.[79] He asked, who chose Houari Boumédiène to rule over Algeria?[80] What about Ghana?[81] Burnham wondered why Western powers accepted the reign of Black despots, but not Whites who brought more prosperity and progress to their regions. The Western chauvinist tried to explain the conflict in a neo-Spenglerian manner: Burnham argued that, for centuries, the people of Europe and subsequently the United States were "historically active," while Asia, Africa, and Latin America remained "historically inert."[82] Recognizing the racial significance of this statement, he wrote that he was not sure if the West's "activity" was due to "accident or fate."[83] Regardless, now Asians and Africans had become historical actors.[84] This sparked a struggle with the West.

To consolidate their control over the country, White settlers passed a constitution that established Rhodesia as a republic in 1969. And it enshrined White political power at the expense of Blacks. The move was denounced around the world. Burnham even followed suit. He called the new constitution "racist and fundamentally despotic," arguing that it created a situation in which Africans were permanently subject to Europeans, "no matter what their increase in literacy, income, virtue or any other quality."[85] This suggested that Burnham did not believe that any group was indefatigably inferior; they could achieve equality, but only gradually.

Again, Burnham demanded immediate action (even violence) to undermine communism, yet he resisted quick, dramatic change (even violence) when it came to decolonization and attempts to spread equality. He did not oppose an Africa where Blacks participated equally with Whites; he just preferred one that occurred organically. He questioned any change produced by the human mind or ideology—change inspired by concepts such as democracy, freedom, or equality. The Burkean insinuated that events in Africa could emulate the French Revolution; he feared that in their quest for equality, Africans may resort to violence.[86] It may be too much change too fast.

Burnham blamed Western powers for the fiasco by contending that Rhodesian settlers acted rationally: knowing that the West would leave them to the wolves, they tended toward self-preservation. What would come next? He wrote that it was now beyond the United States' ability to influence events in Africa because she should not intervene in the affairs of other countries unless her security was at risk. He regretted that the whole situation had become "immoral."[87] This implied too much ideology—reliance on concepts like freedom, democracy, and equality—caused immorality. Only by understanding the true nature of humanity could one act morally.

Burnham also employed ideas that he pronounced in *The Machiavellians* when analyzing decolonization, specifically the importance of power. Africans used words like "liberty" and "equality" merely to acquire power.[88] Events in Africa should be interpreted as an attempt by Black men to usurp power.[89] The careers, homes, possessions, and even the lives of Whites in Africa existed tenuously. Burnham theorized that maybe some economic benefits could emerge if a Black-run Africa became integrated into the Western economy, but that was little consolation for the White settlers.[90] He compared their position to that of Jews in Palestine. Possibly through some courage and political skill, the Whites in Africa could survive, except that Jewish settlers at least had the backing of all Jews. White settlers in Africa were condemned by most of the Whites in the Western world.[91]

Burnham may have lamented decolonization in practice, but he recognized it was inevitable. He viewed America's changing relationship with China similarly; he knew a metamorphosis in Sino-US relations was imminent during the Nixon administration. Lest anyone forget what US formal recognition of Taipei at the expense of China earned the world, however, he wrote a piece in 1971 defending US policy in Asia. Burnham wanted history to remember that rejecting the Peoples Republic of China saved Taiwan from communism. And this saved South Korea because the Chinese delegate would have prevented UN intervention in the Korean War, and thus, the United States would have been unable to act. Africa would have next fallen to Chinese expansion, particularly Western Africa. The United States shielded Japan from Chinese aggression, too. According to Burnham, America's enemy in World War II recovered so quickly because she did not have to protect herself against an invasion from the "Camp of Socialism and Peace."[92] Reversing her position on China did not make America's previous one wrong.

CHAPTER 11

Two months after Burnham wrote "The Balance Sheet," President Richard Nixon visited China. The president believed that establishing cordial relations with the Asian giant would increase American leverage against the Soviets because he knew something that Burnham did not: the Soviet Union and China were not a monolithic bloc. Burnham had minimized the Sino-Soviet split by calling it "verbal only."[93] He stressed the "continuing commitment of the global communist enterprise" to destroy Western civilization.[94] This simplistic holist view of communism prevented him from seeing some crucial nuances, such as the fact that the Soviet Union and China genuinely feared one another, at times even more than they feared the United States. John Lewis Gaddis contended, "Wars among communists . . . were all too real a possibility: the ideological schism between the Soviet Union and the People's Republic of China had become so intense during the Khrushchev years that as they ended his representatives were discussing *with the Americans* plans for a *joint preventative military action* against Chinese nuclear facilities in the Gobi desert."[95] Although China and the Soviet Union were both pursuing communism, they were not unified.[96]

In his analysis of the two communist giants, Burnham made the same mistake that he made in *The Managerial Revolution* when he conflated the USSR and Nazi Germany. Just as managerial societies may conflict, so too might communist societies. Lost on Burnham was the fact that powerful individuals could transcend the system. In the case of the managerial Nazi Germany, it was Hitler and his need for conquest, even if it meant conquering other managerial societies. During the subsequent Cold War, Burnham failed to recognize that personal rifts between Soviet leaders and Mao could divide communist societies. His worldview remained too holistic.

Nixon's overtures to China surprised most of the world. Not Burnham. He had been rankled by Nixon's chess-like statesmanship since he had been vice president. For the hardliner, strategic moves would not win the Cold War. It would be won only by using power. The president, in contrast, sought dialogue and friendly relations. In doing so, he flouted *National Review*'s ideas about conferences and treaties; he dared to negotiate with communists. The editors were furious.

The Nixon administration was concerned. In an effort to pacify them, William F. Buckley, Burnham, and other editors were invited to the White House to discuss the China situation. Nixon aid Pat Buchanan believed Buckley could be persuaded to support the president, but he called Burnham an "anti-Nixon hawk."[97] Buchanan feared *National*

Review would promote a conservative challenger to Nixon, and in fact, several months before the 1972 presidential election, *National Review* suspended its support for Nixon.[98] The angry president deemed the editors at *National Review* "shortsighted," "dumb," and "unimaginative."[99] Nixon demanded that Henry Kissinger "see some of the gurus of the bunch. See Burnham."[100]

Burnham had a personal relationship with Kissinger, as they had met on several occasions while Kissinger served Nixon as secretary of state. After one such meeting in 1973, Burnham wrote to him: "as I continue to reflect on what you explained, I feel that I do now see more clearly both the objectives you keep in mind. . . . If I occasionally have doubts about some of those steps . . . it may quite possibly be, I realize, because my ideas, unlike yours, do not have to meet the daily and pitiless test of action."[101] It seems Burnham recognized that he could more easily preach hardline ideas from afar. At some level, he knew the difference between postulating ideas about nuclear weapons and actually using them. The alleged Machiavellian conceded his ideas were not always practical; his words should not always be taken at face value.

In January 1973, with the support of the Nixon administration, the Paris Peace Accords were signed. US power in Vietnam soon vanished. In January 1975, the communists showed little regard for written treaties that brought peace; North Vietnam sent one hundred and sixty thousand soldiers and four hundred armored vehicles into South Vietnam. Saigon fell several months later. Burnham tries to assign culpability for US failure in Vietnam in an article called "It's All Your Fault." The piece could have been called "It Wasn't My Fault. I Told You So." He recognizes that everyone wanted to blame everyone else. But he asks, blame whom for what? For sending aid to South Vietnam? For sending soldiers there? For ordering aerial bombardment? For not destroying Hanoi and Haiphong? For not using nuclear weapons? For inappropriate military tactics? For permitting disgruntled citizens to sabotage the war effort? For withdrawing too soon? For signing peace accords with an enemy that lies? For being too stingy with support after withdrawal?[102]

Burnham denied any culpability. The Vietnam hardliner declared himself prophetic. Knowing he was occasionally read by Nixon and Kissinger, he reminds his readers what he wrote in 1973:

> To the North Vietnamese, the ceasefire agreement means, in essence, getting rid of the Americans, as before they got rid of the French. . . . With U.S. forces withdrawn from the theater, the

strategic position of the Communists in relation to South Vietnam, in fact to Indochina as a whole, would seem to be overwhelming.... When U.S. power is gone, Communist power will be predominant in the Indochinese equilibrium.... The Communists will not keep their terms of the ceasefire.... It will soon become psychologically and politically impossible for the U.S. to shift back to direct military intervention.[103]

Nixon and Kissinger ignored *National Review*'s advice at their peril.

Burnham did fault the president and his secretary of state for Vietnam failure. At the same time, he maintained that they—along with Congress—were carrying out the will of the American people. Does that mean that the American people were to blame? He claimed that in one sense, yes. The United States grew weary of war. In "It's All Your Fault," Burnham also laments that no US political leader galvanized the public by reviving courage and discipline. In fact, politicians unwittingly encouraged weakness. He concludes the article by bemoaning, "'The President's trips to Peking and Moscow,' I noted in 1973, 'destroyed the political as well as moral foundation for the American anticommunist policy in Indochina.'"[104] He suggests that the United States lost Vietnam because she ignored the primary recommendations of his Cold War polemics: she lacked the will to win. Establishing cordial relations with China demonstrated vacillation. One day, the United States dropped bombs on communists, the next, she shook their hands. By sending mixed messages, US foreign policymakers weakened the resolve of her citizens in the crusade against communism. Inspiring leaders never emerged. America did not do what needed to be done.

In "Go East, Old Man," Burnham interprets the post-Vietnam era by using concepts that he had been advocating for decades, namely that the United States must use power, or it would be used against her. He opines in 1975 that because the United States stopped using power in Vietnam, the world no longer feared US power. This had consequences. Had the United States not quit Vietnam, there would have been no oil embargo, no expropriations of US property, and fewer "gang-up anti-U.S. votes in the UN."[105] The worst could be yet to come. After all, US history for three and a half centuries had been characterized by westward expansion. This culminated in World War II with victory over Japan. But Korea was a stalemate, Vietnam a loss. Now, according to Burnham, the United States was beginning to retreat eastward: "The flag was lowered in Okinawa; the troops began their retreat from South

Korea, and Japan, and Taiwan; the fleet vanished from the Formosa Strait and moved back from China. Then the withdrawal swelled with the half-million soldiers, the planes and ships, from Vietnam, and the following thousands from Laos and Thailand."[106] How long would this retreat continue? The fate of America rested in the balance.

The geopolitical strategist tried to place Vietnam in its proper historical context by showing that it did have to be catastrophic—maybe historical trends were not favoring communism. He tried to curb pessimism (partly his own) by noting that all powerful nations lose wars. Persia lost wars to Greece but remained a regional power for centuries. Rome lost plenty of wars. France, Germany, and Russia had all lost multiple wars, and had done so relatively recently. In "Reflections on Defeat," Burnham maintains that when put in its appropriate historical context, Vietnam was a "minor affair."[107] Casualties were roughly equal to those on US highways each year, and the $150 billion cost was less than two years of health, education, and welfare expenditures.[108] What did America's future hold? Burnham uses principles to predict the future: once a small retreat occurs, all holdings become threatened. The process had already begun. The jettisoning of military bases in Thailand proved this. Burnham reasoned that US military bases in Korea and Japan may soon follow. He contends that Vietnam was a small, trivial battle with consequences that could lead to the decline of the United States.[109]

Burnham predictably rejected any sort of "peaceful coexistence" and the détente policy that emerged during Vietnam because he maintained that this primarily benefited the communists. He insisted that the Cold War had never really been "cold" in the first place, so peaceful coexistence was impossible. Détente was another immoral utopian illusion because fighting always raged somewhere, whether it be in Greece, China, Korea, Cuba, Hungary, Venezuela, Indonesia, Burundi, Vietnam, or the Congo. And peaceful coexistence was one-sided: it was violated when Americans promoted anticommunism abroad yet accepted when one preached communism in the United States.[110] If practiced in the long run, it would inevitably culminate in a final struggle, "that is, in general war, when the time is ripe, that will involve nuclear arms. The general war would most probably be initiated by a communist nuclear strike against decisive noncommunist targets."[111] In *The War We Are In*, he sarcastically suggests that peaceful coexistence would climax when the peace-loving people conquered the militaristic, warmongering people, leading to a zone of peace around the world.[112]

Burnham initially had high hopes that the Ford administration would "imbue détente with more realism and even a dash of skepticism."[113] In a *National Review* article, he reminds his readers that during his time in the House, Ford had become an expert on military systems and strategy. In his first address to Congress, Ford had noted that "weakness invites war" and "a strong defense is the surest way to peace."[114] Whereas Nixon spent too much time wooing China and the USSR with gifts, Burnham hoped that the new administration would actually get something in return for bargaining. Thus far, détente had been "a one-way street with traffic permitted to move only in the Soviet direction."[115] Burnham closes another *National Review* article by asking what benefits the United States got from détente. The American people deserved to know.

His hopes were dashed when Ford signed the Helsinki Accords in August 1975. These recognized Eastern Europe as part of the Soviet sphere and allowed the USSR more access to Western technology. For their part, the Soviets affirmed the importance of human rights. Worrying about the psychological effects more than the practical ones, Burnham maintained that the accords enhanced Soviet prestige and legitimized their control over Eastern Europe.[116] And it was fraught with irony: the clause allowing free movement of people and ideas was signed two weeks after the Soviets denied access to Western journalists and photographers who sought to witness the launching of the Soviet half of a joint manned space mission. Burnham urged the Ford administration to oppose any deal, as least until the Soviet Union stopped trying to export communism to Western Europe.[117]

Burnham argued that by seeking rapprochement with the USSR, the Ford administration effectively colluded against the citizens and nations under Soviet control.[118] He compared it to the era of 1944–1947 when the West gave two million people who had found themselves in Western hands to Stalin.[119] Détente meant that as communists assaulted the borders of Portugal, the United States accepted the new borders of Eastern Europe. Communism expands, and the United States acquiesces. This was the "logic of détente."[120] The Americans perceived it as a trade-off since war was averted. In a piece titled the "Dialectics of Détente," the former philosophy professor theorizes that for communists, the US "mode of conceiving détente is what Communists call bourgeois, Aristotelian, abstract and static. The Communist mode is (they say) proletarian, dialectical, concrete, and dynamic."[121] Applied to current affairs, the dialectical clash was occurring between US imperialists and Soviet workers. The United States must accept détente on Soviet terms because the United States—as a reactionary force—was weakening. America's retreat in Indochina, the oil squeeze, growing dissatisfaction with the North Atlantic Treaty Organization and increased communist influence in Western Europe revealed US weakness. He laments in the article that détente became a green light for Soviet development of Multiple Independent Reentry Vehicle warheads, and a red light for the development of the United States' antimissile defenses. Her politicians complied because they did not have to provide real, courageous leadership; they just preached reducing tensions. What seemed like a win-win for the Americans was actually a no-lose for the Soviets.[122] While communism advanced, American leaders used nice-sounding words.

Burnham declared that Jimmy Carter did not understand the true nature of communism and the Cold War any more than Nixon or Ford. Shortly after his election as president in 1976, Burnham analyzed the new president's professed love for morality. Carter called himself a disciple of Protestant theologian Reinhold Niebuhr's political philosophy. Niebuhr defined politics as "the sad art of establishing justice in a sinful world," a quote Carter liked to use. Carter said government ought to be moral, like people. Even relations with other governments should be based on moral standards. In a piece called "Politics and Morality," Burnham writes that the president's belief that governments must be moral and honest could never have come from Niebuhr. Under the subtitle "Danger Ahead," the international realist calls Carter's delusions "dangerous" and "absurd," especially when it came to foreign policy.[123] Burnham argues that terms like "justice" were emotional, yet empty. Consequently, they would lead to political action, but mistaken political action. If the United States was about to embark on a foreign policy based on love and compassion, it would be a lonely road, and one fraught with peril. Burnham concludes the piece by stating that Carter's "government-is-love" philosophy could not be his real foreign policy, or at least Niebuhr would have hoped so.[124]

Even at the end of his writing career, Burnham maintained that morality must be based on seeing things how they really are. All nations pursue their own interests. The Soviets seek to spread communism. Deniers such as President Carter could not claim the "moral" moniker because they cannot act properly. They ended up appeasing communism, hardly a moral act.

Although the next US president may not have shared Burnham's conception of morality, he did share—partly because of Burnham's influence—his conception of the Cold War: it was a struggle for the world that had to be fought and won. And it *could* be won, if the United States properly displayed force. Despite some popular misconceptions, Ronald Reagan was an avid reader from a young age.[125] He even carried with him a personal library of books about political philosophy when he traveled.[126] Many biographers have noted his photographic memory. Reagan was so passionate about politics in the late 1940s, his ex-wife cited it as a reason for their failed marriage. *National Review* was one of his favorite periodicals. Even before *National Review*, Reagan certainly read some of Burnham's popular Cold War polemics. It is not a matter of whether Reagan read and was influenced by Burnham, but rather how much.

Some of Burnham's influence on Reagan can be directly traced in the mid-to-late 1970s. During this time, the future president hosted a radio show that gave him the opportunity to express his political views. The content occasionally mimicked Burnham's articles in *National Review*. For example, in "The Resonance Differential," Burnham analyzes the leftist Portuguese coup d'état against an oppressive right-wing regime in 1974 known as the Carnation Revolution. He attempts to show how left-wing dictatorships were treated differently by the left and the media than right-wing dictatorships.[127] Burnham creates an imaginary nation called Ruritania where officers staged a coup not against an oppressive right-wing regime, but against a Marxist one. Burnham contends that the world would respond with thousands of meetings, demonstrations, speeches, sit-ins, and sermons denouncing the "fascists."[128] In an August 1975 radio address, Reagan does the same. He explicates Burnham's imaginary scenario by stating: "Imagine military officers stage a successful coup d'état in a mythical land called Ruritania. It frees people from an oppressive Soviet-like regime."[129] How would the world respond? Reagan states: "Student sit-ins would follow, editorials, petitions and TV specials denouncing the fascist, military dictators. Of course the U.N. would get in the act with eloquent speeches thundering through the hall protesting the violation of 'human, civil and political rights of the Ruritanian workers and peasants' . . . Burnham describes the Ad-Hoc committees that would spring up in a dozen countries demanding sanctions and severance of diplomatic relations."[130] Reagan believed the media would follow suit, showing their left-wing bias.

In January 1978, Burnham wrote a piece titled "SALT-Verifiability=0." It contends that Strategic Arms Limitations Talks sounded nice, assuming the limitations were "fair." But what did fair mean? No one, including experts on both sides, could comprehend all of the details concerning nuclear arsenals. And no one on the US side really knew the intentions of Soviet policy. Burnham argues that what mattered about SALT was verifiability: "Granted the general murkiness shrouding strategic arms, there would nevertheless seem to be an essential feature of an acceptable SALT about which even all senators could agree: *verifiability*. No matter what the terms of SALT are, they are meaningless unless their fulfillment can be verified beyond reasonable doubt."[131] SALT was pointless unless the results could be verified.

Two months later, Reagan wrote an address criticizing SALT. It seemed SALT was one-sided: "We have made concessions such as canceling the B-1 Bomber without waiting for the negotiations."[132] Reagan emphasized verifiability, too: "Then there is the matter of *verification*. Yes, our reconnaissance satellites can keep a reasonable count on how many missiles the Soviets have on hand. But there is no way without on site inspection (which the Russians would never agree to) to verify whether the Soviets are indeed complying with the treaty."[133] The idea became part of the fortieth president's manta toward the Soviet Union: *Doveryai no proveryai* (trust but verify). He used the phrase on multiple occasions to General Secretary Gorbachev during their summit meetings, much to Gorbachev's chagrin.[134]

In November 1978, Burnham suffered a serious stroke. It did not incapacitate him, but it did prevent him from writing seriously again. A year later, the Soviets invaded Afghanistan. President Carter called it the greatest threat to peace since World War II. He acknowledged that the Soviets had lied to him. Had he followed Burnham, he would have known that communists were liars who only wanted to spread communism.

President Reagan recognized this. He became one of the determined men whom the optimistic Burnham predicted would emerge in the struggle against communism. In his first official press conference as president, Reagan cribbed Burnham: "Well, so far détente's been a one-way street that the Soviet Union has used to pursue its own aims. I don't have to think of an answer as to what I think their intentions are; they have repeated it."[135] Reagan continued that the Soviets only sought to conquer the world and establish a socialist or communist state. And their only morality involved spreading their system; they would use any means. Reagan noted that communists were guided by a "different set of standards" than everyone else and anyone who negotiates with communists must keep all of this in mind.[136] Consistent with Burnham's prescriptions, over the next several years billions of dollars were spent on new defense projects because Reagan believed the Soviets could not keep up in an arms race. In a 1981 interview, he insisted: "Up until now, we have been making unilateral concessions, allowing our forces to deteriorate, and they have been building the greatest military machine the world has even seen. But now they could be faced with [the fact] that we could go forward with an arms race and they can't keep up."[137] Reagan showed power by flexing American muscles.

Reagan did not, however, share Burnham's belief that victory required some form of violence. The fortieth president insisted in his "evil empire" speech that "while America's military strength is important, let me add here that I've always maintained that the struggle now going on for the world will never be decided by bombs or rockets, by armies or military might."[138] Reagan feared hard power more than apocalyptic Burnham. And the president even dared to negotiate with communists.

Reagan did employ soft power against the Soviet Union because consistent with the first James Burnham, he optimistically believed that—with the proper use of power—democracy could prevail there. Like the author of *The Coming Defeat of Communism*, Reagan proclaimed the existence of inexorable historical trends. He turned Marxism on its head by declaring in a famous 1982 speech that "it is the Soviet Union that runs against the tide of history by denying human freedom and human dignity to its citizens."[139] The president suggested that the Soviets were experiencing insurmountable economic crises that would lead to the collapse of their system. This should be interpreted as a form of political or psychological warfare intended to promote fear and fertilize the Soviet leaders' seeds of doubt. Reagan's denouncement of the USSR as an "evil empire" and his demand that Gorbachev tear down the Berlin Wall should also be understood as forms of soft power that aimed at promoting democracy.

Two weeks before calling the Soviet Union an "evil empire," Reagan awarded Burnham the Presidential Medal of Freedom. He said to Burnham, "As a scholar, writer, historian and philosopher, James Burnham has profoundly affected the way America views itself and the world. Since the 1930s, Mr. Burnham has shaped the thinking of world leaders. His observations have changed society and his writings have become guiding lights in mankind's quest for truth. Freedom, reason and decency have had few greater champions in this century than James Burnham. And I owe him a personal debt, because throughout the years traveling the mash-potato circuit I have quoted you widely."[140]

Epilogue
Burnham Today

James Burnham died in July 1987. The day after his passing, President Reagan stated, "Nancy and I have learned with deep sadness of the passing of James Burnham. Mr. Burnham, the author of seminal works, like 'The Managerial Revolution' and 'The Suicide of the West,' and a senior editor of the *National Review*, was one of those principally responsible for the great intellectual odyssey of our century: the journey away from totalitarian statism and towards the uplifting doctrines of freedom."[1] Burnham's "intellectual odyssey" from Marxist to staunch anticommunist was not unique. Sidney Hook, Max Eastman, Irving Kristol, Frank Meyer, Will Herberg, and John Dos Passos traveled along similar intellectual paths. What separates Burnham from these figures is his enduring influence. Burnham's ideas played an important role in ending the Cold War, but the end of the Cold War did not end his relevance. In fact, current divides within the Republican Party between neoconservatives and paleoconservatives can partly be interpreted as conflicts between the two James Burnhams; each Burnham has influenced a competing sect with its own philosophy of power.

In the late 1990s, for example, so-called neoconservatives William Kristol and Robert Kagan—two students of Burnham's thought—began demanding the ousting of Saddam Hussein by using American force in a piece for the *New York Times* titled "The Bombing of Iraq Isn't Enough."[2] Fearing Iraqi chemical weapons, the authors maintained that the United States had a responsibility to act—something had to be done. In another article, they declared: "A devastating knockout blow against Saddam Hussein, followed by an American-sponsored effort to rebuild Iraq and put it on a path toward democratic governance, would have a seismic impact on the Arab world—for the better."[3] Contending that displays of American power were necessary in the region, Kristol and Kagan believed that violence could regenerate the Middle East—they optimistically believed that democracy could prevail there.[4]

How would Burnham have reacted to US involvement in the Middle East and later, Ukraine? All we can do is speculate. Burnham did demand an aggressive foreign policy aimed at liberating the people of Eastern Europe. *The Struggle for the World*, however, explicitly rejects the notion that all nations should follow the US democratic model. And the mature Burnham was not a universalist. As was shown, Burnham did not believe that parts of the non-Western world were even capable of Western-style democracy, at least not yet. Democracy's inability to thrive in Afghanistan would not have surprised him.

Neither would have Russian expansion in Eastern Europe given that Burnham recognized the geopolitical significance of this region, part of "The Heartland." And he believed that nation-states always pursue their own interests. Whether or not Burnham would have supported giving US aid to the region is difficult to know. Burnham did promote the American national interest, and potential Russian annexation of the Ukraine has not immediately threatened US interests. But no one knows Russia's future aspirations. At least during the Cold War, Burnham had no qualms about giving US aid to those resisting Soviet expansion. The question of whether Burnham would have supported US escapades in foreign parts of the world may be reduced to which Burnham does one champion: the inchoate neocon who believed US force and power could improve the world, or the paleoconservative paragon?

The ideas of the latter are currently more fashionable. Republican presidential candidate Vivek Ramaswamy posted on X in 2024: "The real divide isn't black vs. white or even Democrat vs. Republican. It's the managerial class vs. the everyday citizen."[5] Bemoaning that Burnham's forecasted managerial revolution has come to fruition, Ramaswamy and other writers have argued that corporate managers—not wealthy stockholders and CEOs—wield the power at American corporations.

Examples include Netflix, Amazon, Apple, Disney, and Google, where managers control production (e.g., content produced), and these managers are mostly liberal and sometimes "woke."[6] They use their positions to promote liberal values that are antithetical to American national interests. As Burnham had predicted in *The Managerial Revolution*, those who control the productive forces foist their (liberal) ideology on the people. They shape culture.

Another group of twenty-first-century conservatives have advanced related ideas presented by the more pessimistic Burnham in *The Managerial Revolution* and *The Machiavellians*. This Burnham has been called a "hallowed figure" among national conservatives (NatCons) who form Trump's base.[7] Insisting that globalist elites in Washington, DC, have gained too much power, NatCons believe that the ruling class governs the United States only to promote their own interests, at the expense of the people. NatCons cynically view politics as merely a playground for the globalist elite, and they must be resisted in the name of American democracy.

Trump has encapsulated their demands (at least rhetorically) by pledging to "drain the swamp" or restrict the power of the privileged elite in DC who are not democratically elected and only work to serve their interests. He argued in his inaugural address: "For too long, a small group in our nation's capital has reaped the rewards of government, while the people have borne the cost. Washington flourished, but the people did not share in its wealth. Politicians prospered, but the jobs left and the factories closed. The establishment protected itself, but not the citizens of our country."[8] *Vanity Fair, Washington Post, USA Today, New York Magazine*, and the *New Yorker* all highlighted the "dark" side of this speech. President Trump later insisted that "unelected deep state operatives who defy the voters to push their own secret agendas are truly a threat to democracy itself."[9] And the president warned against "the steady creep of government bureaucracy that drains the vitality and wealth of the people."[10] Trump has embraced some of the ideas that Burnham inherited from Trotsky: bureaucrats hold the power, even though they are not real representatives of the people. Instead, they pursue their own interests. They are the enemies of democracy.

Trump and his base have decried international governing bodies like the United Nations and the World Health Organization (WHO) because their words allegedly do little to improve the homeland. Trump called the United Nations a "club for people to get together, talk and have a good time."[11] He even threatened to pull the United States from the WHO, insisting that communist China has "total control" over the organization.[12] For the president, the national interest transcends everything. Echoing Burnham, he declared, "We reject the ideology of globalism, and embrace the doctrine of patriotism."[13]

Trump shares Burnham's domestic worldview that revolves around elites and the ways that they undermine democracy. They are both unorthodox conservatives. Like Burnham, Trump was not part of the religious right, nor did he embrace the free market to the degree that many conservatives do. Geopolitically, Trump, like Burnham, promoted the national interest above any humanitarian impulses or universal organizations. Of course, Trump and those who share his thinking lean toward isolationism. Burnham never did. Even in the post–Cold War era, Burnham probably would have questioned a foreign policy in which the United States did not take a leadership role; he preached internationalism. Like it or not, according to Burnham, "America is a hegemony, and the hegemon has imperial responsibilities."[14] What about Trump's uncouth style? Attacking, criticizing, and ridiculing others was a hallmark of Burnham writings. It is doubtful he would have faulted a president who did the same, especially against members of the establishment.

Burnham's ideas about power and popular resistance were even displayed during the COVID-19 pandemic, when federal, state, and local governments (political elites with help from the bureaucracy) exercised a virtually unprecedented amount of power against their citizens. Businesses were shuttered, per the recommendation of bureaucratic health officials. Some normal human activities like visiting family and friends or walking on the beach were at best discouraged and at worst became punishable offenses. Even protests (public opposition) in California were banned in April (this was rescinded in early June for protesters on the left who challenged a power structure that they too deemed oppressive). The stated reason for selectively banning protests was humanitarian, or the attempt to limit the spread of COVID-19. Consistent with arguments made in *The Machiavellians*, some people disagreed on the grounds that the elite are never humanitarian—they seek only to exercise authority. For parts of the American right, COVID-19 restrictions were a naked power grab. What was the best way to curb government force? Fight back with power. This explains the protests against California's governor in more conservative parts of the liberal state. Consistent with Burnham, by resisting, the protesters—at least in their minds—were exercising power against the powerful, a requirement for democracy.

These events reveal Burnham's continued significance, especially among conservatives as a power theorist. For neoconservatives, American power (hard and soft) should be exercised abroad to protect or even promote democracy. For paleoconservatives, consciousness must be raised about the raging power struggle between elites and nonelites—democracy depends on it. The reader can decide which (if either) Burnham deserves support, but his continued importance cannot be denied.

NOTES

Introduction

1. James Burnham, *The Machiavellians: Defenders of Freedom* (New York: John Day, 1943), 246.
2. Burnham, *The Machiavellians*, 246.
3. James Burnham, *The Struggle for the World* (New York: John Day, 1947), 230.
4. James Burnham, "Reply to Letters," *National Review*, June 29, 1971, 720.
5. Robert Merry, "Reagan's Geopolitical Genius," *National Interest*, June 25, 2014.
6. William Kristol and Robert Kagan, "Toward a Neo-Reaganite Foreign Policy," *Foreign Affairs*, July/August 1996, 18.
7. Kristol and Kagan, "Toward a Neo-Reaganite Foreign Policy," 20.
8. Kristol and Kagan, "Toward a Neo-Reaganite Foreign Policy," 21.
9. See, for example, Timothy Shenk, "The Dark History of Trump's Right Wing Revolt," *The Guardian*, August 16, 2016, https://www.theguardian.com/news/2016/aug/16/secret-history-trumpism-donald-trump; and Thomas Meany, "Trumpism after Trump," *Harper's*, February 2020, https://harpers.org/archive/2020/02/trumpism-after-trump/.
10. Samuel Francis, "The New Shape of American Politics," *Chronicles: A Journal of American Culture*, January 1998, 30–31.
11. Francis, "The New Shape of American Politics," 30.
12. Christopher Hitchens, "How Neoconservatives Perish," *Harper's*, July 1, 1990, 67.
13. Hitchens, "How Neoconservatives Perish," 67.
14. Binoy Kampmark, "The First Neo-Conservative: James Burnham and the Origins of a Movement," *Review of International Studies* 37, no. 4 (October 2011): 1892.
15. Daniel Kelly, *James Burnham and the Struggle for the World* (Wilmington, DE: ISI Books, 2002), 208.
16. Richard Brookhiser, "Notes and Asides," *National Review*, January 27, 1997, 20.
17. Michael Lind, *The New Class War: Saving Democracy from the Managerial Elite* (New York: Portfolio, 2020), xi.
18. Lind, *The New Class War*, 146.
19. Alan Wald, "From Trotsky to Buckley," *Jacobin*, September 15, 2017.

1. The Young Burnham

1. Daniel Kelly, *James Burnham and the Struggle for the World* (Wilmington, DE: ISI Books, 2002), 1.
2. Kelly, *James Burnham*, 2.
3. Kelly, *James Burnham*, 5.
4. James Burnham, "Do Present Conditions in America Stimulate the Production of Literature?," *Canterbury Quarterly*, June 1923, 25.
5. Burnham, "Present Conditions in America," 25.
6. Burnham, "Present Conditions in America," 27.
7. Paul Charles Kemeny, *Princeton in the Nation's Service: Religious Ideals and Educational Practice, 1868–1928* (New York: Oxford University Press, 1998), 198.
8. Kemeny, *Princeton in the Nation's Service*, 201.
9. The Scopes Monkey Trial also occurred when Burnham was at Princeton. At least on the surface, it pitted those who asserted God's divine providence in the world against those who did not. Although the issues were more complex, for the US public at the time, it was a victory for secularists.
10. F. Scott Fitzgerald, *This Side of Paradise* (Oxford: Oxford University Press, 2009), 34.
11. James Burnham, "Through a Glass, Darkly," *Nassau Literary Magazine*, June 1925, 101–102.
12. Kelly, *James Burnham*, 15.
13. Kelly, *James Burnham*, 10.
14. Kelly, *James Burnham*, 10.
15. H. J. A. Sire, *Father Martin D'Arcy: Philosopher of Christian Love* (Herefordshire, UK: Gracewing, 1997), 28.
16. Thomas Aquinas, *Summa Theologica*, part 1, question 2, article 3.
17. Kelly, *James Burnham*, 24.
18. Stephen Trombley, *Fifty Major Thinkers Who Shaped the Modern World* (London: Atlantic, 2013), 161.
19. Kelly, *James Burnham*, 30.
20. George Santayana, *The Letters of George Santayana*, ed. Daniel Cory (London: Constable, 1955), 264–265.
21. Kelly, *James Burnham*, 31.
22. David Burnham, *This Is Our Exile* (New York: Scribner's, 1931), 239.
23. Burnham, *This Is Our Exile*, 272.
24. Burnham, *This Is Our Exile*, 272.
25. Kelly, *James Burnham*, 23–24.
26. James Burnham and Philip Wheelwright, *Introduction to Philosophical Analysis* (New York: Holt, 1932), 16–17.
27. Burnham and Wheelright, *Introduction to Philosophical Analysis*, 171–178.
28. Comments, *Symposium*, Spring 1932, 132.
29. James Burnham, "The Wondrous World of Architecture of the World," *Symposium*, April 1931, 166.
30. See Sidney Hook, *Out of Step* (New York: Harper and Row, 1987), 218; Daniel Oppenheimer, *Exit Right* (New York: Simon and Schuster, 2016), 87; Kelly, *James Burnham*, 33–34; Jeffrey Hart, *The Making of the American*

Conservative Mind: National Review and Its Enemies (Wilmington, DE: ISI Books, 2005), 20–21.

31. Erik Larson, *In the Garden of the Beasts* (New York: Random House, 2011), 25–26.

32. Martha Dodd Papers, box 4, Manuscript Division, Library of Congress, Washington, DC.

33. Larson, *In the Garden of the Beasts*, 41–42.

34. James Burnham, "Panama or Taiwan," *National Review*, September 16, 1977, 1043.

2. Embracing Marxism

1. Sidney Hook, "Towards the Understanding of Karl Marx," *Symposium*, July 1931, 325–367. It would later be published in book form in 1933.

2. Hook, "Towards the Understanding," 349.

3. Hook, "Towards the Understanding," 351. Hook's emphasis.

4. Hook, "Towards the Understanding," 351.

5. Leon Trotsky, *History of the Russian Revolution*, trans. Max Eastman, vol. 3 (New York: Simon & Schuster, 1933), 166.

6. For a more Hegelian and less dogmatic interpretation of Marx, see György Lukács, *History and Class Consciousness* (1923). Lukács highlighted the philosophical (Hegelian) side of Marx as opposed to the scientific side. It was condemned by many communist leaders.

7. Trotsky, *History of the Russian Revolution*, preface.

8. James Burnham, "Review of *History of the Russian Revolution*, by Leon Trotsky," *Symposium*, July 1932, 371.

9. Burnham, "Review of *History*," 375.

10. Burnham, "Review of *History*," 376–377.

11. James Burnham and Philip Wheelwright, "Thirteen Propositions," *Symposium*, April 1933, 130.

12. Burnham and Wheelwright, "Thirteen Propositions," 131–132.

13. Burnham and Wheelwright, "Thirteen Propositions," 132.

14. James Burnham, "Comment," *Symposium*, July 1933, 259.

15. Burnham, "Comment," 267.

16. Burnham, "Comment," 268.

17. Burnham, "Comment," 272.

18. Burnham, "Comment," 273.

19. Burnham, "Comment," 270.

20. T. S. Eliot, "A Commentary," *The Criterion: A Literary Review*, July 1933, 642–643.

21. James Burnham, "Comment," *Symposium*, October 1933, 408.

22. Burnham, "Comment," October 1933, 408.

23. Burnham, "Comment," October 1933, 404–405.

24. Burnham, "Comment," October 1933, 410.

25. "Personal Statement," James Burnham Papers, box 1, folder 1, Hoover Institution Library and Archives.

26. Burnham, "Comment," October 1933, 405.

27. Burnham, "Comment," October 1933, 413.

28. Beth Thomas Bates, *The Making of Black Detroit in the Age of Henry Ford* (Chapel Hill: University of North Carolina Press, 2012), 160.

29. Marjorie Murphy, *Blackboard Unions: The AFT and the NEA 1900–1980* (Ithaca, NY: Cornell University Press, 1990), 40–41.

30. Sidney Hook, "Radical, Teacher, Technician," *National Review*, September 11, 1987, 32. Burnham's breakup with Wheelwright would be the first of many intellectual fallouts with onetime collaborators.

31. Sidney Hook, *Out of Step* (New York: Harper and Row, 1987), 192.

32. Hook, *Out of Step*, 193.

33. American Workers Party (AWP), Statement of Programmatic Orientation, New York: The Provisional Organizing Committee of the American Workers Party, 21.

34. AWP, Statement of Programmatic Orientation, 24.

35. AWP, Statement of Programmatic Orientation, 4.

36. A. J. Muste, *The Essays of A. J. Muste*, ed. Nat Hentoff (New York: Simon and Schuster, 1970), 179–180.

37. Muste, *The Essays of A. J. Muste*, 180.

38. Muste, *The Essays of A. J. Muste*, 181.

39. In 1935, Burnham had a falling out with Muste over the best way to promote socialism in the United States. Not long after this, Muste left the socialist party.

40. Hook, *Out of Step*, 202–203.

41. Hook, *Out of Step*, 204.

42. James Cannon, *Struggle for the Proletarian Party* (New York: Pioneer, 1943), 15.

43. Hook, *Out of Step*, 203.

44. Hook, *Out of Step*, 204.

45. Daniel Kelly, *James Burnham and the Struggle for the World* (Wilmington, DE: ISI Books, 2002), 50.

46. Kelly, *James Burnham*, 50.

47. Burnham to Hook, January 11, 1949, box 8, Sidney Hook Papers, Hoover Institution Library and Archives.

48. James Burnham, "Was Europe a Success?," *The Nation*, October 3, 1934, 375.

49. Burnham, "Was Europe a Success?," October 3, 1934, 375.

50. It is worth noting that Martha Dodd's father William Dodd was appointed by Roosevelt as the American ambassador to Adolf Hitler's Germany in 1933. Martha followed him there and lived a public life as a dilettante. Burnham's relentless attacks on Roosevelt could be interpreted as attacks on the entire Roosevelt administration—and by extension Martha Dodd.

51. James Burnham, "THEIR Government," *Labor Action*, December 1, 1934, 4.

52. James Burnham, "THEIR Government," *Labor Action*, March 15, 1934, 3.

53. Burnham, "THEIR Government," March 15, 1934, 3.

54. V. I. Lenin, *What Is to Be Done?*, trans. S. V. and Patricia Utechin (Oxford: Oxford University Press, 1963), 169.

55. James Burnham, "His Place in History," review of *Lenin*, by Ralph Fox, *New Masses*, January 23, 1934, 15.

56. Burnham, "His Place in History," 15.

57. James Burnham, "THEIR Government," *Labor Action*, November 15, 1934, 5.

58. Cannon, *Struggle for the Proletarian Party*, 7-8.

59. Christopher Phelps, *Young Sidney Hook: Marxist and Pragmatist* (Ithaca, NY: Cornell University Press, 1997), 121.

60. Leon Trotsky, "How to Conduct a Political Discussion," in *The Writings of Leon Trotsky*, 2nd ed., ed. Naomi Allen and George Breitman, vol. 10 (New York: Pathfinder, 1976), 106.

61. Allan Wald, *The New York Intellectuals: The Rise and Decline of the Ant-Stalinist Left from the 1930s to the 1980s*, 2nd ed. (Chapel Hill: University of North Carolina Press, 2017), 178.

62. Joseph Stalin, "The Possibility of Building Socialism in Our Country," in *J.V. Stalin: Works*, vol. 8 (Moscow: Foreign Language Publishing House, 1954), 101-104.

63. Leon Trotsky, *The Permanent Revolution* and *Results and Prospects*, trans. John G. Wright, revised by Brian Pearce (New York: Pioneer, 1965).

64. Trotsky, *The Permanent Revolution* and *Results and Prospects*, 9.

65. James Burnham (as John West), "The Question of Organic Unity," *New International*, February 1936, 17.

66. Fearing German expansion, in 1935, the Soviets and French concluded a mutual assistance treaty. It was ratified in early 1936. Hitler used it to justify expansion into the Rhineland. The Nazi-Soviet Pact of 1939 effectively ended it.

67. See, for example, Mussolini's "Speech on Rome," March 18, 1934.

68. James Burnham (as John West), "Non-Violence," review of *The Power of Non-Violence*, by Richard B. Gregg, *New International*, December 1934, 159.

69. Burnham, "Non-Violence," 159.

70. Burnham, "Non-Violence," 159.

71. Marx did suggest at times that socialism could be ushered in peacefully in certain parts of the world. See, for example, Marx's speech in Amsterdam in September 1872.

72. James Burnham (as John West), "The Nature and Causes of Modern War," *New Militant*, January 26, 1935, 3.

73. James Burnham (as John West), "The Struggle against War," *New Militant*, February 2, 1935, 3.

74. Burnham, "The Struggle against War," 3.

75. Burnham, "The Struggle against War," 3.

76. These ideas continued Saint Augustine's just war theory. The Christian philosopher argued that if war brings peace, it is a just war.

77. Mathew Josephson, *Infidel in the Temple* (New York: Knopf, 1967), 108.

78. Cited in *The Writings of Leon Trotsky*, ed. Evelyn Reed and George Breitman, vol. 6 (New York: Pathfinder, 1969), 300.

79. Cited in *Writings of Leon Trotsky*, 300.

80. Cited in *Writings of Leon Trotsky*, 304.

81. James Burnham (as John West), "The Bands Are Playing," *New International*, July 1935, 115.

82. Both Lenin and Trotsky emphasized the importance of force and violence in the wake of the Russian Revolution. See, for example, Lenin's "The Proletarian Revolution and the Renegade Kautsky" (1918) and Trotsky's "Terror and Communism" (1920).

83. James Burnham (as John West), "War and the Workers," originally published in 1936 by the Workers Party, 4.

84. Burnham, "War and the Workers," 35.

85. Burnham, "War and the Workers," 35.

86. Burnham, "War and the Workers," 13.

87. V. I. Lenin, "Military Programme of Proletarian Revolution," in *Lenin: Collected Works*, trans. M. S. Levin (Moscow: Progress, 1964), 23: 81.

88. Lenin, "Military Programme," 81.

89. Burnham, "War and the Workers," 18.

90. Burnham, "War and the Workers," 21.

91. Burnham, "War and the Workers," 21.

92. Burnham, "War and the Workers," 16.

93. Burnham, "War and the Workers," 16.

94. Burnham, "War and the Workers," 17.

95. Burnham, "War and the Workers," 17.

96. Burnham, "War and the Workers," 17.

97. Trotsky, "How to Conduct a Political Discussion," 106.

98. Max Eastman, *Marx, Lenin and the Science of Revolution* (Westport, CT: Hyperion, 1973), 81.

99. Christopher Irmscher, *Max Eastman: A Life* (New Haven, CT: Yale University Press, 2017), 214. Both Hook and Eastman were students of John Dewey's, one of America's foremost pragmatists.

100. James Burnham (as John West), "Max Eastman's Straw Man," *New International*, December 1935, 220.

101. Browder tried to recruit Burnham to the Communist Party in 1933, but Burnham believed that US social conditions differed from those in the USSR, so different ideas and practices were required for revolution.

102. James Burnham, "Browder Defends Imperialism," *Socialist Appeal*, February 5, 1938, 4.

103. Burnham, "Browder Defends Imperialism," 4.

104. James Burnham, "Anti-Semitic Pogroms are a By-Product of Capitalism," *Socialist Appeal*, November 26, 1938, 3.

105. James Burnham (as John West), "U.S. Imperialism at Work," *New Militant*, February 15, 1936, 4.

106. Burnham, "U.S. Imperialism at Work," 4.

3. Leaving Marxism

1. Leon Trotsky, *The Revolution Betrayed: What Is the Soviet Union and Where Is It Going?* (New York: Pioneer, 1945), 8.

2. James Burnham, "From Formula to Reality," in *Neither Capitalism nor Socialism: Theories of Bureaucratic Collectivism*, ed. Ernest Haberkern (Atlantic Highlands, NJ: Humanities, 1996), 7–8.

3. Burnham, "From Formula to Reality," 8.
4. Burnham, "From Formula to Reality," 15–16.
5. Burnham, "From Formula to Reality," 16.
6. Burnham, "From Formula to Reality," 18.
7. George Breitman, ed., *The Founding of the Socialist Workers Party: Minutes and Resolutions, 1938–1939* (New York: Monad, 1982), 221–222.
8. James Burnham to Sydney Hook, August 2, 1938, box 8, Sidney Hook Papers, Hoover Institution Library and Archives.
9. Burnham to Hook, August 2, 1938.
10. Burnham to Hook, August 2, 1938.
11. Max Eastman, "Against the Marxist Dialectic," *The New Republic*, February 21, 1934, 35–39.
12. Max Eastman, "Russia and the Socialist Ideal," *Harper's Monthly Magazine*, March 1938, 374–375.
13. Eastman, "Russia and the Socialist Ideal," 376.
14. Eastman, "Russia and the Socialist Ideal," 375.
15. Eastman, "Russia and the Socialist Ideal," 378.
16. Eastman, "Russia and the Socialist Ideal," 384.
17. James Burnham, "Max Eastman as Scientist," *New International*, June 1938, 178.
18. Burnham, "Max Eastman," 178.
19. Burnham, "Max Eastman," 178.
20. Max Eastman, "Burnham Dodges," *New International*, August 1938, 244.
21. Eastman, "Burnham Dodges," 244.
22. In a private letter, Burnham panned most of the article. See "Burnham to Hook," n.d., box 8, folder 5, Sidney Hook Papers, Hoover Institution Library and Archives.
23. Sidney Hook, "Reflections on the Russian Revolution," *The Southern Review*, January 1, 1938, 431.
24. Hook, "Reflections on the Russian Revolution," 457.
25. Hook, "Reflections on the Russian Revolution," 452.
26. Hook, "Reflections on the Russian Revolution," 450.
27. Selden Rodman, "Violence, For and Against: A Symposium on Marx, Stalin and Trotsky," *Common Sense*, January 1938, 19.
28. Henry A. Wallace, "Jefferson Kept His Sense of Balance," in Rodman, "Violence, For and Against," 19.
29. Cited in Joshua Rubenstein, *Leon Trotsky, A Revolutionaries Life* (New Haven, CT: Yale University Press), 190.
30. Leon Trotsky, "Their Morals and Ours," *The New International*, June 1938, 163.
31. Trotsky, "Their Morals and Ours," 163.
32. Trotsky, "Their Morals and Ours," 172.
33. James Burnham and Max Shachtman, "Intellectuals in Retreat," *The New International*, January 1939, 3.
34. Burnham and Shachtman, "Intellectuals in Retreat," 5.
35. Burnham and Shachtman, "Intellectuals in Retreat," 4.
36. Burnham and Shachtman, "Intellectuals in Retreat," 9.

37. Burnham and Shachtman, "Intellectuals in Retreat," 13.
38. Burnham and Shachtman, "Intellectuals in Retreat," 7.
39. Burnham and Shachtman, "Intellectuals in Retreat," 8.
40. Burnham and Shachtman, "Intellectuals in Retreat," 8.
41. Leon Trotsky, "A Petty-Bourgeois Opposition in the Socialist Workers Party," in *In Defence of Marxism* (London: New Park, 1942), 60.
42. Terry A. Cooney, *The Rise of the New York Intellectuals: Partisan Review and Its Circle, 1934–1945* (Madison: University of Wisconsin Press, 1986), 50.
43. Alan Wald, *The New York Intellectuals*, 2nd ed. (Chapel Hill: University of North Carolina Press, 2017), 78.
44. Wald, *New York Intellectuals*, 78.
45. Leon Trotsky, "Art and Politics," *Partisan Review*, August–September 1938, 10.
46. With articles from Arthur Koestler and George Orwell, the magazine began to take an anticommunist stance in the mid-1940s. The journal experienced some financial difficulties in the 1950s. To help, the journal received financial assistance from the CIA, precisely when Burnham was there.
47. James Burnham, "'A Belated Dialectician,' Review of *The Marxist Philosophy and the Sciences* by J. B. S. Haldane," *Partisan Review*, Spring 1939, 120–123.
48. Burnham, "A Belated Dialectician," 121.
49. Burnham, "A Belated Dialectician," 121.
50. Burnham, "A Belated Dialectician," 122.
51. Daniel Kelly, *James Burnham and the Struggle for the World* (Wilmington, DE: ISI Books, 2002), 79.
52. Kelly, *James Burnham*, 79.
53. Kelly, *James Burnham*, 79.
54. Leon Trotsky, "The USSR in War," in *In Defence of Marxism* (London: New Park, 1942), 22–23. Trotsky's emphasis.
55. Leon Trotsky, "A Letter to Max Shachtman," in *In Defence of Marxism* (London: New Park, 1942), 51.
56. James Burnham, "On the Character of the War and the Perspective of the Fourth International," September 5, 1939, cited in *Internal Bulletin Issued by the Socialist Workers Party*, November 6, 1939, 10–11.
57. Burnham, "On the Character of the War," 10.
58. James Cannon, *Struggle for the Proletarian Party* (New York: Pioneer, 1943), 175.
59. Trotsky, "Petty-Bourgeois Opposition," 63.
60. Trotsky, "Petty-Bourgeois Opposition," 64–65.
61. Trotsky, "Petty-Bourgeois Opposition," 68.
62. Trotsky, "Petty-Bourgeois Opposition," 57.
63. Trotsky, "Petty-Bourgeois Opposition," 57.
64. Leon Trotsky, "An Open Letter to Comrade Burnham," in *In Defence of Marxism* (London: New Park, 1942), 91.
65. Trotsky, "Open Letter to Comrade Burnham," 91.
66. Trotsky, "Petty-Bourgeois Opposition," 56.
67. James Burnham, "Politics of Desperation," *New International*, April 1940, 75–80.

68. Kelly, *James Burnham*, 83.

69. John P. Diggins, *Up from Communism: Conservative Odysseys in American Intellectual History* (New York: Columbia University Press, 1993), 163.

70. James Burnham, "Science and Style: A Reply to Comrade Trotsky," in *In Defense of Marxism* (London: New York Park, 1942), 233.

71. Burnham, "Science and Style," 233–234.

72. Burnham, "Science and Style," 237.

73. Cannon, *Struggle for the Proletarian*, 242.

74. Cannon, *Struggle for the Proletarian*, 241.

75. Kelly, *James Burnham*, 85. Burnham also resigned as an editor for the short-lived *Marxist Quarterly* in 1937.

76. James Burnham, "Letter of Resignation from the Workers Party," in *In Defence of Marxism* (London: New Park, 1942), 257.

77. Burnham, "Letter of Resignation," 258.

78. Burnham, "Letter of Resignation," 261.

79. Leon Trotsky, "Balance Sheet of the Finnish Events," in *In Defence of Marxism* (London: New Park, 1942), 221.

80. Cited in Kelly, *James Burnham*, 79.

4. The New Elite

1. James Burnham, *The Managerial Revolution: What is Happening in the World?* (New York: John Day, 1941), 4.

2. Burnham, *The Managerial Revolution*, 31.

3. Burnham, *The Managerial Revolution*, 31.

4. Burnham, *The Managerial Revolution*, 31–32.

5. Burnham, *The Managerial Revolution*, 34.

6. Burnham, *The Managerial Revolution*, 32.

7. Burnham, *The Managerial Revolution*, 35.

8. Burnham, *The Managerial Revolution*, 36.

9. Burnham, *The Managerial Revolution*, 42.

10. Burnham, *The Managerial Revolution*, 82.

11. Burnham, *The Managerial Revolution*, 95.

12. Burnham, *The Managerial Revolution*, 66–67.

13. Burnham, *The Managerial Revolution*, 67.

14. Burnham, *The Managerial Revolution*, 72.

15. Burnham, *The Managerial Revolution*, 59. Burnham's description of this era is simplistic. In fact, a series of complicated arrangements characterize this era, partially depending on where in Europe one lived.

16. Burnham, *The Managerial Revolution*, 71.

17. Burnham, *The Managerial Revolution*, 137.

18. Burnham, *The Managerial Revolution*, 154.

19. Burnham, *The Managerial Revolution*, 126.

20. Burnham, *The Managerial Revolution*, 126.

21. Burnham, *The Managerial Revolution*, 133.

22. Burnham, *The Managerial Revolution*, 133.

23. Burnham, *The Managerial Revolution*, 135.
24. Burnham, *The Managerial Revolution*, 135.
25. Burnham, *The Managerial Revolution*, 190–191.
26. Burnham, *The Managerial Revolution*, 191.
27. Burnham, *The Managerial Revolution*, 155–156.
28. Burnham, *The Managerial Revolution*, 156.
29. Burnham, *The Managerial Revolution*, 147.
30. Burnham, *The Managerial Revolution*, 147.
31. Burnham, *The Managerial Revolution*, 147.
32. Leon Trotsky, *The New Course: The Struggle for the New Course*, trans. Max Shachtman (Ann Arbor: University of Michigan Press, 1965), 91–92.
33. Robert V. Daniels, *The Rise and Fall of Communism in Russia* (New Haven, CT: Yale University Press, 2007), 184.
34. Leon Trotsky, *The Revolution Betrayed: What Is the Soviet Union and Where Is It Going?* (New York: Pioneer, 1945), 93–94.
35. Leon Trotsky, "The USSR in War," in *In Defence of Marxism* (London: New Park, 1942), 10.
36. James Burnham, "From Formula to Reality," in *Neither Capitalism nor Socialism: Theories of Bureaucratic Collectivism*, ed. Ernest Haberkern (Atlantic Highlands, NJ: Humanities, 1996), 17.
37. Burnham, "From Formula to Reality," 22–23.
38. Burnham, *The Managerial Revolution*, 156.
39. Burnham, *The Managerial Revolution*, 225.
40. Burnham, *The Managerial Revolution*, 225.
41. Burnham, *The Managerial Revolution*, 225.
42. Burnham, *The Managerial Revolution*, 253.
43. Burnham, *The Managerial Revolution*, 255–256.
44. Burnham, *The Managerial Revolution*, 257.
45. Burnham, *The Managerial Revolution*, 273.
46. Burnham, *The Managerial Revolution*, 25.
47. Burnham, *The Managerial Revolution*, 161.
48. Burnham, *The Managerial Revolution*, 161.
49. Burnham, *The Managerial Revolution*, 152.
50. Burnham, *The Managerial Revolution*, 144.
51. Burnham, *The Managerial Revolution*, 167.
52. Burnham, *The Managerial Revolution*, 167.
53. Burnham, *The Managerial Revolution*, 167.
54. Burnham, *The Managerial Revolution*, 168.
55. Burnham, *The Managerial Revolution*, 168–169.
56. Burnham, *The Managerial Revolution*, 169.
57. Burnham, *The Managerial Revolution*, 170.
58. Burnham, *The Managerial Revolution*, 171.
59. Lawrence Dennis's *The Coming of Fascism to America* (New York: Harper, 1936) and Anne Lindberg's *The Wave of the Future* (New York: Harcourt Brace, 1940) are two right-wing examples. Burnham admitted reading the first and he was certainly familiar with the second.

60. Leon Trotsky, "A Petty-Bourgeois Opposition in the Socialist Workers Party," in *In Defence of Marxism* (London: New Park, 1942), 68.

61. Bruno Rizzi, *The Bureaucratization of the World* (New York: Free Press, 1985), 50.

62. See "Introduction" to *Neither Capitalism Nor Socialism*, and Daniel Bell, "The Strange Tale of Bruno R.," in *New Leader*, September 28, 1959, 19. Rizzi may have been influenced by Burnham's 1937 piece "From Formula to Reality." In this case, plagiarism is too strong a word to apply to Burnham's *The Managerial Revolution*.

63. "Letter to Silva Norkela," James Burnham Papers, box 1, folder 2, Hoover Institution Library and Archives.

64. Bell, "The Strange Tale of Bruno R.," 20.

65. "Rizzi Letter to James Burnham," James Burnham Papers, box 7, folder 21, Hoover Institution Library and Archives.

66. "Rizzi Letter to James Burnham," James Burnham Papers.

67. "Rizzi Letter to James Burnham," James Burnham Papers.

68. Daniel Kelly, *James Burnham and the Struggle for the World* (Wilmington, DE: ISI Books, 2002), 93.

69. Thorstein Veblen, *The Engineers and the Price System* (New York: Huebsch, 1921), 142.

70. Veblen expanded on this idea in *Absentee Ownership and Business Enterprise in Recent Times: The Case of America* (New York: Huebsch, 1923), a work that influenced Berle and Means.

71. Lincoln Gordon, "Review of *The Managerial Revolution: What Is Happening in the World?*, by James Burnham," *American Economic Review*, September 1942, 626.

72. Ralph Thompson, "Books of the Times," *New York Times*, May 5, 1941.

73. "Coming Rulers of the U.S.," *Fortune* 24, no. 5 (1941): 100.

74. *Time*, "The Year in Books," December 15, 1941, 108.

75. Robert Gale Woolbert, "Recent Books on International Relations," *Foreign Affairs*, January 1942, 373.

76. Dwight Macdonald, "The Burnhamian Revolution," *Partisan Review*, January 1942, 81.

77. Macdonald, "The Burnhamian Revolution," 76.

78. Macdonald, "The Burnhamian Revolution," 80.

79. Albert Gates, "Burnham and His Managers," *New International*, July 1941, 144.

80. Paul Sweezy, "The Illusion of the 'Managerial Revolution,'" *Science and Society*, January 1, 1942, 9.

81. Sweezy, "Illusion Managerial Revolution," 11.

82. Joseph Hansen, "Burnham's Managerial Revolution," *Fourth International*, June 1941, 157.

83. J. K. Galbraith, "Radical, Teacher, Technician," *National Review*, September 11, 1987, 35. Other important liberal academics who later drew from *The Managerial Revolution* include C. Wright Mills and Daniel Bell. In his review of the book, the future elite theorist Mills called Burnham a "Marx for Managers." Bell argued that the managerial revolution was merely a contradiction within capitalism, not a replacement society.

84. Peter Drucker, "The Rulers of Tomorrow," *The Saturday Review*, May 10, 1941, 9.

85. Peter Drucker, *The Future of Industrial Man* (New York: John Day, 1942), 13–14.

86. Drucker, *The Future of Industrial Man*, 144–146.

87. Ludwig von Mises, *Bureaucracy* (New Haven, CT: Yale University Press, 1944), 11.

88. von Mises, *Bureaucracy*, 12.

89. von Mises, *Bureaucracy*, 17–18.

90. von Mises, *Bureaucracy*, 64.

91. Friedrich August Hayek, "Review of *The Managerial Revolution* by James Burnham," *Economica*, November 1942, 401–402.

92. Friedrich August Hayek, *The Road to Serfdom* (London: Routledge, 2001), 227.

93. The idea of planned economies was fashionable at this time. Other popular examples that Hayek was attempting to refute include Sidney and Beatrice Webb's *Soviet Communism* (1935), Karl Manheim's *Man and Society in and Age of Reconstruction* (1940), and H. G. Wells's *The New World Order* (1940).

94. Hayek, *Road to Serfdom*, 95.

95. Karl Popper, *The Open Society and Its Enemies* (Princeton, NJ: Princeton University Press, 1950), 6.

96. James Burnham, "Is Democracy Possible?," in *Whose Revolution: A Study of the Future Course of Liberalism in the United States*, ed. Irving DeWitt Talmadge (New York: Howell, Soskin, 1941), 213.

97. Burnham, "Is Democracy Possible?," 214.

98. Burnham, "Is Democracy Possible?," 215.

99. Burnham, "Is Democracy Possible?," 217.

100. Burnham, "Is Democracy Possible?," 216.

101. Burnham, "Is Democracy Possible?," 202.

5. The Truth about the Elite

1. Burnham, now thirty-six, was married to Marcia Lightner with children. He held a 2A draft classification, exempting him from military service.

2. James Burnham, *The Machiavellians: Defenders of Freedom* (New York: John Day, 1943), 246.

3. Niccolò Machiavelli, *Discourses on Titus Livius,* trans. Ninian Hill Thomson (London: Kegan Paul, Trench & Co. 1883), 19.

4. Burnham, *The Machiavellians*, 3.

5. Burnham, *The Machiavellians*, 1.

6. Burnham, *The Machiavellians*, 20.

7. Burnham, *The Machiavellians*, 9. Leo Strauss presented similar concepts in a 1941 essay titled "Persecution and the Art of Writing." This essay argued that a hidden meaning permeated philosophical texts. Strauss distinguished between the words philosophers used and the real meaning of the text where truth was "presented exclusively between the lines." Like Burnham, Strauss exerted influence on various conservative sects—albeit precisely how and over

whom remains debated. See Paul Gottfried's *Leo Strauss and the Conservative Movement in America* (Cambridge: Cambridge University Press, 2011).
8. Burnham, *The Machiavellians*, 10.
9. Burnham, *The Machiavellians*, 24.
10. Burnham, *The Machiavellians*, 24.
11. Burnham, *The Machiavellians*, 24.
12. Burnham, *The Machiavellians*, 5.
13. Burnham, *The Machiavellians*, 25.
14. Burnham, *The Machiavellians*, 66.
15. Burnham, *The Machiavellians*, 81–82.
16. Burnham, *The Machiavellians*, 82.
17. "Letter to Silva Norkela," James Burnham Archive, box 1, folder 2, Hoover Institution Archives.
18. Burnham, *The Machiavellians*, 87.
19. Burnham, *The Machiavellians*, 88.
20. Burnham, *The Machiavellians*, 91.
21. Burnham, *The Machiavellians*, 91.
22. Burnham, *The Machiavellians*, 96.
23. Burnham, *The Machiavellians*, 97.
24. Burnham, *The Machiavellians*, 97.
25. Burnham, *The Machiavellians*, 93.
26. Burnham, *The Machiavellians*, 102.
27. Burnham, *The Machiavellians*, 102–103.
28. Burnham, *The Machiavellians*, 103–104.
29. Burnham, *The Machiavellians*, 103.
30. Burnham, *The Machiavellians*, 103.
31. Burnham, *The Machiavellians*, 104.
32. Burnham, *The Machiavellians*, 108.
33. Burnham, *The Machiavellians*, 109.
34. Burnham, *The Machiavellians*, 111.
35. Burnham, *The Machiavellians*, 111.
36. Burnham, *The Machiavellians*, 112.
37. Burnham, *The Machiavellians*, 112.
38. Burnham, *The Machiavellians*, 112.
39. Burnham, *The Machiavellians*, 113.
40. Burnham, *The Machiavellians*, 119.
41. Burnham, *The Machiavellians*, 119.
42. Burnham, *The Machiavellians*, 121.
43. Burnham, *The Machiavellians*, 121.
44. Burnham, *The Machiavellians*, 122.
45. Burnham, *The Machiavellians*, 127.
46. Burnham, *The Machiavellians*, 126–127.
47. Burnham, *The Machiavellians*, 126.
48. Burnham, *The Machiavellians*, 129.
49. Burnham, *The Machiavellians*, 129–130.
50. Burnham, *The Machiavellians*, 131.
51. Burnham, *The Machiavellians*, 131.

52. Burnham, *The Machiavellians*, 131.
53. Burnham, *The Machiavellians*, 132.
54. Burnham, *The Machiavellians*, 132.
55. Burnham, *The Machiavellians*, 135.
56. Burnham, *The Machiavellians*, 142.
57. Burnham, *The Machiavellians*, 145.
58. Burnham, *The Machiavellians*, 146.
59. Burnham, *The Machiavellians*, 159–160.
60. Burnham, *The Machiavellians*, 167–168
61. Burnham, *The Machiavellians*, 167.
62. Burnham, *The Machiavellians*, 171.
63. Burnham, *The Machiavellians*, 171.
64. Burnham, *The Machiavellians*, 172.
65. Burnham, *The Machiavellians*, 175.
66. Burnham, *The Machiavellians*, 175.
67. Burnham, *The Machiavellians*, 208.
68. Burnham, *The Machiavellians*, 209.
69. Burnham, *The Machiavellians*, 208.
70. Burnham, *The Machiavellians*, 176.
71. Burnham, *The Machiavellians*, 177.
72. Burnham, *The Machiavellians*, 176.
73. Burnham, *The Machiavellians*, 177–178.
74. Burnham, *The Machiavellians*, 177–178.
75. James Burnham, preface to second edition of *The Machiavellians: Defenders of Freedom* (New York: Gateway, 1963), xx.
76. Burnham, *The Machiavellians*, 135.
77. Burnham, *The Machiavellians*, 135.
78. Burnham, *The Machiavellians*, 135.
79. Burnham, *The Machiavellians*, 195.
80. See Murray Rothbard, *The Betrayal of the American Right* (Auburn, AL: Ludwig von Mises Institute, 2007), 167; or Michael Malice *The New Right: A Journey to the Fringe of American Politics* (New York: St. Martin's, 2019), 119.
81. Sidney Hook, "On James Burnham's *The Machiavellians*," *Society*, March 1988, 68.
82. Brian Crozier, "Activist, Strategist," *National Review*, September 11, 1987, 36.
83. Burnham, *The Machiavellians*, 236.
84. Burnham, *The Machiavellians*, 238.
85. Burnham, *The Machiavellians*, 239.
86. Burnham, *The Machiavellians*, 239.
87. Burnham, *The Machiavellians*, 244.
88. Burnham, *The Machiavellians*, 244.
89. Burnham, *The Machiavellians*, 245.
90. Machiavelli, *Discourses*, 24.
91. Burnham, *The Machiavellians*, 245.
92. Burnham, *The Machiavellians*, 246.
93. Burnham, *The Machiavellians*, 246.
94. Burnham, *The Machiavellians*, 248.

95. Burnham, *The Machiavellians*, 244. Burnham's emphasis.
96. Burnham, *The Machiavellians*, 247.
97. Burnham, *The Machiavellians*, 248.
98. Burnham, *The Machiavellians*, 248.
99. Burnham, *The Machiavellians*, 248.
100. Burnham, *The Machiavellians*, 247.
101. Burnham, *The Machiavellians*, 251.
102. Burnham, *The Machiavellians*, 249.
103. Burnham, *The Machiavellians*, 252.
104. Burnham, *The Machiavellians*, 252.
105. Burnham, *The Machiavellians*, 252.
106. Burnham, *The Machiavellians*, 69.
107. Burnham, *The Machiavellians*, 69.
108. Burnham, *The Machiavellians*, 70.
109. Burnham, *The Machiavellians*, 77.
110. Burnham, *The Machiavellians*, 77.
111. Burnham, *The Machiavellians*, 74.
112. Hook, "On James Burnham's *The Machiavellians*," 68.
113. Sidney Hook, "The Fetishism of Power," *The Nation*, May 13, 1939.
114. Hook, "The Fetishism of Power," 562.
115. Hook, "The Fetishism of Power," 562.
116. Hook, "The Fetishism of Power," 563.
117. "The Atlantic Bookshelf," *The Atlantic*, June 1943, 129.
118. Benedetto Croce, "Political Truth and Popular Myths," in *My Philosophy: Essays on the Moral and Political Problems of Our Time* (London: George Allen, 1949), 89.
119. Croce, "Political Truth and Popular Myths," 89.
120. Reinhold Niebuhr, "Study in Cynicism," *The Nation*, May 1, 1943, 637.
121. Niebuhr, "Study in Cynicism," 637.
122. "Is Democracy Possible?," *Time*, May 17, 1943, 90.

6. Samuel Francis, George Orwell, the Bureaucratic Elite, and Power

1. James Burnham, "The Federal Bureaucracy: The Fourth Branch of Government," *Human Events*, June 3, 1959, 2. Burnham's emphasis.
2. Burnham, "The Federal Bureaucracy," 2.
3. Burnham, "The Federal Bureaucracy," 2.
4. Burnham, "The Federal Bureaucracy," 2.
5. Mike Lofgren, *The Deep State* (New York: Viking, 2016), 32–33.
6. Lofgren, *The Deep State*, 33.
7. Lofgren, *The Deep State*, 36.
8. Lofgren, *The Deep State*, 14.
9. Milovan Djilas employs the concept of the "managerial revolution" in *The New Class* (San Diego, CA: Harcourt Brace, 1983), although he does not cite Burnham.
10. See Samuel Francis, *Power and History: The Political Thought of James Burnham* (Lanham, MD: University Press of America, 1984), chap. 2.

11. Patrick Buchanan, foreword to *Shots Fired: Sam Francis on America's Culture War* (Vienna, VA: Fitzgerald Griffin Foundation, 2006).
12. Howard Kurtz, "Washington Times Clips Its Right Wing," *Washington Post*, October 19, 1995, D.
13. Samuel Francis, "Crossfire of Culture Camps," *Washington Times*, September 1, 1992.
14. Samuel Francis, *Beautiful Losers: Essays on the Failures of American Conservatism* (Columbia: University of Missouri Press, 1993), 31.
15. Samuel Francis, "From Household to Nation," *Chronicles*, March 1996, 13.
16. Samuel Francis, "Principalities and Powers," *Chronicles*, November 1, 1996, 41.
17. Samuel Francis, *Leviathan and Its Enemies* (Arlington, VA: Washington Summit, 2016), 52.
18. Francis, *Leviathan and Its Enemies*, 52.
19. Francis, *Leviathan and Its Enemies*, 35.
20. Karl Marx and Friedrich Engels, "Manifesto of the Communist Party," in *Karl Marx and Friedrich Engels: Collected Works*, VI (London: Lawrence & Wishart, 1996), 482.
21. Francis, "From Household to Nation," 13.
22. Francis, "From Household to Nation," 13.
23. William Steinhoff, *George Orwell and the Origins of 1984* (Ann Arbor: University of Michigan Press, 1976), 43.
24. George Orwell, "As I Please," February 2, 1945, James Burnham Papers, box 1, folder 10, Hoover Institution Library and Archives.
25. James Burnham, "Letter to Tribune," February 19, 1944, James Burnham Papers, box 1, folder 10, Hoover Institution Library and Archives.
26. Burnham, "Letter to Tribune."
27. Burnham, "Letter to Tribune."
28. Burnham, "Letter to Tribune."
29. Burnham, "Letter to Tribune."
30. Orwell, "As I Please," cited in *Orwell, As I Please 1943–1945*, ed. Sonia Orwell and Ian Angus (Boston: Godine, 2000), 328.
31. Orwell, "As I Please," 328.
32. Orwell, "Second Thoughts on James Burnham," *Published by Polemic*, May 1946, https://www.orwell.ru/library/reviews/burnham/english/e_burnh.
33. Orwell, "Second Thoughts."
34. Orwell, "Second Thoughts."
35. Orwell, "Second Thoughts."
36. John Atkins, *George Orwell: A Literary Study* (London: Calder and Boyars, 1954), 238.
37. Orwell's emphasis. Orwell expanded on how words get used, misused, and abused in a 1946 essay titled "Politics and the English Language," *Horizon*, April 1946, 252–265.
38. George Orwell, *1984* (New York: Penguin, 1983), 182.
39. Orwell, *1984*, 182.
40. Orwell, *1984*, 183.

41. Orwell, *1984*, 183.
42. Orwell, *1984*, 183–184.
43. Orwell, *1984*, 234.
44. For other sources of Orwell's concept of power, see chapter 4 of William R. Steinhoff, *George Orwell and the Origins of 1984* (Ann Arbor: University of Michigan Press, 1975).

7. Using Power against Communism

1. Francis Sempa, "Foundation for Victory," Claremont Review of Books, March 18, 2019, https://claremontreviewofbooks.com/digital/foundation-for-victory/.
2. Robert Merry, "James Burnham: Reagan's Geopolitical Genius," *The National Interest*, June 25, 2014, https://nationalinterest.org/feature/james-burnham-reagans-geopolitical-genius-10741?page=0%2C1.
3. George H. Nash, *The Conservative Intellectual Movement in America* (New York: Basic Books, 1976), 91.
4. James Burnham, *The War We Are In* (New Rochelle, NY: Arlington House, 1967), 10.
5. John B. Diggins, *Up from Communism* (New York: Columbia University Press, 1994), 319.
6. James Burnham, "The Sixth Turn of the Communist Screw," *Partisan Review*, Summer 1944, 365.
7. ELAM was the military wing of the Greek Communist Party. While Greece was still under Axis control, the British assisted its primary opponent, the National Greek Republic League.
8. James Burnham, "Sixth Turn of the Communist Screw," 366.
9. James Burnham, "Stalin and the Junkers: The Logic of the New Line-up," *The Commonweal*, September 15, 1944, 514.
10. Burnham, "Stalin and the Junkers," 516.
11. James Burnham, "Lenin's Heir," *Partisan Review*, Winter 1945, 70.
12. Burnham, "Lenin's Heir," 72.
13. Burnham, "Lenin's Heir," 64.
14. According to Daniel Kelly, Burnham later admitted that parts of the article were a put-on. Maybe taking the piece too literally, Dwight Macdonald wrote in *Partisan Review* that the essay demonstrated Burnham's need for a father figure. First Aquinas, then Trotsky, then Hitler, and now as Hitler neared defeat, Stalin. Burnham retorted in a *Partisan Review* piece that Macdonald resembled a whiny child who complained when he did not get his way.
15. Burnham, "Lenin's Heir," 67.
16. Burnham, "Lenin's Heir," 67.
17. Burnham, "Lenin's Heir," 67.
18. James Burnham, "On Eisenstein's Mea Culpa," *New Leader*, January 4, 1947, 12.
19. Burnham, "Eisenstein's Mea Culpa," 12.
20. Burnham, "Eisenstein's Mea Culpa," 12.

21. Burnham, "Eisenstein's Mea Culpa," 12.
22. Burnham, "Eisenstein's Mea Culpa," 12.
23. Martha Dodd was by now an active communist spy. She worked for the Soviet secret police in an effort to promote communism in America. Burnham's attacks on communism may partly be interpreted as attacks on Dodd.
24. Burnham to Hook, August 19, 1946, box 8, Sidney Hook Papers, Hoover Institution Library and Archives.
25. Victor Kravchenko, *I Chose Freedom* (London: Robert Hale, 1946), 478.
26. James Burnham, *The Struggle for the World* (New York: John Day, 1947), 1.
27. Burnham, *The Struggle for the World*, 6.
28. Burnham, *The Struggle for the World*, 6.
29. Burnham, *The Struggle for the World*, 7.
30. Burnham, *The Struggle for the World*, 9.
31. Burnham, *The Struggle for the World*, 12.
32. Burnham, *The Struggle for the World*, 12.
33. Burnham, *The Struggle for the World*, 10.
34. Burnham, *The Struggle for the World*, 11.
35. Burnham, *The Struggle for the World*, 62.
36. Burnham, *The Struggle for the World*, 62.
37. Burnham, *The Struggle for the World*, 65.
38. Burnham, *The Struggle for the World*, 72.
39. Burnham, *The Struggle for the World*, 74.
40. Burnham, *The Struggle for the World*, 74.
41. Burnham, *The Struggle for the World*, 109.
42. Burnham, *The Struggle for the World*, 110.
43. Burnham, *The Struggle for the World*, 110.
44. Burnham, *The Struggle for the World*, 110.
45. Burnham, *The Struggle for the World*, 119.
46. Burnham, *The Struggle for the World*, 120.
47. Burnham, *The Struggle for the World*, 122.
48. Burnham, *The Struggle for the World*, 123.
49. Burnham, *The Struggle for the World*, 124.
50. Burnham, *The Struggle for the World*, 125.
51. Burnham, *The Struggle for the World*, 125.
52. Burnham, *The Struggle for the World*, 125.
53. Burnham, *The Struggle for the World*, 127.
54. Burnham, *The Struggle for the World*, 127–128.
55. Burnham, *The Struggle for the World*, 128–129.
56. Burnham, *The Struggle for the World*, 128.
57. Burnham, *The Struggle for the World*, 141.
58. Burnham, *The Struggle for the World*, 141.
59. Burnham, *The Struggle for the World*, 142.
60. Burnham, *The Struggle for the World*, 143.
61. Burnham, *The Struggle for the World*, 143.
62. Burnham, *The Struggle for the World*, 181.
63. Burnham, *The Struggle for the World*, 189.
64. Burnham, *The Struggle for the World*, 8.

65. Burnham, *The Struggle for the World*, 178.
66. Burnham, *The Struggle for the World*, 178.
67. Burnham, *The Struggle for the World*, 182.
68. Burnham, *The Struggle for the World*, 53.
69. Burnham, *The Struggle for the World*, 212.
70. Burnham, *The Struggle for the World*, 213–214.
71. Burnham, *The Struggle for the World*, 187–188.
72. Burnham, *The Struggle for the World*, 188.

73. As Burnham would have noted, terms must be defined. What makes someone a neoconservative must be clarified for anyone making an argument. Certainly, neoconservatives recommend an activist US foreign policy to promote and protect democracy. But there is more to neoconservatism than this. Burnham critiques other aspects of neoconservatism in a May 12, 1972 *National Review* article titled "Selective, Yes. Huamnism, Maybe."

74. Burnham, *The Struggle for the World*, 230.
75. Burnham, *The Struggle for the World*, 229.
76. Burnham, *The Struggle for the World*, 229.
77. Burnham, *The Struggle for the World*, 229.
78. Burnham, *The Struggle for the World*, 212.

79. Daniel Kelly, *James Burnham and the Struggle for the World* (Wilmington, DE: ISI Books, 2002), 393, n33.

80. Burnham, *The Struggle for the World*, 239–240.
81. Burnham, *The Struggle for the World*, 240.
82. Burnham, *The Struggle for the World*, 240.
83. Burnham, *The Struggle for the World*, 240.
84. Burnham, *The Struggle for the World*, 240–241.
85. Burnham, *The Struggle for the World*, 243.
86. Burnham, *The Struggle for the World*, 244.
87. Burnham, *The Struggle for the World*, 244.
88. Burnham, *The Struggle for the World*, 244.
89. Burnham, *The Struggle for the World*, 35.
90. Burnham, *The Struggle for the World*, 243.
91. Burnham, *The Struggle for the World*, 244.
92. Burnham, *The Struggle for the World*, 244–245.
93. Burnham, *The Struggle for the World*, 245.
94. Burnham, *The Struggle for the World*, 245–246.
95. Burnham, *The Struggle for the World*, 246.
96. Burnham, *The Struggle for the World*, 246.
97. Burnham, *The Struggle for the World*, 246.
98. Burnham, *The Struggle for the World*, 244–245.
99. Burnham, *The Struggle for the World*, 223.
100. Kelly, *James Burnham*, 129.

101. Roughly the same percentage of Americans perished in World War II as have died from COVID-19 between 2020 and 2024.

102. Former Soviet Ambassador William C. Bullitt's *The Great Globe Itself* (New York: Scribner, 1946), Kennan's "long telegram" (more in note 110) and John Foster Dulles's two articles in *Life* magazine titled "Thoughts on Soviet

Foreign Policy and What to Do About It" are some examples that Burnham was familiar with. Dean Acheson stated that the United States was not ready for world leadership, Ambassador Averell Harriman argued that the Soviet economy was weak, and Secretary of State James F. Byrnes demanded a US monopoly of nuclear weapons before Burnham's book.

103. Andrew Swanberg, *Luce and His Empire* (New York: Scribner, 1972), 254.

104. "The Truman-Burnham Parallel," *Christian Century*, June 4, 1947, 702.

105. *Life Magazine*, March 31, 1937, 52–80.

106. Swanberg, *Luce and His Empire*, 254.

107. *New York Times*, Best Seller List, April 20, 1947, Non-Fiction.

108. Louis Menand, *The Free World: Art and Thought in the Cold War* (New York: Farrar, Straus and Giroux, 2021), 9.

109. Menand, *The Free World*, 9.

110. George Kennan, "Long Telegram," February 22, 1946, https://digitalarchive.wilsoncenter.org/document/116178.pdf.

111. Sarah-Jane Corke, *US Covert Operations and Cold War Strategy: Truman, Secret Warfare and the CIA, 1945–1953* (New York: Routledge, 2007), 193, n95.

112. Corke, *US Covert Operations*, 193, n95. Burnham would later skewer Bohlen and Davies while writing for *The Freeman*. More in chapter 9.

113. John Lewis Gaddis, *George Kennan* (New York: Penguin, 2011), 258–259.

114. George Orwell, "Burnham's View of the Contemporary Struggle," cited in *The Collected Essays, Journalism and Letter of George Orwell*, 1945–1950, vol. 4, ed. Sonia Orwell and Ian Angus (New York: Harcourt Brace, 1968), 313.

115. Orwell, "Burnham's View," 317.

116. Orwell, "Burnham's View," 317.

117. Orwell, "Burnham's View," 324.

118. Orwell, "Burnham's View," 325.

119. Orwell, "Burnham's View," 325.

120. Arthur Schlesinger, "World War III," *The Nation*, April 5, 1947, 398.

121. Schlesinger, "World War III," 398.

122. Arthur Schlesinger, *The Vital Center* (Brunswick, NJ: Transaction, 2018), 236.

123. Schlesinger, *The Vital Center*, 236.

124. Schlesinger, *The Vital Center*, 239.

125. Schlesinger, *The Vital Center*, 240.

126. Joseph Romano, "James Burnham in France: The Export-Import of the 'Managerial Revolution' after 1945," *Revue française de science politique* 53, no. 2 (April 2003): 261.

127. Romano, "James Burnham in France," 261.

128. Michael Curtis, "Raymond Aron and *La France libre*," in *Political Reason in the Age of Ideology: Essays in Honor of Raymond Aron*, ed. Bryan-Paul Frost and Daniel J. Mahoney (New York: Routledge, 2007), 168.

129. Carlos Gasper, "Raymond Aron and the Origins of the Cold War," in *Political Reason in the Age of Ideology*, 179.

130. Gasper, "Raymond Aron and the Origins," 184.

131. Andre Malraux and James Burnham, *The Case for De Gaulle: A Dialogue Between Andre Malraux and James Burnham* (New York: Random House, 1948), 45.

132. Malraux and Burnham, *Case for De Gaulle*, 46.
133. Malraux and Burnham, *Case for De Gaulle*, 43.
134. Malraux and Burnham, *Case for De Gaulle*, 53.
135. Burnham, "What Is the Purpose of the United Nations?," *ANNALS of the American Academy of Political and Social Science*, July 1947, 1.
136. Burnham, "What Is the Purpose," 2.
137. Burnham, "What Is the Purpose," 7.
138. Burnham, "What Is the Purpose," 7.
139. Burnham, "What Is the Purpose," 8. The United Nations was a Cold War battleground almost from the outset. An early proxy war occurred over Iran. During World War II, the British, Americans, and Soviets stationed troops there. After World War II, the British and Americans left per an agreement, but Soviet troops remained. Iran demanded a UN investigation. Soviet representative to the UN Andrei Gromyko used procedural maneuvers to delay the process.
140. Burnham, "What Is the Purpose," 10.
141. Hearings on Proposed Legislation to Curb or Control the Communist Party of the United States: Hearings, US Government Printing Office, 1948, 380.
142. Hearings on Proposed Legislation, 380.
143. John Parnell Thomas, Hearings Regarding the Communist Infiltration of the Motion Picture Industry: Hearings Before the Committee on Un-American Activities, House of Representatives, Eightieth Congress, First Session, Public Law 601 (section 121, subsection Q(2)), US Government Printing Office, 1947, 217.

8. A Strategy for Liberation

1. Daniel Kelly, *James Burnham and the Struggle for the World* (Wilmington, DE: ISI Books, 2002), 138.
2. "Burnham to Hook," January 11, 1949, Sidney Hook Papers, box 8, folder 5, Hoover Institution Library and Archives.
3. "Burnham to Hook," January 11, 1949.
4. James Burnham, *The Coming Defeat of Communism* (New York: John Day, 1950), 9.
5. See, for example, Lenin's "The Latest Word in Bundist Nationalism," in *Lenin: Collected Works*, VI (Moscow: Progress, 1903), 518.
6. Burnham, *The Coming Defeat of Communism*, 2.
7. Burnham, *The Coming Defeat of Communism*, 17–18.
8. Burnham, *The Coming Defeat of Communism*, 28.
9. Burnham, *The Coming Defeat of Communism*, 29.
10. Burnham, *The Coming Defeat of Communism*, 34.
11. Burnham, *The Coming Defeat of Communism*, 34.
12. Burnham, *The Coming Defeat of Communism*, 21. A February 1948 communist coup in Czechoslovakia was followed by purges and restrictions of basic rights, such as competitive elections. The coup helped inspire passage of the Marshall Plan. Two months after the coup, President Truman put into effect

a trade agreement that was arranged before the coup. It involved basic home goods, clothes, and food. Burnham was not alone in his criticism.

13. Burnham, *The Coming Defeat of Communism*, 23.
14. Burnham, *The Coming Defeat of Communism*, 24.
15. Burnham, *The Coming Defeat of Communism*, 27.
16. Burnham, *The Coming Defeat of Communism*, 27.
17. Burnham, *The Coming Defeat of Communism*, 36–37.
18. Burnham, *The Coming Defeat of Communism*, 36.
19. After reading Lippmann's work, Kennan came to believe that he overstated his case for US intervention through the policy of containment.
20. Walter Lippmann, *The Cold War* (New York: Harper, 1947), 16–17. Burnham stressed the importance of ideology and the Red Army. He related to the two in "Stalin and the Junkers: The Logic of the New Line-up," *The Commonweal*, September 15, 1944.
21. Lippmann, *The Cold War*, 18–19.
22. Lippmann, *The Cold War*, 33–34.
23. Lippmann, *The Cold War*, 61.
24. Lippmann, *The Cold War*, 61.
25. Burnham, *The Coming Defeat of Communism*, 44.
26. Burnham, *The Coming Defeat of Communism*, 44.
27. Burnham, *The Coming Defeat of Communism*, 44.
28. Burnham, *The Coming Defeat of Communism*, 58.
29. Burnham, *The Coming Defeat of Communism*, 136.
30. Burnham, *The Coming Defeat of Communism*, 107.
31. Burnham, *The Coming Defeat of Communism*, 110.
32. Burnham, *The Coming Defeat of Communism*, 130.
33. Burnham, *The Coming Defeat of Communism*, 146.
34. Burnham, *The Coming Defeat of Communism*, 132.
35. Burnham, *The Coming Defeat of Communism*, 133.
36. Burnham, *The Coming Defeat of Communism*, 140.
37. Burnham, *The Coming Defeat of Communism*, 23.
38. Burnham, *The Coming Defeat of Communism*, 145.
39. Burnham, *The Coming Defeat of Communism*, 146–147.
40. Burnham, *The Coming Defeat of Communism*, 147.
41. Burnham, *The Coming Defeat of Communism*, 24.
42. Burnham, *The Coming Defeat of Communism*, 148.
43. Burnham, *The Coming Defeat of Communism*, 165.
44. Burnham, *The Coming Defeat of Communism*, 165.
45. Burnham, *The Coming Defeat of Communism*, 169.
46. Burnham, *The Coming Defeat of Communism*, 169.
47. Burnham, *The Coming Defeat of Communism*, 177.
48. Burnham, *The Coming Defeat of Communism*, 177.
49. George Kennan, "The Inauguration of Organized Political Warfare," National Archives and Records Administration, Record group 59, entry A1 558-B, Policy Planning Staff/Council, Subject files, 1947–1962, box 28, https://digitalarchive.wilsoncenter.org/document/208714.pdf?v=0dcd3b6b5638d938 57f6ba75cee7c0cf.

50. Kennan, "Inauguration of Organized Political Warfare," memorandum, April 1948.
51. Kennan, "Inauguration of Organized Political Warfare."
52. Burnham, *The Coming Defeat of Communism*, 150.
53. Burnham, *The Coming Defeat of Communism*, 152.
54. Burnham, *The Coming Defeat of Communism*, 152.
55. Burnham, *The Coming Defeat of Communism*, 153.
56. Burnham, *The Coming Defeat of Communism*, 152-153.
57. Burnham, *The Coming Defeat of Communism*, 151.
58. Burnham, *The Coming Defeat of Communism*, 153-154.
59. Burnham, *The Coming Defeat of Communism*, 154.
60. Burnham, *The Coming Defeat of Communism*, 154.
61. Burnham, *The Coming Defeat of Communism*, 154.
62. Burnham, *The Coming Defeat of Communism*, 227.
63. Burnham, *The Coming Defeat of Communism*, 227.
64. Burnham, *The Coming Defeat of Communism*, 254.
65. Burnham, *The Coming Defeat of Communism*, 255.
66. Burnham, *The Coming Defeat of Communism*, 272-273.
67. Burnham, *The Coming Defeat of Communism*, 275.
68. Burnham, *The Coming Defeat of Communism*, 273-274.
69. Burnham, *The Coming Defeat of Communism*, 278.
70. The initial divide was between reform-minded communists led by Mikhail Gorbachev and hardliners who resisted change, such as Erich Honecker.
71. Pope John Paul II, in particular, inspired anticommunist forces in Poland. It is not a coincidence that the first popular protests and free elections that brought down a communist regime occurred in Eastern Europe's most Catholic country.
72. Numerous Soviet sources suggest that the US military buildup in the early 1980s helped provoke reform by showing how far the Soviets lagged in the arms race. Always a key component in determining who was winning the Cold War, Soviet failures in this area showed that change was needed. Other issues that inspired reforms include Soviet military failure in Afghanistan, a stagnated economy and rising discontent among satellite states.
73. Christian F. Ostermann, *Between Containment and Rollback: The United States and Cold War History* (Stanford, CA: Stanford University Press, 2021), 169.
74. Stefan Creuzberger, *Kampf für die Einheit: Das gesamtdeutsche Ministerium und die Politische Kultur des Kalten Krieges 1949-1969* (Düsseldorf: Droste Verlag, 2008), 53.
75. Cited in Benjamin Tromly, *Cold War Exiles and the CIA: Plotting to Free Russia* (Oxford: Oxford University Press, 2019), 279.
76. Tromly, *Cold War Exiles and the CIA*, 281.
77. Franklin Burdette, "Review of *The Coming Defeat of Communism* by James Burnham," *Social Science* 25, no. 4 (October 1950): 269.
78. John P. Diggins, *Up from Communism* (New York: Columbia University Press, 1994), 12.
79. Charles Poore, "Books of the Times," review of *The Coming Defeat of Communism* by James Burnham, *New York Times*, February 16, 1950, 21.

80. James Reston, "A Chart for Taming the Russians," review of *The Coming Defeat of Communism* by James Burnham, *New York Times*, February 19, 1950, Section BR.

81. "Talk with James Burnham," *New York Times*, February 26, 1950, Section BR.

82. A 2000 book argued that Kennan favored rollback, too. See Peter Grose, *Operation Rollback: America's Secret War Behind the Iron Curtain* (Boston: Houghton Mifflin, 2000).

83. "Burnham versus Kennan," *Washington Post*, March 25, 1950.

84. "Burnham versus Kennan."

85. Paul Nitze, *From Hiroshima to Glasnost: At the Center of the Decision* (New York: Grove Weidenfeld, 1989), 93.

86. National Security Council Report 68 (NSC-68), Report to the National Security Council by the Executive Secretary on United States Objectives and Programs for National Security, April 11, 1950, https://digitalarchive.wilsoncenter.org/document/116191.pdf?v=2699956db534c1821edefa61b8c13ffe.

87. NSC-68.

88. NSC-68.

89. Editorial, "For the Sake of Koreans," *New York Times*, July 1, 1950.

90. Townsend Hoopes, *The Devil and John Foster Dulles* (Boston: Little, Brown, 1973), 118.

91. Hoopes, *Devil and John Foster Dulles*, 118.

92. John Foster Dulles, *War or Peace* (New York: Macmillan, 1950), 2.

93. Dulles, *War or Peace*, 32.

94. Dulles, *War or Peace*, 162.

9. Thought and Action

1. Daniel Kelly, *James Burnham and the Struggle for the World* (Wilmington, DE: ISI Books, 2002), 138. It would become a permanent leave.

2. Kelly, *James Burnham*, 151.

3. Kelly, *James Burnham*, 152.

4. Kelly, *James Burnham*, 152.

5. Kelly, *James Burnham*, 154.

6. CIA, "Project Outline," QKDROOP, August 28, 1950, 7, https://www.cia.gov/readingroom/docs/QKDROOP_0001.pdf.

7. CIA, "Project Outline," 8.

8. CIA, "Project Outline," 7.

9. "Catholic Jubilee Year," December 1, 1949, James Burnham Papers, box 11, folder 1, Hoover Institution Library and Archives.

10. Anne Applebaum, *Iron Curtain* (New York: Knopf Doubleday, 2013), 303.

11. "The 35th Anniversary of Lenin's Death, December 6, 1949, James Burnham Papers, box 11, folder 1, Hoover Institution Library and Archives.

12. "Lenin's Anniversary," December 8, 1949, James Burnham Papers, box 11, folder 1, Hoover Institution Library and Archives.

13. "Cartoons," December 8, 1949, James Burnham Papers, box 11, folder 1, Hoover Institution Library and Archives.

14. Niccolò Machiavelli, *Discourses on Livy* (New York: Open Road Media, 2020), 249.

15. Miles Copeland, "Activist, Strategist," *National Review*, September 11, 1987, 37. Roosevelt makes no mention of Burnham in his *Countercoup: The Struggle for Control of Iran* (New York: McGraw Hill, 1979).

16. Kelly, *James Burnham*, 183.

17. Kelly, *James Burnham*, 183-184.

18. Kelly, *James Burnham*, 184.

19. "Psychological Warfare in China," December 13, 1949, James Burnham Papers, box 11, folder 1, Hoover Institution Library and Archives.

20. "Psychological Warfare in China."

21. "Psychological Warfare in China."

22. James Burnham, "Psychological Warfare or Else," James Burnham Papers, box 2, folder 18, Hoover Institution Library Archives.

23. Burnham, "Psychological Warfare or Else."

24. Burnham, "Psychological Warfare or Else."

25. Burnham, "Psychological Warfare or Else."

26. Burnham, "Psychological Warfare or Else."

27. CIA, "Information Report on Cultural and Scientific Conference for World Peace," May 2, 1949, https://www.cia.gov/readingroom/docs/CIA-RDP80-00926A001100030004-4.pdf.

28. CIA, "Information Report."

29. CIA, "Information Report."

30. CIA, "Information Report."

31. CIA, "Information Report."

32. Cited in Sarah Miller Harris, *CIA and the Congress for Cultural Freedom* (New York: Routledge, 2018), 68.

33. Cited in Harris, *CIA and the Congress*, 69.

34. James Burnham, "Rhetoric and Peace," *Partisan Review*, November-December 1950, 861.

35. Burnham, "Rhetoric and Peace," 863.

36. Burnham, "Rhetoric and Peace," 863.

37. Burnham, "Rhetoric and Peace," 866.

38. Burnham, "Rhetoric and Peace," 868.

39. Kelly, *James Burnham*, 134.

40. James Burnham, "Philosophy of Communism," *Naval War College Information Service for Officers*, March 1952, 73-75.

41. Burnham, "Philosophy of Communism," 77.

42. James Burnham, *Containment or Liberation: An Inquiry into the Aims of United States Foreign Policy* (New York: John Day, 1953), 31.

43. Burnham, *Containment or Liberation*, 31.

44. Burnham, *Containment or Liberation*, 34.

45. Burnham, *Containment or Liberation*, 34-35.

46. Burnham, *Containment or Liberation*, 61.

47. Burnham, *Containment or Liberation*, 64.

48. Burnham, *Containment or Liberation*, 65.

49. Burnham, *Containment or Liberation*, 68.
50. Burnham, *Containment or Liberation*, 69.
51. Burnham, *Containment or Liberation*, 70.
52. Burnham, *Containment or Liberation*, 80.
53. Burnham, *Containment or Liberation*, 98.
54. Burnham, *Containment or Liberation*, 95.
55. Burnham, *Containment or Liberation*, 112.
56. Burnham, *Containment or Liberation*, 112.
57. Burnham, *Containment or Liberation*, 183.
58. Burnham, *Containment or Liberation*, 185.
59. Burnham, *Containment or Liberation*, 189.
60. Burnham, *Containment or Liberation*, 189.
61. Burnham, *Containment or Liberation*, 192-193. The US Air Force helped thousands of stranded Muslims in Beirut reach Mecca in 1952.
62. Burnham, *Containment or Liberation*, 191.
63. Burnham, *Containment or Liberation*, 208.
64. Burnham, *Containment or Liberation*, 208.
65. Burnham, *Containment or Liberation*, 217.
66. Burnham, *Containment or Liberation*, 217.
67. Burnham, *Containment or Liberation*, 218.
68. George Kennan, "The Sources of Soviet Conduct," *Foreign Affairs*, July 1947, 582.
69. George F. Kennan, "Preparedness as Part of Foreign Relations," Armed Services Committee Washington, DC, January 8, 1948.
70. V. I. Lenin, "Letter to Central Committee Members," October 24, 1917.
71. Burnham, *Containment or Liberation*, 220.
72. Burnham, *Containment or Liberation*, 222.
73. Burnham, *Containment or Liberation*, 225.
74. Burnham, *Containment or Liberation*, 225.
75. Burnham, *Containment or Liberation*, 226. Burnham spent much time trying to help organize the American-sponsored The Free Europe College in the early 1950s. See box 9, folder 2 for a host of his recommendations to leaders at the university.
76. Burnham, *Containment or Liberation*, 227.
77. Burnham, *Containment or Liberation*, 240-241.
78. Burnham, *Containment or Liberation*, 242.
79. James Burnham, "Can America Liberate the World?," *This Week Magazine*, February 8, 1953; James Burnham Papers, box 1, folder 8, Hoover Institution Library and Archives.
80. Burnham was referring to the Egyptian Revolution and the Iraqi intifada, both in 1952.
81. Burnham, "Can America Liberate the World?"
82. Burnham, "Can America Liberate the World?"
83. Burnham, "Can America Liberate the World?"
84. Arthur Schlesinger Jr., "Middle Aged Man with a Horn," *New Republic*, March 16, 1953, 17. Burnham was in the process of having a falling out with the Harvard historian over the issue of Joseph McCarthy. More later in this chapter.

85. George F. Kennan, *Memoirs 1950–1963* (Boston: Little, Brown, 1972), 100.
86. "Nomination of Charles E. Bohlen," March 2, 1953, US Senate Committee on Foreign Relations.
87. CIA Deputies Meeting, February 26, 1953, https://www.cia.gov/readingroom/docs/CIA-RDP80B01676R002300120032-1.pdf.
88. Martha Dodd and her husband Alfred K. Stern were two figures accurately accused of communism by McCarthy. This may help explain why Burnham refused to condemn the senator.
89. James Burnham, "Editor Meets Senator," *The Freeman*, June 15, 1953, 661.
90. Sidney Hook, *Out of Step* (New York: Harper and Row, 1987), 422.
91. Kelly, *James Burnham*, 190.
92. Kelly, *James Burnham*, 187.
93. Kelly, *James Burnham*, 189.
94. John P. Diggins, *Up from Communism* (New York: Columbia University Press, 1994), 328.
95. Diggins, *Up from Communism*, 328.
96. James Burnham, "A Letter of Resignation," *Partisan Review*, November–December 1953, 716.
97. Burnham, "Letter of Resignation," 716.
98. Burnham, "Letter of Resignation," 716.
99. Diggins, *Up from Communism*, 328.
100. Kelly, *James Burnham*, 192.
101. Kelly, *James Burnham*, 204.
102. Kelly, *James Burnham*, 204.
103. James Burnham, *Web of Subversion* (New York: John Day, 1954), 19.
104. Burnham, *Web of Subversion*, 15, 18–19.
105. Burnham, *Web of Subversion*, 18.
106. Burnham, *Web of Subversion*, 19–20.
107. Burnham, *Web of Subversion*, 20.
108. Burnham, *Web of Subversion*, 20.
109. Burnham, *Web of Subversion*, 22.
110. Burnham, *Web of Subversion*, 36.
111. Burnham, *Web of Subversion*, 36–37.
112. Burnham, *Web of Subversion*, 71.
113. Burnham, *Web of Subversion*, 72.
114. Burnham, *Web of Subversion*, 160.
115. Burnham, *Web of Subversion*, 71.
116. Burnham, *Web of Subversion*, 75.
117. Burnham, *Web of Subversion*, 139–140.
118. Burnham, *Web of Subversion*, 169.
119. Burnham, *Web of Subversion*, 224. Racism has been described in the same way by scholars. See María del Carmen Salazar and Jessica Lerner, *Teacher Evaluation as Cultural Practice: A Framework for Equity and Excellence* (New York: Routledge, 2019), chap. 3; or Malcolm Cross and Michael Keith, eds., *Racism, the City and the State* (New York: Routledge, 1993), 207.
120. See, for example, Cotton Mather, *More Wonders of the Invisible World* (1693).
121. Burnham, *Web of Subversion*, 219.

122. Burnham, *Web of Subversion*, 219.
123. Burnham, *Web of Subversion*.
124. Schlesinger, "Freedom's Enemies," *The Saturday Review*, March 20, 1954, 16.
125. Schlesinger, "Freedom's Enemies," 16.
126. Irving Kristol, "Web of Realism," *Commentary*, June 1954, 609.
127. Kristol, "Web of Realism," 610.
128. Kristol, "Web of Realism," 610.
129. James Burnham, "Was Bohlen a Blunder?," *The Freeman*, May 4, 1953, 551–552.
130. James Burnham, "How the IPR Helped Stalin Seize China," *The Freeman*, June 30, 1952, 645–650.
131. James Burnham, "No Firecrackers Allowed," *The Freeman*, October 1955, 684.
132. Burnham, "No Firecrackers Allowed," 686.

10. *National Review, Congress and the American Tradition*, and *Suicide of the West*

1. "Publisher's Statement," *National Review*, November 19, 1955, 5–7.
2. That does not mean it tolerated all right-wing voices. With Burnham's support, Buckley generally excluded John Birchers and Ayn Randians.
3. William F. Buckley, "James Burnham," *National Review*, September 11, 1987, 31.
4. James Burnham, "Down Stalin, Up Lenin, ? ? Trotsky," *National Review*, July 25, 1956, 8.
5. James Burnham (unsigned), "End the Masquerade," *National Review*, July 18, 1956, 5.
6. Burnham, "End the Masquerade," 5.
7. Anne Applebaum, *Iron Curtain* (New York: Knopf Doubleday, 2013), 460.
8. Daniel Kelly, *James Burnham and the Struggle for the World* (Wilmington, DE: ISI Books, 2002), 232.
9. James Burnham, "The Week," *National Review*, November 24, 1956, 3.
10. James Burnham, "The Week," *National Review*, December 8, 1956, 3.
11. James Burnham, *Suicide of the West: An Essay on the Meaning and Destiny of Liberalism* (New York: John Day, 1964), 306.
12. James Burnham (unsigned), "Earthquake at Suez," *National Review*, August 11, 1956, 4.
13. Burnham, "Earthquake at Suez," 4.
14. Burnham, "Earthquake at Suez," 4.
15. Burnham, "The Third World War," *National Review*, November 26, 1955, 20. The 1955 Baghdad Pact, an alliance between Turkey, Iraq, Iran, Pakistan, and the United Kingdom, helped trigger the arms sale. It was designed to counter Soviet influence in the region, but Egypt interpreted the pact as aggressive.
16. Burnham, "The Third World War," 20.
17. James Burnham, "Abstractions Kill the West," *National Review*, December 8, 1956, 6.
18. Burnham, "Abstractions Kill the West," 6.

19. Burnham, "Abstractions Kill the West," 6.
20. Lippman had made a similar proposal in 1947. Kennan would too.
21. James Burnham, "Sighting the Target," *National Review*, December 29, 1956, 12.
22. The description of the conflict between Burnham and Schlamm is based on Daniel Kelly's account in *James Burnham*, 234-236.
23. James Burnham, "Disinformation Bureaus," *National Review*, November 30, 1957, 488.
24. Burnham, "Disinformation Bureaus," 488.
25. James Burnham, "The Burnt Child Jumps Into the Fire," *National Review*, October 5, 1957, 300.
26. James Burnham, "Words East and West," in *The War We Are In: The Last Decade and the Next* (New Rochelle, NY: Arlington House, 1967), 263.
27. James Burnham, "Horns of a Nuclear Dilemma," *National Review*, August 31, 1957, 187.
28. Burnham, "Horns of a Nuclear Dilemma," 187.
29. Burnham, "Horns of a Nuclear Dilemma," 187.
30. Burnham, "Horns of a Nuclear Dilemma," 189.
31. Burnham, "Horns of a Nuclear Dilemma," 189.
32. Burnham wrote a 1962 piece for *NR* that scolded then-ambassador Galbraith for not representing American interests. Like Schlesinger, Burnham and Galbraith were one-time friends. Galbraith sent Burnham a get-well note after a stroke in the late 1970s.
33. Galbraith to Burnham, August 6, 1971, James Burnham Papers, box 6, folder 27, Hoover Institution Library and Archives.
34. John Kenneth Galbraith, *The New Industrial State* (New York: Penguin, 1991), 126-127, n5.
35. James Burnham, "Books in Brief," *National Review*, May 3, 1959, 430.
36. Burnham was not alone in his criticism at this point. Kennan's lectures may have been widely reported, but that does not mean that the contents were widely supported.
37. James Burnham (unsigned), "At Home," *National Review Bulletin*, December 13, 1958, 4. Kennan had to have known that Burnham wrote this unsigned piece.
38. George Kennan, "Letter to the Editor," *National Review Bulletin*, December 27, 1958, 2.
39. George Kennan, "Draft of Unused Letter to Mr. W. Buckley," April 11, 1960, George F. Kennan Papers. 1861-2014, Series 4, writings 1879-2004, subseries 4D, Major Unused Drafts, box 241, folder 21, Mudd Library, Princeton, NJ.
40. Kennan, "Draft of Unused Letter."
41. Burnham adopted this concept from Oswald Spengler who predicted the rise of "Caesarism" in *The Decline of the West* (New York: Knopf, 1926).
42. James Burnham, *Congress and the American Tradition* (Chicago: Henry Regnery, 1959), 23.
43. Burnham, *Congress and the American Tradition*, 23.
44. Burnham, *Congress and the American Tradition*, 23.

45. Burnham, *Congress and the American Tradition*, 25.
46. Burnham, *Congress and the American Tradition*, 36.
47. Burnham, *Congress and the American Tradition*, 34.
48. Burnham, *Congress and the American Tradition*, 127.
49. Burnham, *Congress and the American Tradition*, 130.
50. Burnham, *Congress and the American Tradition*, 150.
51. Burnham, *Congress and the American Tradition*, 54.
52. Burnham, *Congress and the American Tradition*, 157.
53. Burnham, *Congress and the American Tradition*, 160.
54. Burnham, *Congress and the American Tradition*, 163.
55. Burnham, *Congress and the American Tradition*, 29.
56. Burnham, *Congress and the American Tradition*, 61.
57. Burnham, *Congress and the American Tradition*, 120.
58. Burnham, *Congress and the American Tradition*, 221.
59. Burnham, *Congress and the American Tradition*, 223–224.
60. Burnham, *Congress and the American Tradition*, 224.
61. Burnham, *Congress and the American Tradition*, 234.
62. Burnham, *Congress and the American Tradition*, 252.
63. Burnham, *Congress and the American Tradition*, 234–235.
64. Burnham, *Congress and the American Tradition*, 333.
65. Burnham, *Congress and the American Tradition*, 333–334.
66. Burnham, *Congress and the American Tradition*, 334.
67. Burnham, *Congress and the American Tradition*, 336.
68. Burnham, *Congress and the American Tradition*, 335.
69. Burnham, *Congress and the American Tradition*, 336.
70. Burnham, *Congress and the American Tradition*, 349.
71. Burnham, *Congress and the American Tradition*, 344.
72. Burnham, *Congress and the American Tradition*, 344.
73. Samuel Francis, "Burnham Agonistes," *Chronicles: A Magazine of American Culture*, July 2002.
74. James Burnham, "The Dulles Record: An Appraisal," *National Review*, May 9, 1959, 44.
75. Burnham, "Dulles Record: An Appraisal," 44.
76. Burnham, "Dulles Record: An Appraisal," 44.
77. James Burnham, "A Foreign Policy for the Republican Party," in *The War We Are In*, 124.
78. Burnham, "Foreign Policy for the Republican Party," 124.
79. Burnham, "Foreign Policy for the Republican Party," 126.
80. Burnham, "Foreign Policy for the Republican Party," 126.
81. James Burnham, "Needed: A Blow," *National Review*, April 22, 1961, 248.
82. Burnham, "Needed: A Blow," 248.
83. Burnham, "Who Gives a Whoop?," *National Review*, April 9, 1963, 279.
84. James Burnham, "The Choking Point," *National Review*, March 27, 1962, 203.
85. Burnham, "Choking Point," 203.
86. Burnham, "Who Gives a Whoop?," 279.
87. James Burnham, "Can't Make a Policy without Breaking Some Eggheads," *National Review*, February 26, 1963, 141.

88. In early April 1961, the State Department released a pamphlet about Cuba. It was extensively revised by Schlesinger and contended "we are confident that the Cuban people, with their passion for liberty, will continue to strive for a free Cuba." US Department of State, Office of the Historian, Foreign Relations of the United States, 1961–1963, vol. X, Cuba, January 1961–September 1962, https://history.state.gov/historicaldocuments/frus1961-63v10/d79.

89. Burnham, "Can't Make a Policy," 141.

90. James Burnham, "What Lessons, What Profit?," *National Review*, May 6, 1961, 276.

91. Burnham, "What Lessons," 82.

92. James Burnham, "On the Horns of Our Dilemma," *National Review*, October 21, 1961, 265.

93. James Burnham, "The Gentle Khrushchev," *National Review*, December 31, 1962, 505.

94. James Burnham, "Turn of the Kaleidoscope," *National Review*, February 26, 1963, 154.

95. Burnham, "Turn of the Kaleidoscope," 154.

96. James Burnham (unsigned), *National Review Bulletin*, December 10, 1963, 1.

97. James Burnham, "Operation Will-o'the-Wisp," *National Review* supplement, November 5, 1960, 6.

98. Burnham, "Operation Will-o'the-Wisp," 8.

99. Burnham, "Operation Will-o'the-Wisp," 8.

100. Lee Edwards, *Barry Goldwater: The Man Who Made a Revolution* (Washington, DC: Regnery, 1995), 129.

101. Barry Goldwater, *The Conscience of a Conservative* (Princeton, NJ: Princeton University Press, 2007), 9.

102. Goldwater, *The Conscience of a Conservative*, 81–82.

103. Goldwater, *The Conscience of a Conservative*, 82.

104. Goldwater, *The Conscience of a Conservative*, 84.

105. James Burnham, "Foreign Affairs," *National Review*, July 14, 1964, 589.

106. James Burnham, "What to Do about the UN," *National Review*, April 24, 1962, 284.

107. Burnham, "What to Do about the UN," 284.

108. Burnham, "What to Do about the UN," 284.

109. Burnham, "What to Do about the UN," 284.

110. James Burnham, "Ideology and Foreign Aid," *National Review*, April 10, 1962, 243.

111. Burnham, "Ideology and Foreign Aid," 243.

112. Burnham, "Ideology and Foreign Aid," 243.

113. James Burnham, "Foreign Aid: Distinctions Needed," in *The War We Are In*, 164.

114. Burnham, "Foreign Aid," 164.

115. Burnham, "Foreign Aid," 164.

116. Cited in Kelly, *James Burnham*, 245.

117. Edmund Burke, *Reflections on the French Revolution* (New York: Dutton, 1951), 58.

118. Edmund Burke, *An Appeal from the New to the Old Whigs* (New York: Bobbs-Merrill, 1962), 134.

119. Edmund Burke, "A Letter to Sir Hercules Langrishe, Bart., M.P," in *Works of the Right Honourable Edmund Burke* (London: Nimmo, 1887), 4: 301.

120. Brent Bozell, "Freedom or Virtue," *National Review*, September 11, 1962, 181-187.

121. Frank Meyer, "The Twisted Tree of Liberty," *National Review*, January 16, 1962, 25-26.

122. Burnham, *Suicide of the West*, 5.
123. Burnham, *Suicide of the West*, 40-42.
124. Burnham, *Suicide of the West*, 126.
125. Burnham, *Suicide of the West*, 129.
126. Burnham, *Suicide of the West*, 136.
127. Burnham, *Suicide of the West*, 136.
128. Burnham, *Suicide of the West*, 136.
129. Burnham, *Suicide of the West*, 127.
130. Burnham, *Suicide of the West*, 148.
131. Burnham, *Suicide of the West*, 137.
132. Burnham, *Suicide of the West*, 138.
133. Burnham, *Suicide of the West*, 69.
134. Burnham, *Suicide of the West*, 69.
135. Burnham, *Suicide of the West*, 70.
136. Burnham, *Suicide of the West*, 71.
137. Burnham, *Suicide of the West*, 135.
138. Burnham, *Suicide of the West*, 141.
139. Burnham, *Suicide of the West*, 107-108.
140. Burnham, *Suicide of the West*, 123.
141. Burnham, *Suicide of the West*, 123.
142. Burnham, *Suicide of the West*, 132.
143. Burnham, *Suicide of the West*, 145.
144. Burnham, *Suicide of the West*, 145.
145. Burnham, *Suicide of the West*, 145.
146. Burnham, *Suicide of the West*, 109.
147. Burnham, *Suicide of the West*, 109.
148. Burnham, *Suicide of the West*, 106.
149. Burnham, *Suicide of the West*, 107.
150. Burnham, *Suicide of the West*, 107.
151. Burnham, *Suicide of the West*, 108. In the early 1960s, clean-up drives were launched to improve the Bowery area of New York City.

152. Burke, *Reflections on the French Revolution*, 46.
153. Burnham, *Suicide of the West*, 188.
154. Burnham, *Suicide of the West*, 189.
155. Burnham, *Suicide of the West*, 203.
156. Burnham, *Suicide of the West*, 190-191.
157. Burnham, *Suicide of the West*, 204.

158. Burnham's views of the bureaucracy as presented in *The Managerial Revolution* are briefly discussed in the book.

159. Russell Kirk, *Conservative Mind: From Burke to Santayana* (Chicago: Regnery, 1953), 444.
160. Kirk, *Conservative Mind*, 444.
161. Burnham, *Suicide of the West*, 281.
162. Burnham, *Suicide of the West*, 288.
163. Burnham, *Suicide of the West*, 282.
164. Michael Oakeshott, *Rationalism in Politics and Other Essays* (Indianapolis, IN: Liberty Fund, 1991), 54.
165. "Russel-Einstein Manifesto," July 9, 1955, Atomic Heritage Foundation, https://www.atomicheritage.org/key-documents/russell-einstein-manifesto.
166. Burnham, *Suicide of the West*, 227.
167. Burnham, *Suicide of the West*, 227.
168. Burnham, *Suicide of the West*, 292.
169. Burnham, *Suicide of the West*, 292.
170. Burnham, *Suicide of the West*, 294.
171. Burnham, *Suicide of the West*, 288.
172. Burnham, *Suicide of the West*, 289-290.
173. Burnham, *Suicide of the West*, 289.
174. Burnham, *Suicide of the West*, 289.
175. Burnham, *Suicide of the West*, 305.
176. *The War We Are In* (1967) is mostly a collection of past essays.
177. Burnham, *Suicide of the West*, 193.
178. Burnham, *Suicide of the West*, 194.
179. Irving Howe, "Bourbon on the Rocks," *New York Review*, May 14, 1964, 12.
180. Gerhart Niemeyer, "Ideology as Fate," *Modern Age*, Summer 1964, 320.
181. Henry Kissinger, "Begeht Der Westen Selbstmord," Henry A. Kissinger Papers, part II, series VI, press clippings, German reviews of writings by Henry Kissinger, Yale University Digital Collections.

11. Vietnam Failure and the Non-Western World

1. James Burnham, "What Are We Doing in Vietnam?," *National Review*, March 23, 1965, 232.
2. James Burnham, "The Weakest Front," *National Review*, June 15, 1965, 499.
3. Burnham, "The Weakest Front," 499.
4. George F. Kennan, "The Conceptual Element in Recent American Foreign Policy," lecture at the Charles Warren Center at Harvard University, April 19, 1967.
5. Hans Morgenthau, *In Defense of the National Interest* (New York: Knopf, 1951), 242.
6. Hans Morgenthau, *A New Foreign Policy for the United States* (New York: Praeger, 1969), viii.
7. James Burnham, "Whose National Interest," *National Review*, May 6, 1969, 442.
8. Burnham, "Whose National Interest," 443.
9. Burnham, "Whose National Interest," 443.

10. James Burnham, "Bell for the Next Round," *National Review*, July 13, 1965, 583.

11. Burnham, "Bell for the Next Round," 583.

12. James Burnham, "Knots of Our Own Tying," *National Review*, September 7, 1965, 762.

13. Burnham, "Knots of Our Own Tying," 762.

14. Burnham, "Knots of Our Own Tying," 762.

15. Burnham, "Knots of Our Own Tying," 762.

16. Burnham, "Knots of Our Own Tying," 762.

17. Leon Trotsky, *The Permanent Revolution* and *Results and Prospects*, trans. John G. Wright, revised Brian Pearce (New York: Pioneer, 1965).

18. Different protests across the country had different immediate causes. The Vietnam War is just part of the broader context.

19. James Burnham, "Whose Peace," in *The War We Are In: The Last Decade and the Next* (New Rochelle, NY: Arlington House, 1967), 274.

20. Burnham, "Whose Peace," 274.

21. Burnham, "Whose Peace," 276.

22. Burnham, "Whose Peace," 276.

23. James Burnham, "Student Riots and Blanqui's Legacy," *National Review*, June 18, 1960, 392.

24. James Burnham, "From Ho, With Love," *National Review*, March 8, 1966, 203.

25. James Burnham, "While in That Corner," *National Review*, March 9, 1969, 186.

26. Burnham, "While in That Corner," 186.

27. Burnham, "Globalism," in *The War We Are In*, 137–138.

28. Burnham, "Globalism," 138.

29. Burnham, "Globalism," 138.

30. Burnham, "Globalism," 138–139.

31. James Burnham, "Joys and Sorrows of Empire," *National Review*, July 13, 1971, 748.

32. Burnham, "Joys and Sorrows," 748.

33. Burnham, "Joys and Sorrows," 748.

34. Burnham, "Joys and Sorrows," 748.

35. This treaty banned nuclear testing in the atmosphere, outer space, and under water.

36. James Burnham, "Questions Begging," *National Review*, August 27, 1963, 148.

37. Burnham, "Questions Begging," 148.

38. Burnham," Questions Begging," 148.

39. James Burnham, "Is Disarmament Possible?," in *The War We Are In*, 151.

40. James Burnham, "A War Distorted," *New York Times*, April 9, 1971.

41. Burnham, "A War Distorted," 31.

42. Burnham, "A War Distorted," 31.

43. Before the late 1960s, elements of both parties supported these ideas.

44. James Burnham, "Reply to Letters," *National Review*, June 29, 1971, 720.

45. James Burnham, "Rhetoric and Medicare," *National Review*, August 24, 1965, 720.

46. James Burnham, "Logical Steps Forward," *National Review*, April 6, 1957, 323-324.

47. James Burnham, *Suicide of the West* (New York: John Day, 1964), 167-168.

48. James Burnham, "Why Not Investigate the Court?," *National Review*, July 20, 1957, 84.

49. James Burnham, "Earl Warren: Ideologue," *National Review*, July 4, 1956, 5.

50. James Burnham, "Utopia and Civil Rights," *National Review*, August 3, 1957, 127.

51. Burnham, "Utopia and Civil Rights," 127.

52. Editorial, "Why the South Must Prevail," *National Review*, August 24, 1957, 148-149.

53. Editorial, "Why the South Must Prevail," 148.

54. Daniel Kelly, *James Burnham and the Struggle for the World* (Wilmington, DE: ISI Books, 2002), xix.

55. James Burnham, "Parakeets and Parchesi: An Indian Memorandum," *Partisan Review*, September-October 1951, 559.

56. Burnham, "Parakeets and Parchesi," 561.

57. Burnham, "Parakeets and Parchesi," 561.

58. Daniel Kelly attributed Burnham's sentiments about India to his distaste for its prime minister Jawaharlal Nehru, whom Burnham believed was not pro-Western enough.

59. James Burnham, "In Tribute to Sir John Kotelawala," in *The War We Are In*, 213.

60. Burnham, "In Tribute to Sir John Kotelawala," 213.

61. Burnham, "In Tribute to Sir John Kotelawala," 213.

62. James Burnham, "Rising Expectations of What?," in *The War We Are In*, 228.

63. James Burnham, "Too Much Too Soon," *National Review*, August 27, 1960, 107.

64. Burnham, "Rising Expectations," 229.

65. Burnham, "Rising Expectations," 229.

66. Frantz Fanon, *The Wretched of the Earth*, trans. Richard Philcox (New York: Grove, 1963), 1.

67. James Burnham, "Are Americans Black Natives?," *National Review*, February 9, 1971, 133.

68. Burnham, "Are Americans Black Natives?," 133.

69. James Burnham, "The Explosion of Africa," in *The War We Are In*, 218.

70. James Burnham, "What Is Ahead for Black Africa?," in *The War We Are In*, 221.

71. Burnham, "What Is Ahead for Black Africa?," 221.

72. James Burnham, "The Week," *National Review*, March 12, 1960, 164.

73. James Burnham, "Danger! Ideologues at Large!," in *The War We Are In*, 229.

74. James Burnham, "The Loneliest Men," *National Review*, March 12, 1960, 164.

75. James Burnham, "Fire Burn, Cauldron Bubble," *National Review*, November 30, 1965, 1062-1063.

76. Burnham, "Fire Burn, Cauldron Bubble," 1063.
77. Burnham, "Fire Burn, Cauldron Bubble," 1063.
78. Burnham, "Fire Burn, Cauldron Bubble," 1063.
79. James Burnham, "Global Apartheid?," *National Review*, October 18, 1966, 1036.
80. Boumédiène came to power through a bloodless coup and then abolished the constitution and parliament.
81. Ghana became a one-part state in 1964.
82. Burnham, "Global Apartheid," 1036. Although he recognized that all groups are part of history, Spengler distinguished between ahistorical people and those who had world historical consciousness.
83. Burnham, "Global Apartheid," 1036.
84. Burnham, "Global Apartheid," 1036.
85. James Burnham (unsigned), "Closing the Doors," *National Review*, June 17, 1969, 578.
86. Burnham, "Closing the Doors," 578.
87. Burnham, "Closing the Doors," 578.
88. Burnham, "The Loneliest Men," 164.
89. Burnham, "The Loneliest Men," 164.
90. Burnham, "The Loneliest Men," 164.
91. Burnham, "The Loneliest Men," 164.
92. James Burnham, "The Balance Sheet," *National Review*, May 18, 1971, 518.
93. James Burnham, "Who Shall Be Master?," *National Review*, August 11, 1964, 688.
94. James Burnham, "How Blows the East Wind," *National Review*, March 24, 1964, 230.
95. John Lewis Gaddis, *We Now Know: Rethinking Cold War History* (New York: Oxford University Press, 1997), 218. Gaddis's emphasis.
96. Burnham seemed to have grasped this at the very end of his writing career. In a letter to Buckley in 1978, he questioned the loyalty of the Chinese to the Soviets.
97. Patrick J. Buchanan, memorandum to Attorney General H. R. Haldeman, December 3, 1971, Richard Nixon Presidential Library, "Contested Materials Collection," box 3, folder 56.
98. Laurence Jurdem, *Paving the Way for Reagan* (Lexington: University Press of Kentucky, 2018), 73.
99. Jurdem, *Paving the Way*, 73.
100. Jurdem, *Paving the Way*, 73.
101. James Burnham to Henry Kissinger, December 7, 1973, Henry Kissinger Papers, part II, MS 1981, Yale University Library, New Haven, CT.
102. James Burnham, "It's All Your Fault," *National Review*, April 25, 1975, 441.
103. Burnham, "It's All Your Fault," 441.
104. Burnham, "It's All Your Fault," 441.
105. James Burnham, "Go East, Old Man," *National Review*, May 23, 1975, 549.

106. Burnham, "Reflections on Defeat," 549.
107. Burnham, "Reflections on Defeat," 549.
108. Burnham, "Reflections on Defeat," 549.
109. Burnham, "Reflections on Defeat," 549.
110. Burnham, *The War We Are In*, 20.
111. Burnham, *The War We Are In*, 20.
112. Burnham, *The War We Are In*, 20.
113. James Burnham, "A Ford Foreign Policy," *National Review*, August 30, 1974, 959.
114. Burnham, "A Ford Foreign Policy," 959.
115. James Burnham, "Détente, the Tarnished Banner," *National Review Bulletin*, May 2, 1975, B57.
116. James Burnham, "Helsinki, Here We Come," *National Review*, August 1, 1975, 813.
117. Burnham, "Helsinki, Here We Come," 813.
118. James Burnham, "The Logic of Détente," *National Review*, August 15, 1975, 873.
119. Burnham, "The Logic of Détente," 873.
120. Burnham, "The Logic of Détente," 873.
121. James Burnham, "The Dialectics of Détente," *National Review*, August 29, 1975, 928.
122. Burnham, "The Dialectics of Détente," 928.
123. James Burnham, "Politics and Morality," *National Review*, November 12, 1976, 1226.
124. Burnham, "Politics and Morality," 1226.
125. See Ron Reagan, *My Father at 100* (New York: Viking, 2011) for a personal account of Reagan's love of reading.
126. Thomas W. Evans, *The Education of Ronald Reagan* (New York: Columbia University Press, 2006), 9.
127. James Burnham, "The Resonance Differential," *National Review*, June 6, 1975, 602.
128. Burnham, "Resonance Differential," 602.
129. Ronald Reagan, *Reagan, In His Own Hand* (New York: Free Press, 2001), 130.
130. Reagan, *In His Own Hand*, 130.
131. James Burnham, "Salt—Verifiability 0," *National Review*, January 6, 1978, 22.
132. Reagan, *In His Own Hand*, 76.
133. Reagan, *In His Own Hand*, 78. Reagan's emphasis.
134. The "trust but verify" idea has played an important role in twenty-first century American politics. Regarding the Iran deal, President Obama stated: "This deal is not built on trust. It is built on verification." Republican critic of the Iran deal, Senator James Inhofe (R-OK) said, "President Reagan's method to diplomatic negotiations was trust but verify. This deal has no guarantee of verification." President Joe Biden has insisted that verification be part of any extension of the Strategic Arms Reduction Treaties (START). Verification, in fact, has been part of all START treaties.

230   NOTES TO PAGES 185–189

135. Ronald Reagan, "The President's News Conference," January 29, 1981, Ronald Reagan Presidential Library and Museum, https://www.reaganlibrary.gov/archives/speech/presidents-news-conference-1.

136. Reagan, "The President's News Conference."

137. Interview with the President, October 16, 1981, *Presidential Documents*, 1160–1161, Ronald Reagan, "Remarks and a Question-and-Answer Session at a Working Luncheon with Out-of-Town Editors," October 16, 1981, Ronald Reagan Presidential Library and Museum, https://www.reaganlibrary.gov/archives/speech/remarks-and-question-and-answer-session-working-luncheon-out-town-editors.

138. Ronald Reagan, "Remarks at the Annual Convention of the National Association of Evangelicals in Orlando, FL," March 8, 1983, Ronald Reagan Presidential Library and Museum, https://www.reaganlibrary.gov/archives/speech/remarks-annual-convention-national-association-evangelicals-orlando-fl.

139. Ronald Reagan, "Address to Members of the British Parliament," June 8, 1982, Ronald Reagan Presidential Library and Museum, https://www.reaganlibrary.gov/archives/speech/address-members-british-parliament. These ideas should not be labeled as merely the thoughts of the president's speechwriters. Their speeches were based on ideas that Reagan has been publicly expressing for many years. And Reagan always carefully edited his important presidential speeches.

140. Ronald Reagan, "Remarks at the Presentation Ceremony for the Presidential Medal of Freedom," February 23, 1983, Ronald Reagan Presidential Library and Museum, https://www.reaganlibrary.gov/archives/speech/remarks-presentation-ceremony-presidential-medal-freedom.

Epilogue

1. Ronald Reagan, "Statement on Death of James Burnham," July 29, 1987, Ronald Reagan Presidential Library and Museum, https://www.reaganlibrary.gov/archives/speech/statement-death-james-burnham.

2. William Kristol and Robert Kagan, "Bombing Iraq Isn't Enough," *New York Times*, January 30, 1998, Section A.

3. Robert Kagan and William Kristol, "What to Do about Iraq?," *Weekly Standard*, January 21, 2002, 23.

4. Robert Kagan wrote a 2002 piece titled "Power and Weakness" for *Policy Review*, no. 113 (June and July 2002). It examines European and US conceptions of power in the international arena. The twenty-five-page essay uses the word "power" 156 times.

5. Vivek Ramaswamy, @VivekGRamaswamy, "The real divide isn't black vs. white or even Democrat vs. Republican. It's the managerial class vs. the everyday citizen," X, January 21, 2024.

6. See, for example, Malcom Kyeyune, "Wokeness, the Highest Stage of Managerialism," *City Journal*, Spring 2022, https://www.city-journal.org/article/wokeness-the-highest-stage-of-managerialism; or Julius Krein, "James Burnham's Managerial Elite," *American Affairs*, Spring 2017, https://americanaffairsjournal.org/2017/02/james-burnhams-managerial-elite/.

7. Thomas Meany, "Trumpism after Trump," *Harper's Magazine*, February 2020, https://harpers.org/archive/2020/02/trumpism-after-trump/.

8. Donald Trump, inaugural address, January 20, 2017, Washington, DC, https://trumpwhitehouse.archives.gov/briefings-statements/the-inaugural-address/.

9. Donald Trump, speech, Billings, MT, September 6, 2018, https://www.presidency.ucsb.edu/documents/remarks-make-america-great-again-rally-billings-montana.

10. Donald Trump, speech, Warsaw, Poland, July 6, 2017, https://www.cnn.com/2017/07/06/politics/trump-speech-poland-transcript/index.html.

11. Donald J. Trump, @realDonaldTrump, "The United Nations has such great potential but right now it is just a club for people to get together, talk and have a good time. So sad!," Twitter, December 26, 2016.

12. Donald Trump, "Remarks by Donald Trump on Actions against China," May 29, 2020, https://trumpwhitehouse.archives.gov/briefings-statements/remarks-president-trump-actions-china/.

13. Donald Trump, "Remarks to the United Nations General Assembly," September 25, 2018, New York City, https://2017-2021.state.gov/president-trump-addresses-the-73rd-un-general-assembly/.

14. James Burnham, "Joys and Sorrows of Empire," *National Review*, July 13, 1971, 748.

Index

Abt, John, 130
Acheson, Dean, 125, 142, 146, 211–212n102
Adamic, Louis, 38
Adams, John Quincy, 143
Afghanistan, 185, 188, 215n72
Africa, 116, 139, 141, 147, 149, 153, 174–77; North, 126; South Africa, 167, 175. *See also* Algeria; Rhodesia
Algeria, 175–76
Alsop, Stewart, 138
American Committee of Cultural Freedom (ACCF), 128
American Workers Party (AWP), 21, 24
Angola, 166
Argentina, 87
Aristotle, 12, 42, 64
Aron, Raymond, 100
Asia, 107, 116, 139, 149, 174, 176
Atkins, John, 80
Ayer, A. J., 120

Bay of Pigs, 147–49, 169
Bell, Daniel, 128, 203n83
Bentham, Jeremy, 58
Berle, Adolf, 19–20, 57
Berlin, 116, 120–23; Berlin Airlift, 105; Berlin Wall, 107, 149
Bernstein, Eduard, 90
Biden, Joe, 229n134
Blanqui, Louis, 169
Blum, Leon, 30
Bohlen, Charles "Chip," 98, 128, 134
Bolivia, 29, 154
Bolshevik Revolution, 25, 84, 111, 157
Bolsheviks, 17, 25, 29, 34, 37, 38, 69, 84, 107, 137
Boumédiène, Houari, 176, 228n80
bourgeoisie, 18, 20, 25–26, 29, 34, 57, 122
Bozell, Brent, 151, 155
Brazil, 154

Breit, Harvey, 114
Britain, 48, 72, 79–80, 83, 92, 97, 126, 139, 175, 220n15
Brookhiser, Richard, 8
Browder, Earl, 30, 31–32, 134, 198n101
Bruno, Giordano, 72
Buchanan, Pat, 7, 77, 178
Buckley, William F., 4–5, 136, 140, 178
Bukharin, Nikolai, 51
Bullitt, William C., 211–212n102
bureaucracy, 7, 51, 51–52, 58, 64, 76, 78, 110–111; in government, 76, 189; power of, 64, 76–77, 144
Burke, Edmund, 5, 8, 154–55, 160, 163, 176
Burnham, Claude, 10
Burnham, David, 13–14
Burnham, James, writings of: "Abstraction Kills the West," 139; "The Balance Sheet," 178; "The Bands Are Playing," 27; "A Belated Dialectician," 40; book reviews, 19–20, 23–24, 26, 30, 39–40, 84–85, 141–42, 167; "Browder Defends Imperialism," 31–32; "On the Character of the War and the Perspective of the Fourth Internationalists," 41; *The Coming Defeat of Communism*, 82, 104–16, 118, 122, 162, 186; *Congress and the American Tradition*, 143–46, 162; *Containment or Liberation*, 82, 116, 122–23, 125–28, 162; *The Deep State*, 76; "Disinformation Bureaus," 140–41; "The Dulles Record: An Appraisal," 146; "Editor Meets Senator," 128; "From Formula to Reality," 34, 203n62; "From Ho, With Love," 169; "Intellectuals in Retreat," 38, 39; *Introduction to Philosophical Analysis* (with Wheelwright), 14, 19; "Is Democracy Possible?," 59; "It's All Your Fault," 179–80; "Joys and Sorrows of Empire," 170; "Lenin's Heir," 83–85; *The Machiavellians*, 1, 2–3, 6, 61–70, 74, 76,

Burnham, James (*continued*)
77, 80, 86–87, 130, 143, 146, 162, 174, 177, 189–90; *The Managerial Revolution*, 1–6, 8, 47, 48, 51, 52–61, 71, 74, 76–77, 79–80, 85–86, 89, 114, 116, 130, 143, 146, 162, 178, 187, 189; "Max Eastman as Scientist," 35; "Max Eastman's Straw Man," 31; "Politics and Morality," 183; "The Politics of Desperation," 43; "Psychological Warfare or Else," 119–20; "The Question of Organic Unity," 25; *Reflection on the French Revolution*, 159; "Reflections on Defeat," 180–81; "The Resonance Differential," 184; "Rhetoric and Peace," 121; "SALT-Verifiability=0," 184–85; "Science and Style," 43; "The Sixth Turn of the Communist Screw," 82, 85; "Stalin and the Junkers," 83, 85; *The Struggle for the World* (Burnham), 3, 6, 82, 86–93, 95–104, 116, 122, 123, 162, 188; *Suicide of the West*, 5, 6, 154–64, 187; "THEIR Government," 23, 24; "Thirteen Propositions" (with Wheelwright), 19, 20; "Through a Glass, Darkly," 12; "War and the Workers," 28–29; "A War Distorted," 171; *The War We Are In*, 181; *The Web of Subversion*, 129–34, 150; "What Is the Purpose of the United Nations?," 101; "What to Do About the UN," 152; "Why the South Must Prevail," 173; "Words of East and West," 141
Burnham, Mary Mae Gillis, 10
Burnham, Phillip, 83
Bush, George H. W., 78

Calhoun, John C., 143–44
Cannon, James, 22, 24, 41–42
capitalism, 20, 22–24, 26, 28, 31, 42, 50, 53, 55, 57–58, 63, 81, 112–13, 130; vs. communism, 17, 22, 122, 127, 168; demise of, 49–51; failings of, 19, 32, 48, 90, 98, 100; and imperialism, 28, 32; laissez-faire, 73, 134, 160, 172; and managerialism, 49, 53, 142, 203n83; vs. Marxism, 30, 41; vs. socialism, 37, 44–45, 48, 52, 81
Carter, James "Jimmy," 183, 185
Carter, John Vincent, 133
Castro, Fidel, 147–48, 169
Catholic Church, 4, 10, 12, 62, 111–12, 118, 155

Central Intelligence Agency (CIA), 4, 8, 76, 110, 114, 117–19, 128, 136, 200n46
Chamberlain, John, 38
Chamberlain, Neville, 32
Chambers, Whittaker, 131
Chaplin, Charlie, 120
Chiang Kai-shek, 131
China, 47, 119, 177, 190, 228n96; communism in, 105, 119, 123–26, 132–34, 141, 149–50, 166, 168, 174, 178, 181; and the United States, 87, 132, 177–78, 180, 182; and the Soviet Union, 83, 150, 178
Christianity, 11, 21, 22, 66, 90, 155, 159
Churchill, Winston, 133
civil rights, 37, 151, 154–55, 172–73
class struggle/warfare, 26, 28–29, 31–32, 43, 66, 89–90, 122, 137
Clausewitz, Carl von, 122
Clay, Henry, 143
Clinton, William "Bill," 78
Cold War, 3, 82, 84, 93–94, 96, 100, 105, 108–9, 111–15, 121, 123–24, 130, 137, 140, 141, 149, 168, 173, 178, 181, 187, 215n72; American failures, 105–6, 116, 151–52; American successes, 4, 105, 127; understanding of, 183–84
communism, 3–5, 17, 22, 34–35, 47, 59, 76–77, 84–85, 88, 90, 101–2, 109, 113–14, 116, 121–22, 128, 132, 134, 137, 141, 147, 150, 152, 162, 168, 215n70, 219n88; in Africa, 116, 139; vs. capitalism, 17, 22, 122, 127, 168; in China/Asia, 102, 105, 116, 119, 123, 125, 126, 132–33, 134, 139, 141, 150, 166, 168, 174, 178, 180; defeat of, 95, 110–11, 113; in Europe, 22, 83, 101, 107, 116, 126, 133, 138, 166, 168, 213–214n12; fighting, 3, 91–92, 94, 112, 115, 117, 121, 123, 127, 139, 146, 153, 161, 176; latent, 130, 132; vs. Nazism, 52, 57, 137; negotiation with, 87, 140, 178, 186; opposition to, 19, 73, 85, 99, 101, 118, 136, 162, 173; possible responses to, 91–92; power as objective of, 87–88; promotion of, 130, 131, 134, 210n23; Soviet, 4, 19, 97, 123–24, 150, 166, 168, 178; spread of, 83, 107, 161, 183, 185; as threat, 3, 5, 102, 117, 146, 154, 161–62, 168; in the United States, 25, 88–89, 97, 128, 130–33, 150, 210n23; and US

policies, 93, 108, 132; use of terror by, 88, 102, 137. *See also* Soviet Union
Communist League of America (CLA), 24
Communist Party, 4, 20, 25, 83, 89, 122, 134, 138, 198n101; British, 138; French, 138; Greek, 209n7; Italian, 138; in the United States (CPUSA), 21, 31, 102
Congo, 148, 181
Congress for Cultural Freedom (CCF), 4, 120, 128, 148
conservatism, 3, 77, 79, 82, 144, 155–56, 172, 189, 191. *See also* neoconservatism; paleoconservatism
containment, 5, 6, 7, 100, 107, 114–15, 122–23, 125, 126, 128, 138, 143, 146, 166, 214n19
Costello, Frank, 8
Counts, George S., 38
Croce, Benedetto, 74, 120
Cuba, 147–48, 149, 161–62, 169–70, 181, 223n88
Czechoslovakia, 112, 139, 213–214n12

Dante Alighieri, 14, 62
D'Arcy, Martin, 12–13, 45
Davies, John Paton, 98, 134
de Gaulle, Charles, 100, 149
decolonization, 155, 174–77
deep state, 76, 189
Dellingshausen, Ewert Freiherr von, 113–14
Dennis, Lawrence, 202n59
Department of All-German Affairs (West Germany), 114
détente, 5, 182–83
Dewey, John, 37–38, 120, 198n99
dialectic, 2, 35, 36, 39, 42–45, 122. *See also* materialism, dialectical
Dickinson, John, 143
Diggins, John P., 114
Djilas, Milovan, 76–77
Dodd, Martha, 15, 196n50, 210n23, 219n88
Dodd, William, 196n50
Dole, Bob, 78
Dos Passos, John, 187
Drucker, Peter, 57, 58
Du Bois, W. E. B., 120
Dulles, Allen, 128
Dulles, John Foster, 115–16, 146, 211–212n102

Eastern Europe, 53, 111, 113, 124, 137, 140, 162; communism in, 116, 126, 138, 168; liberation of, 85–86, 93, 115, 123–25, 127–28, 138, 188; Soviet Union in, 83, 147, 157, 182, 188
Eastman, Max, 30, 35–36, 38, 42, 136, 187
Egypt, 138–39, 154, 157, 175, 220n15
Einstein, Albert, 22, 72, 120, 160
Eisenhower, Dwight D., 134, 139, 146, 149, 165, 167, 172
Eisenstein, Sergei, 84
ELAM, 83, 209n7
Eliot, T. S., 20, 40
elite(s): 7, 32, 66, 73, 77, 79, 82, 111, 113, 190; bureaucratic, 2, 7, 34, 51, 62, 81, 146; globalist, 78, 189; managerial, 50, 77–78, 82, 146; power of, 8, 50, 63–64, 68, 70, 191; ruling, 1, 2, 7, 67
Engels, Friedrich, 40, 51; *The Communist Manifesto*, 78
England. *See* Britain
Enlightenment, 12, 154, 160
Esthonia, 126
Ethiopia, 28, 29, 175
Eurasia, 83–84, 91, 94, 107, 139
Europe, 3, 22–23, 25–26, 29, 83, 92, 94, 107, 146; Central, 47, 57, 107, 116, 140; Western, 47, 64, 100, 107, 123–24, 127, 168, 171. *See also* Eastern Europe
Evans, Medgar, 129

Fairbanks, John K., 133
Fanon, Frantz, 174–75
Farrell, James, 38
fascism, 29, 38, 41, 47, 55, 69, 70, 184
Fitzgerald, F. Scott, 10–13
Ford, Gerald, 182–83
Ford Hunger March, 21
foreign aid, 153–54, 188
Foreign Economic Association, 131
Foreign Service, 76, 110
Fourier, Charles, 35
Fox, Ralph, 23
France, 48, 91, 97, 101, 126, 139, 181, 197n66
Francis, Samuel, 6, 7, 77–78, 79, 146
Franco, Francisco, 162, 167
Free Germany Committee, 83
French Revolution, 34, 67, 109, 143, 154, 176

INDEX

Gaddis, John Lewis, 98, 178
Galbraith, John Kenneth, 57, 142, 221n32
Gates, Albert, 57
Germany, 26, 31, 51, 53, 55, 58, 61, 72, 79–80, 88, 101, 114, 157, 181, 196n50, 197n66; East, 83, 88, 114, 118; under the Nazis, 32, 51, 53, 57, 79, 118, 178; rearmament of, 29, 108–9; West, 88, 97, 114, 140; in World War II, 80, 83, 99, 149. *See also* Berlin; Hitler, Adolf
Ghana, 157, 176, 228n81
Gibbons, Edward, 145
globalism, 170, 189, 190
Glotzer, Albert, 57
Goldwater, Barry, 1, 5, 150–52
Gorbachev, Mikhail, 185, 215n70
Gramsci, Antonio, 78
Great Depression, 14, 16, 21, 23–24, 39, 55
Greece, 83, 86, 97, 105, 108, 166, 170, 181
Gregg, Richard B., 26
Gromyko, Andrei, 102, 213n139

Hackes, Louis, 38
Haiti, 6
Haldane, J. B. S., 40
Hansen, Joseph, 57
Harriman, Averell, 211–212n102
Harrison, Charles Yale, 38
Hayek, Fredrich, 57, 58–59, 204n93
Hegel, G. W. F., 44, 113
Hegelianism, 31, 40, 113, 150
Helsinki Accords, 182
Herberg, Will, 187
Hickenlooper, Bourke, 128
Hiss, Alger, 130–31, 132, 150
Hitchens, Christopher, 7, 93
Hitler, Adolf, 24, 26, 32, 52, 57, 70, 80, 83, 87, 118, 120, 137, 167, 178, 196n50, 197n66, 209n14; confronting, 87, 108, 167; and German expansion, 26, 178, 197n66; and Russia, 33, 41; vs. Stalin, 38, 70, 80, 118, 137
Ho Chi Minh, 126, 169
Hobbes, Thomas, 58
holism, 25, 28, 150, 178
Honecker, Erich, 215n70
Hook, Sydney, 16–17, 19, 21, 22, 24, 34, 36–37, 42, 120, 187; Burnham's disagreements with, 38–39, 41, 45; writings of, 30–31, 36, 40, 70, 73–74
Hoopes, Townsend, 116

Hoover, Herbert, 162
Hopkins, Harry, 131
House Un-American Activities Committee (HUAC), 131, 162
Howe, Irving, 163
Hungary, 138, 139, 146, 161, 181
Hussein, Saddam, 7, 188
Huxley, Aldous, 22

India, 107, 123, 139, 149, 173–74
Indochina, 123, 126, 170, 180, 183
Indonesia, 157, 181
Inhofe, James, 229n134
Institute of Pacific Relations, 134
Iran, 8, 78, 119, 213n139, 220n15, 229n134
Iraq, 8, 220n15
isolationism, 3, 6, 31, 92, 94–96, 100, 154, 170, 190
Israel, 139
Italy, 26, 28–29, 31, 138

Jackson, Henry "Scoop," 152–53
Japan, 3, 29, 31, 47, 53, 55, 61, 80, 83, 92, 141, 149, 157, 177, 180–81
Jefferson, Thomas, 37, 87
John Birch Society, 133, 162
Johnson, Lyndon B., 161, 167
Josephson, Matthew, 27
Junkers, 83

Kagan, Robert, 6, 7, 187–88
Kamenev, Lev, 125
Kampmark, Binoy, 93
Kant, Immanuel, 58
Kazakhstan, 160
Kelly, Daniel, 7, 13, 96, 140, 173, 209n7
Kendall, Willmoore, 136
Kennan, George, 98, 107, 115, 124, 138, 142–43, 166, 167–68; writings of, 98, 110, 124–25, 127–28, 142, 168, 211–212n201, 221n32
Kennedy, John F., 10, 147–50, 161
Kent, Sherman, 128
Khrushchev, Nikita, 137–38, 141, 149–50, 161, 178
Kirk, Russel, 136, 159–60
Kissinger, Henry, 141–42, 163–64, 179
Koestler, Arthur, 40, 121, 200n46
Korea, 123–24, 126, 181; North, 115; South, 115, 153, 177, 180–81

INDEX 237

Korean War, 114–15, 128, 170, 177, 180
Kotelawala, John, 174
Kravchenko, Victor, 85
Kristol, Irving, 6, 128, 133–34, 187
Kristol, William "Bill," 6, 7, 187–88
Kronstadters, 37
Krutch, Joseph, 22

Laos, 148, 181
Latin America, 32, 116, 160, 166, 174, 176, 181
Lattimore, Owen, 131, 134
League of Nations, 27, 29–30, 32, 101
Lenin, Vladimir I., 8, 17, 27–29, 34, 39, 48, 51, 88, 117, 125, 137, 168–69, 198n82; Burnham's admiration for, 23–24, 27, 111; death of, 24–25, 37, 118; writings of, 30, 47, 118
Leninism, 8, 47, 113, 117, 149, 168, 173
Lewis, C. I., 44
liberalism, 48, 64, 69, 137, 141–42, 145, 154, 155–56, 158–59, 160, 162, 170, 175, 189
Liberia, 175
libertarianism, social, 134
Lightner, Marcia, 204n1
Lincoln, Abraham, 72
Lind, Michael, 8
Lindberg, Anne, 202n59
Lippman, Walter, 106, 165, 167–68
Litvinov, Maxim, 30
Lofgren, Mike, 76
Luce, Henry, 97
Lundberg, Ferdinand, 38
Luxemburg, Rosa, 17, 28
Lyons, Eugene, 38

Macdonald, Dwight, 40, 56, 128, 209n7
Machiavelli, Nicolo, 8, 61, 72, 87, 154, 163; *Discourses*, 62, 70, 119; *The Prince*, 61, 72
Machiavellianism, 167, 179
Mackinder, Halford, 53, 139
Malaya, 166
Malraux, Andre, 100–101
managerial class, 2, 19, 49, 50, 54, 58, 78, 81, 142, 188–89
managerial revolution, 142, 145, 203n83
managerialism, 44, 49, 50–51, 53–54, 58–59, 76
Manheim, Karl, 204n93

Mao Zedong, 123, 150, 178
Mapplethorpe, Robert, 77
Marshall, George, 99
Marshall Plan, 100, 105, 167, 170, 213–214n12
Marx, Karl, 2, 8, 14, 17, 27, 30, 31, 33, 36, 48–51, 66, 78, 79, 173
Marxism, 2, 8, 13–14, 47, 54, 73, 113, 117, 122, 149, 150, 152, 168, 170, 186; and the 1917 revolution, 84; Burnham and, 14–32; vs. capitalism, 30; and Christianity, 21; and class struggle, 31; *Das Kapital*, 33; as Freudian psychology, 30; goals of, 33; influence of, 78; jargon of, 40; neo-, 58; as philosophy, 35, 40; revolutionary, 15; and the Russian question, 33; scientific nature of, 36; in the Soviet Union, 33; theory of surplus value, 20; theory of the state, 25; Trotsky and, 2, 18; and violence, 21. *See also* dialectic
Marxists, 2, 16, 17, 26, 27, 30, 40, 43, 57, 117, 125; Burnham's criticism of, 48–49, 113, 128, 137; on class struggle, 31, 38, 62; intellectuals, 22, 25, 30, 55, 58, 78, 90; philosophy of, 14, 18, 33, 35–36, 39–40, 44, 73, 84, 150; on the Soviet Union, 33, 35, 40
materialism: dialectical, 39–40, 44, 158; historical, 18
Mazzini, Giuseppe, 66
McCarthy, Joseph, 3, 4–5, 128–29, 134, 143, 155, 162, 218n84, 219n88
McCarthy, Mary, 128
McCarthyism, 4, 129
Means, Gardiner, 19–20, 57
Mencken, H. L., 22
Mensheviks, 24
Meyer, Frank, 155, 187
Michels, Robert, 3, 63, 67–68, 73
Middle East, 6, 123, 126, 138–40, 147, 161–62, 188
Mihailović, Draža, 87, 132
Mills, C. Wright, 1, 76, 203n83
Morgenthau, Hans, 166–67, 168
Morocco, 175
Mosca, Gaetano, 3, 63–65, 73
Mossadegh, Muhammad, 119
Muslims, 124, 141, 218n61
Mussolini, Benito, 26
Muste, A. J., 21, 196n39

Mỹ Lai massacre, 171
myths, 20, 66, 68, 89

Nagy, Imre, 138
Nash, George, 82
Nasser, Gamal, 138–39
national conservatives (NatCons), 189
National Council of the Arts, Sciences and Professions, 120
National Endowment for the Arts, 77
National Greek Republic League, 209n7
National Labor Relations Board, 131
National Review (*NR*), 1, 3, 4–5, 134, 136–37, 140, 168, 178–79, 184, 187; Burnham's colleagues at, 15–52, 155, 160, 172; *National Review Bulletin*, 143
National Security Council Report 68 (NSC-68), 115
Nazis and Nazism, 22, 27, 32, 41, 47, 51–55, 57, 59, 72, 79, 83, 86, 118, 125, 137, 168, 178
Nazi-Soviet Pact, 2, 41, 52, 197n66
neoconservatism, 6, 7, 8, 93, 187–88, 191, 211n73
neo-isolationism, 6, 154. *See also* isolationism
neo-Marxism, 58. *See also* Marxism
New Deal, 15, 19, 47, 51, 53, 55, 58, 102, 152
New York University (NYU), 13–14, 16, 21, 117
Niebuhr, Reinhold, 74, 183
Niemeyer, Gerhart, 163
Nietzsche, Friedrich, 84
Niles, David, 131
Nitze, Paul, 115
Nixon, Richard, 102, 144, 147, 177, 178; and China, 178, 180, 182; and the Cold War, 183; and the *National Review*, 179–80; *National Review*'s disagreements with, 178–79; and the USSR, 180, 182
North Atlantic Treaty Organization (NATO), 123, 126, 142, 183
nuclear weapons, 89, 95–96, 99–100, 115, 120, 128, 132, 141, 142–43, 147, 149, 151–52, 155, 160–61, 167–68, 171, 179, 181, 185, 211–212n102; MIRV, 183. *See also* arms race

Oakeshott, Michael, 160
Obama, Barack, 229n134
October Revolution, 37

Office of Policy Coordination (OPC), 98, 117–18
Office of Production Management, 51
Office of Strategic Services (OSS), 82, 131
Oppenheimer, J. Robert, 141
optimism, 67, 73, 74, 104, 112
Orwell, George, 1, 37, 40, 79, 200n46; *1984*, 3, 80–81, 99; and Burnham, 79–80; "As I Please," 79, 80; reviews of Burnham's books, 80, 99; "Second Thoughts of James Burnham," 99
Oswald, Lee Harvey, 150
Owen, Robert, 35
Oxford University, 12–13, 142

pacifism, 26, 58, 66–67, 99, 109, 121, 161, 167–69; and capitalism, 28; condemnation of, 67, 91; humanitarian, 66; opposition to, 26–27, 29
Paine, Tom, 99
Pakistan, 220n15
paleoconservatism, 6, 7, 8, 77, 146, 187–88, 191
Palestine, 177
Paraguay, 29
Pareto, Vilfredo, 3, 63, 68–69, 73
Partisan Review, 4, 39, 41, 45, 82, 128, 129, 200n46
peace, 67, 69, 152; Berlin conference, 120–21; concept of, 106, 121, 126, 150, 161, 168, 170; desire for, 31; global zone of, 181; movements, 28, 67, 169
Peace Leagues, 26, 27
Perlo, Victor, 130
Peron, Juan, 87
pessimism, 7, 13, 74, 77, 181; of Burnham, 59, 67, 73, 95, 143, 146, 152, 156, 161, 174, 181, 189
Philippines, 3, 92, 166
philosophy, 73, 204–205n7; of Burnham, 80; and the capitalist class, 112; of communism, 122; economic, 5, 59; end of, 31; Enlightenment, 12, 154, 160; Marxist, 14, 18, 33, 35, 36, 39–40, 44, 73, 84, 150; metaphysical, 31; political, 35, 45, 73, 183–84; of power, 72, 187; pragmatist, 42; scientific, 31, 36; of Trotsky, 44; utopian, 68
Poland, 106, 125, 126; anticommunist protests, 137–38; anticommunists in,

215n71; Nazi invasion of, 41; Soviet occupation of, 2, 45–46, 87, 123
Popper, Karl, 1, 36, 39, 57, 59
Portugal, 182, 184
power: as abstract concept, 73; balance of, 144; of the bureaucracy, 7, 51, 64, 76, 144; Burnham's ideas on, 190; in capitalism, 49–50; and the Cold War, 178; against communism, 3, 92, 93, 108, 115, 162; communist, 87–88, 122, 152, 180; of Congress, 143, 145; corrupting influence of, 151; cultural, 77; in democracy, 59, 67–68, 186; demonstration of, 140; desire for, 65, 72, 73; economic, 55; of the elites, 2–3, 7, 8; of empire, 92; of government, 62, 70, 190; hard, 110, 113, 191; human need for, 6; importance of, 165, 177; independent, 76; for its own sake, 81; of liberals, 145; Machiavelli's philosophy of, 72; machinery of, 78; maintaining, 63, 88; in Marxism, 73; military, 76, 96; monopoly of, 87, 122; nature of, 61, 74, 77; necessity for, 17, 167, 178; nuclear, 96; obsession with, 99; of the people, 66–67; philosophy of, 187; political, 17, 45, 51; of the presidency, 143; relations of, 63; relationship to freedom, 151; social, 55; under socialism, 66; soft, 110, 113, 119, 191; of the sovereign, 143; Soviet, 82–83, 115; of the state, 71, 151; state as a tool of, 79; struggle for, 3, 17, 50, 60, 61, 71, 73, 78–79, 166, 191; of the United States, 85–86, 148, 150–51, 170, 180, 188; use of, 7; use of to restrain power, 70, 80, 140, 190; vacuum, 160; in Vietnam, 179; violence and, 66; of the Western world, 164; wielders of, 62, 80; worshippers of, 80
power theorists, 63, 70–71, 78–79, 149, 164, 191
praxis, 117
Pressman, Lee, 130
Princeton University, 11–13, 98
proletariat, 2, 17, 18, 29, 31, 49, 113, 122, 161
propaganda: anticommunist, 92, 114, 118; and the Cold War, 109–10; communist, 85, 89, 130, 161, 169; *Managerial Revolution* as, 56; nationalist, 66; political cartoons, 118; psychological, 147; Soviet, 83, 98, 118, 120, 147; variation in, 118. *See also* warfare, psychological

Rahv, Philip, 38, 41, 128
Ramaswamy, Vivek, 188
Reagan, Ronald, 1, 5–6, 77, 102–3, 184–87, 229n134, 230n139
religious Right, 77, 190
Reston, James, 114
revolution, 15, 18, 21, 23, 25, 27–28, 37, 57, 122, 169, 198n101; Bolshevik, 17, 25, 33, 37, 84, 111, 157; Hungarian, 138, 146; international, 26, 28, 37, 41; in Russia, 18, 22, 24, 142, 198n82; social/socialist, 2, 36, 48, 49, 66
Rhodesia, 175–77
Rizzi, Bruno, 55–56, 57
Robeson, Paul, 120
Rockefeller, Nelson, 5, 152
Rodman, Selden, 37
Roosevelt, Franklin D. (FDR), 15, 19–20, 23–24, 31, 32, 58, 62–63, 68, 97, 131, 144, 161
Roosevelt, Kermit, 119
Roper, Hugh-Trevor, 120
Rorty, James, 38
Rosenberg, Ethel and Julius, 150
Rousseau, Jean-Jacques, 67, 173
Rumania, 126
Russell, Bertrand, 22, 44, 120, 160
Russia, 18, 22, 33, 37, 44, 49, 39, 72, 126, 181, 188. *See also* Soviet Union

Saint-Simon, Henri de, 35
Santayana, George, 13
Schachtman, Max, 24, 25, 38–39, 42
Schlamm, Willi, 136, 140
Schlesinger, Arthur Jr., 1, 120, 125, 128, 145, 148, 223n88; writings of, 99, 100, 127, 133
Scientific and Cultural Conference for World Peace, 120
skid row, 159, 163
Smith, Ian, 175
socialism, 17, 18, 22, 25, 28–30, 32, 35, 40, 45, 51, 55, 57, 63, 66, 73, 90, 122, 196n39, 197n71; vs. capitalism, 37, 44–45, 48, 52, 81; in Europe, 16, 23, 25, 41; in the Soviet Union, 18, 25, 33–34, 36, 57

Socialist Unity Party, 88
Socialist Workers Party (SWP), 34, 41, 44
Sorel, Georges, 3, 63, 65–67
Southeast Asia, 80, 166–169. *See also* Vietnam
Soviet Union, 2, 5, 6, 30, 33, 34, 40, 47, 51, 53, 54, 61, 73–74, 83, 87, 93, 97, 100, 110–11, 113, 116, 119, 127, 134, 136, 141, 149, 151, 163, 167, 178, 182, 186, 228n96; in Afghanistan, 185, 215n72; in Africa, 153; bureaucracy in, 51–52, 55; censorship in, 84–85; and China, 83, 150, 178; communism in, 4, 19, 97, 123–24, 150, 166, 168, 178; desire for world conquest, 91–92, 97, 106, 115, 152, 183; in Eastern Europe, 83, 147, 182, 188; Empire, 84, 85, 89, 90. 92, 96–97, 107, 110, 114, 119, 121, 123, 125, 127, 138; and Europe, 27, 33, 41, 79, 80, 83, 116, 197n66; expansion of, 3, 84, 86, 107, 125, 146, 188; in Poland, 2, 41, 45–46, 87, 123, 106, 137–138; rift satellite nations, 108, 110–112, 115, 123–24; socialism in, 25, 33–34, 36, 57; as threat, 3–5, 98, 105, 151, 162; U2 spy plane in, 148–149; U.S. relations with, 3, 85, 97, 128, 180, 182; weakness of, 107–108, 114, 137. *See also* Cold War; communism; Russia
Spengler, Oswald, 94, 154, 176
Sri Lanka, 174
Stalin, Joseph, 2, 4, 25–26, 27, 30, 33, 37–39, 47, 52, 70, 80, 82, 84, 85, 88, 105, 118, 137, 146, 182; vs. Trotsky, 2, 24–25, 34, 37–39, 83–84. *See also* Soviet Union
Stalinism, 24, 25, 30, 31, 53, 55, 79
Steinhoff, William, 79
Stern, Alfred K., 219n88
Stolberg, Benjamin, 38
Strategic Arms Limitations Talks (SALT), 184–185
Strategic Arms Reduction Treaties (START), 229n134
Strauss, Leo, 204–205n7
Suez Canal, 138–139
Sweezy, Paul, 57
Symposium (journal), 14, 16, 18, 19, 20–21

Taft, Robert A., 96
Taipei, 177
Taiwan, 153, 177, 181

Thailand, 181
Thomas Aquinas, 8, 12, 13–14, 156
Tito, Josip Broz, 87, 111, 114, 116, 132–133
Toynbee, Arnold, 94, 96, 154, 163
Treaty of Moscow, 171
Trilling, Diana, 128
Trotsky, Leon, 2, 8, 18, 27, 28, 39–45, 51, 77, 83–84, 101, 137, 189; in exile, 25, 30, 37, 38; *History of the Russian Revolution*, 17–18, 30, 43; influence on Burnham, 1, 8, 17–18, 23, 24, 26, 27, 31, 34–35, 168; on revolution, 25, 28, 48; vs. Stalin, 24–25, 34, 37–39; writings of, 2, 24, 27, 30, 33, 35, 36, 38, 41–42, 43, 47, 52, 168
Trotskyites, 2, 6–8, 24, 25, 26, 28, 31, 34–35, 47, 57, 114, 168
Troy, William, 45
Truman, Harry S., 97, 144, 168, 213–214n12
Truman Doctrine, 170
Trump, Donald, 6, 7, 8, 77, 189–90
Turkey, 97, 108, 220n15

Ukraine, 126, 149, 188
United Kingdom. *See* Britain
United Nations, 29, 87, 101, 116, 139, 149, 152–53, 170, 175, 180, 189, 213n139
United States, 31, 32, 48, 51, 53, 61, 64, 76, 80, 95–96, 100, 110, 112, 120, 123, 130, 131, 170, 177, 180; and American empire, 7, 92–94, 99, 101; armed forces, 131, 132, 147, 181; capitalism in, 20, 42; vs. communism, 85–86, 92, 108; communism in, 88–89, 128; Constitution, 54, 144, 172; Declaration of Independence, 54, 119; foreign policy, 3, 4, 7, 76–77, 82, 93, 95, 98, 99–100, 106, 110–111, 125–126, 131–132, 139, 141, 147–48, 150–52, 155, 166, 169, 180, 188; Pentagon, 114, 153; State Department, 76, 114, 120, 126, 131, 133; Supreme Court, 145, 172. *See also* Cold War
USSR. *See* Soviet Union

Veblen, Thorstein, 56
Vietnam, 153, 161, 166–70, 179–81; North, 161, 171, 179; South, 169, 179
Vietnam War, 5, 8, 161, 165–71, 179–81
Voice of America, 109, 120
von Mises, Ludwig, 5, 57, 58, 172

INDEX

Wade, Benjamin, 145
Wald, Alan, 8, 24
Wallace, Henry, 37, 97, 100, 120
Ware, Harold, 130, 150
Warren, Earl, 145, 172
Warsaw Pact, 138
Wasserman, Lew, 77
Webb, Beatrice, 204n93
Webb, Sidney, 204n93
Weber, Max, 76
Webster, Daniel, 143
Wells, H. G., 204n93
Wheelwright, Philip E., 14, 19, 21, 45
Whitehead, A. N., 44
Wilson, Edmund, 38

Wilson, Woodrow, 120, 144–45, 147
Wisner, Frank, 98
Witt, Nathan, 130
Workers Party of the United States (WPUS), 24
World Health Organization (WHO), 189–90
World War II, 27, 28, 41, 47, 55, 61, 67, 80, 96, 107, 132, 149, 167, 171, 180
World War III, 147

Yalta conference, 82, 106, 131, 134
Yugoslavia, 6, 116, 133, 166

Zhdanov, Andrei, 84
Zinoviev, Grigory, 125